Paul and the Synagogue

Paul and the Synagogue

Romans and the Isaiah Targum

Delio DelRio

☙PICKWICK *Publications* • Eugene, Oregon

PAUL AND THE SYNAGOGUE
Romans and the Isaiah Targum

Copyright © 2013 Delio DelRio. All rights reserved. Except for brief quotations in critical publications or reviews, no part of this book may be reproduced in any manner without prior written permission from the publisher. Write: Permissions, Wipf and Stock Publishers, 199 W. 8th Ave., Suite 3, Eugene, OR 97401.

Pickwick Publications
An Imprint of Wipf and Stock Publishers
199 W. 8th Ave., Suite 3
Eugene, OR 97401

www.wipfandstock.com

ISBN 13: 978-1-62032-197-3

Cataloguing-in-Publication data:

DelRio, Delio.

Paul and the synagogue : Romans and the Isaiah targum / Delio DelRio, with a foreword by Bruce D. Chilton.

xxii + 134 pp. ; 23 cm. Includes bibliographical references.

ISBN 13: 978-1-62032-197-3

1. Bible. N.T. Romans I, 17—Criticism, interpretation, etc. 2. Bible. O.T. Isaiah. Aramaic—Criticism, interpretation, etc. 3. Rabbinical literature—Relation to the New Testament. I. Title.

BS2665.52 D45 2013

Manufactured in the U.S.A.

To my wife, Kimberly,
and my three children, Michael, Cayden, and Savannah
without who's support and sacrifice over the years
this work would not have been possible.

Contents

Foreword by Bruce D. Chilton | ix
Acknowledgments | xv
Introduction | xvii

1. Romans, Targums, and Intertextuality | 1
2. Inclusivism and Particularism in Isaiah | 23
3. Particularism in Isaiah Targum | 48
4. Inclusivism in Romans | 70
5. An Intertextual Dialogue | 99

Conclusion | 119
Appendix | 123
Bibliography | 127

Foreword

IN THIS BOOK DELIO DelRio places a critical assessment of Aramaic translations of the Hebrew Bible at the center of an appreciation of Pauline theology. The term "targum" in the subtitle simply means "translation" in Aramaic, but the type and purpose of targumic renderings from Hebrew into Aramaic varied widely. Dr. DelRio has mastered those primary sources in order to understand St. Paul.

By the first century CE Aramaic emerged as the common language of Judea, Samaria and Galilee (where distinctive dialects were spoken). The linguistic situation in Judea and Galilee demanded that translation be effected, for the purposes of popular study and worship.

In that the aim of targumic production was to give the *sense* of the Hebrew Scriptures, not merely literal translation, paraphrase is characteristic of the Rabbinic Targumim. Theoretically, a passage of scripture was to be rendered orally by an interpreter (*meturgeman*), after the reading in Hebrew (cf. Mishnah Megillah 4:4–10 and Talmud Megillah 23b–25b). Although the renderings so delivered were oral in principle, over the course of time, traditions in important centers of learning became fixed, and coalescence became possible.

The Targumim divide up among those of the Torah (the Pentateuch), those of the Prophets (both "Former Prophets," or the so-called historical works, and the "Latter Prophets," or the Prophets as commonly designated in English), and those of the Writings (or Hagiographa, of too late a date to feature here), following the conventional designations of the Hebrew Bible in Judaism. Although the Hebrew Bible is almost entirely rendered by the Targumim in aggregate, there was no single moment, and no particular movement, which produced a comprehensive Bible in Aramaic. The Targumim are irreducibly complex in proveniences, purposes, and dialects of Aramaic.

Foreword

Among the Targumim to the Pentateuch, Targum Onqelos appears to correspond best of all the Targumim to Rabbinic ideals of translation. Although paraphrase is evident, especially in order to describe God and his revelation in suitably reverential terms, the high degree of correspondence with the Hebrew of the Masoretic Text (and, presumably, with the Hebrew text current in antiquity) is striking. Onqelos reflects a linguistic period of Transitional Aramaic (200 BCE–200 CE) embracing the various dialects (Hasmonaean, Nabataean, Palmyrene, Arsacid, Essene, as well as Targumic) that came to be used during the period after the Imperial Aramaic of the Persians ceased to be an agreed standard. What followed was a strong regionalization in dialects of Aramaic (200 CE–700 CE).

Various Targumim were produced in Transitional Aramaic even after its demise as a common language, because it remained understandable even after it was current. For that reason, the year 200 CE is not a firm date, after which a Targum in Transitional Aramaic cannot have been composed. Onqelos should probably be dated during the third century, in the wake of similar efforts to produce new Greek renderings during the second century.

The Targum Neophyti I was discovered in 1949 by Alejandro Díez Macho in the Library of the Neophytes in Rome. The paraphrases of Neophyti are substantially different from those of Onqelos. Entire paragraphs are added, as when Cain and Abel argue in the field prior to the first case of murder (Genesis 4:8); such "renderings" are substantial additions, and it is impossible to predict when remarkable freedom of this kind is to be indulged. The dialect of Neophyti is a frankly Regional Aramaic, while Onqelos appears in a Transitional Aramaic that is on the way to becoming Regional. The chronology of the two Targums is about the same, although Neophyti appears somewhat later; the differences between them are a function more of program than dating.

The latest representative of the type of expansive rendering found in Neophyti is Targum Pseudo-Jonathan. Its reference to the names of Muhammad's wife and daughter in Genesis 21:21 put its final composition sometime after the seventh century CE. This oddly designated Targum is so called in that the name "Jonathan" was attributed to it during the Middle Ages, because its name was abbreviated with a *yod*. But the letter probably stood for "Jerusalem," although that designation is also not established critically. The title "Pseudo-Jonathan" is therefore a tacit admission of uncertainty.

Both the Former and the Latter Prophets are extant in Aramaic in a single collection, although the date and character of each Targum within the collection needs to be studied individually. The entire corpus, however, is ascribed by Rabbinic tradition (Talmud Megillah 3a) to Jonathan ben Uzziel, a disciple of Hillel, the famous contemporary of Jesus. On the other hand, there are passages of the Prophets' Targum which accord precisely with renderings given in the name of Joseph bar Hiyya, a rabbi of the fourth century (see Isaiah Targum 5:17b and Talmud Pesahim 68a). As it happens, the Isaiah Targum (which has been subjected to more study than any of the Prophets' Targumim) shows signs of a nationalistic eschatology which was current just after the destruction of the Temple in 70 CE, and of the more settled perspective of the Rabbis in Babylon some three hundred years later. It appears that Targum Jonathan as a whole is the result of two major periods of collecting and editing interpretations by the Rabbis, the first period being Tannaitic, and the second, Amoraic (a term that refers to the Amoraim, "interpreters," who succeeded the Tannaim). During that long period of composition, interpretations contemporaneous with Jesus, Paul, and other contributors to the New Testament were incorporated, and scholars have identified many such cases.

New Testament scholarship has long been aware that Rabbinic literature, including the Targums, can illuminate the context and meaning of events within the New Testament. Jesus' action in the Temple is a telling example.

The location of the vendors of animals was usually on the Mount of Olives (Josephus, *Jewish War* 5.12.2, §§504–505; Yerushalmi tractate Taanit 7:4; Mishnah Sheqalim 5:3-4). An arrangement in which they were actually sited in the Great Court would have been controversial. According to the Babylonian Talmud (Abodah Zarah 8b), around 30 CE, Caiaphas indeed imposed drastic changes, "forty years prior to the destruction of the Temple the Sanhedrin went out into exile from the Temple and held its sessions in a stall." The counterpart of exiling the Sanhedrin from the Temple to *Hanuth*, the word for market stall in Aramaic, is what Mark focuses on: the introduction of trade into the Temple. Jesus is depicted as protesting the new siting of the animals, rather than the exile of the Sanhedrin, which is the concern of the Talmud.

His protest is depicted as mounted in prophetic terms (Isaiah 56:7; Jeremiah 7:11) and incorporates the symbolism of the fig (Proverbs 27:18; Babylonian Talmud Erubin 54a-b). The use of force, not an overt attack on the Temple, is precedented in Tosefta Hagigah 2:11, where a rabbi named Baba b. Buta drove animals *into* the Temple to protest high prices in Jerusalem—by offering them for free. The last chapter of the Targum Zechariah

Foreword

predicts that God's Kingdom will be manifested over the entire earth when the offerings of Sukkoth are presented both by Israelites and non-Jews at the Temple. It further predicts that these worshippers will prepare and offer their sacrifices themselves without the intervention of middlemen (Targum Zechariah 14:21). The thrust of the targumic prophecy brought on the dramatic confrontation that Jesus provoked in the Temple, and Mark preserves the recollection of the circumstances beneath the surface of the text.

Delio DelRio's *Paul and the Synagogue* extends the comparative ambit of New Testament exegesis by setting out the occasion and purpose of Paul's usage of the phrase "obedience of faith" in Romans 1:5 within the context of Targumic language and theology. The monograph does so by attending to issues of history and literature in respect of the considerable secondary discussion that the passage has generated. The Aramaic Isaiah Targum is introduced as a particularly important cultural factor, and this leads into an intertextual analysis involving the Hebrew Book of Isaiah, the Isaiah Targum, and Paul's Letter to the Romans.

To develop a framing context, the book opens with a consideration of Paul in relation to the culture of the synagogue prior to engaging in an exposition of the state of research. As Dr. DelRio observes, the dispute over whether the genitive is objective or subjective has been conducted apart from an appreciation of the Targumic context of the New Testament. He deals with that in a masterful way, proposing an augmentation of analysis guided by study of the Targumim with intertextuality. This possibility has long been latent in research, but Dr. DelRio is the first scholar to have seen its importance, and to explain how a program of reading might be developed on this basis. Intertextuality has typically been treated as if it were merely a modern possibility in reading: Dr. DelRio demonstrates that it was also an ancient practice, for which exegetes of every epoch need to adjust.

Both Hebrew Isaiah and the Targum of Isaiah develop trenchant profiles in regard to the relationship between Israel and the nations. Notably, each work articulates perspectives that vary between inclusion and particularism, to use the categories that Dr. DelRio deploys. He elucidates the issue by attending to key passages in the Masoretic Text and the Targum. He shows decisively, in agreement with the critical discussion, that the Targum's particularism is enhanced, above all at its early, Tannaitic level of development. The claim that the *"kingdoms will be obedient"* to the Messiah (Targum Isaiah 11:10, an innovative phrase, as italics here represent) is especially evocative.

Foreword

But how would Paul feature within the spectrum of inclusion and particularism? Chapter 4 takes up that question, with systematic reference to the passages that emerged in the treatment of Isaiah (in both Hebrew and Aramaic). The echo of Targum Isaiah 11:10 in Romans 1:5 is shown to be a governing concern of Romans as a whole by DelRio's skillful deployment of categories of *Hellenistic* rhetoric. His ability to correlate Hellenistic and Judaic categories marks an unusual level of maturity and acumen. Chapter 5 expands his finding into a treatment of "Intertextual Dialogue" in which Paul is shown, in effect, to behave as a *meturgeman* of Isaiah, in a direction that sometimes departs from that of the Targum and sometimes coheres with it. This chapter is outstanding in its mastery of the thematic issues by means of specific texts. The focal issue of obedience is brought home to any serious reader of Romans, and of the Pauline corpus as a whole.

The conclusion finds that the genitive of the phrase, "obedience of faith," is to be taken as epexegetical. Further, Dr. DelRio suggests a supplementation of the theme of "consolation" to the characteristic *theologoumena* of the Isaiah Targum identified in previous research. The place of intertextual analysis, suitably contexted, is the final suggestion, which offers to bridge the rift between historical and literary approaches that has long plagued recent discussion of the New Testament.

In aggregate, this monograph is not only a satisfying and complete discussion of its topic, but an original contribution to learning. Dr. DelRio has crafted a genuine thesis, and at the highest level of acumen. Its prose, logic, and presentation contribute cogently to the understanding of Paul, and to the methods by which the New Testament might be related to its Aramaic and Targumic environments.

Bruce D. Chilton

Acknowledgments

THE ACCOMPLISHMENT OF THIS monograph would not have been possible without the support of so many. I would like to thank the faculty of New Orleans Baptist Theological Seminary for their Christlike guidance throughout my educational career. I would like especially to thank my doctoral committee, Dr. Charlie Ray, Dr. Bruce D. Chilton, and Dr. Gerald L. Stevens. Thanks to Dr. Ray for introducing me to the field of intertextual studies and exposing me to the possibilities for further biblical understanding. Thanks to Dr. Chilton for graciously accepting me as a doctoral student and offering me access to his expertise in Targum literature through many enriching dialogues. Special thanks also to Dr. Stevens for his tireless efforts, continuous availability, and inspiring academic excellence. Dr. Stevens has passed on to me a love for the text; and as he promised, I have found that the text has indeed loved me back.

I would like also to thank my church families at Mt. Zion Baptist Church and First Baptist Church of Lutz. Both congregations supported me prayerfully as well as financially throughout my educational endeavor. I learned much about Christian love from many of you, and I am indebted to you for your friendship and support.

Finally, I would like to thank my family. To my children, Michael, Cayden, and Savannah, thank you for your inspiration and love through this entire experience. To my wife, Kimberly, thank you for your many sacrifices, constant partnership, and encouraging support over the years. You have been more than I deserve.

Introduction

IN THE OPENING ADDRESS of Romans, Paul described the purpose of his apostolic call to the gospel as "for the obedience of faith among all the Gentiles" (Rom 1:5).[1] The significance of Paul's programmatic statement concerning his apostolic call to the argument in Romans has been recognized within Pauline scholarship. Given the significance of Paul's programmatic statement concerning the Gentiles to the letter of Romans, one is not surprised by the amount of scholarly attention concerning the meaning and rhetorical function of the phrase ὑπακοὴν πίστεως ("obedience of faith") in Rom 1:5. The scholarly discussion has led to a number of suggested meanings but with no significant consensus to date.

What makes this debate even more intriguing is the uniqueness of the phrase, which is found only in Rom 1:5 and 16:26 within the whole of ancient literature. The uniqueness of the phrase justifiably has led some scholars to describe the phrase coined by Paul.[2] The question remains: What was the genesis for Paul's coinage of the phrase in Romans?

Though scholars have investigated a variety of contextual avenues for the genesis of Paul's use of the phrase, one specific context has remained largely unexplored, namely the first-century synagogue. A number of observations supporting a contextual relationship between Paul and the first-century synagogue suggest that an investigation of the context is justified. For example, Paul's pre-conversion Pharisaic background, his post-conversion programmatic ministry pattern of starting with the synagogue upon his arrival in cities, and his ministry strategy as expressed in Romans with his emphasis upon the "Jew first" all suggest that the synagogue context

---

1. Translations and italics of biblical texts are the writer's own unless otherwise stated. All biblical Hebrew texts are from *Biblia Hebraica Stuttgartensia*. All biblical Greek texts are from *Novum Testamentum Graece*. All Septuagint (LXX) texts are from *Septuaginta*.

2. Garlington, *Obedience of Faith*, 4. Jewett, *Romans*, 110.

Introduction

both influenced and remained significant for Paul.[3] The specific research question presented here is, What is Paul's hermeneutic of ὑπακοὴν πίστεως in the context of the first-century synagogue traditions?[4]

Discovering the meaning of the phrase ὑπακοὴν πίστεως in a synagogue context will require consideration of two subproblems. The first subproblem is rhetorical and concerns the literary relationship of the *peroratio* (summation) and the Isaiah citation in the *probatio* (proof) and their mutual relationship to ὑπακοὴν πίστεως in the *exordium* (introduction).[5] What impact do the *peroratio* and the Isaiah citation in the *probatio* have upon the meaning of the phrase ὑπακοὴν πίστεως in Rom 1:5? Concerning the literary context of Romans, the phrase occurs within the *exordium* of the rhetorical structure of the letter. The close rhetorical relationship between the *exordium* and the *peroratio* and the close literary proximity of scriptural catena, which includes the citation of Isa 11:10 in Rom 15:12 at the end of the *probatio*, also warrants close consideration. Furthermore, Paul's rhetorical use of Isaiah in Romans must also be considered in order to understand fully the impact of the Isaiah citation in the *probatio*.

The second sub-problem concerns the historical context of the first-century Christian and Jewish discussions concerning the inclusion of the Gentiles into each respective covenant community. What impact does the larger first-century discussion concerning the inclusion of the Gentiles

---

3. In reference to Paul's Pharisaic background, see Acts 23:6; 26:5; and Phil 3:5. In reference to Paul's programmatic ministry pattern, see Acts 13:14; 14:1; 17:2, 17; 18:4; and 19:8. In reference to Paul's expressed ministry strategy, see Rom 1:16 and 2:9–10. For general discussion of Paul and his Jewish background, see Watson, *Paul*, 1–6; and Witherington III, *Paul Quest*, 53–56. For discussion of Paul's pre-conversion synagogue involvement and later programmatic ministry pattern, see Jewett, *Romans*, 56, 74–75.

4. Hermeneutic usually is defined in biblical studies as the science of interpretation. In keeping with this established definition, here the term refers to Paul's definition of the phrase ὑπακοὴν πίστεως. For further discussion of the term *hermeneutic* in reference to biblical studies, see Schodde, "Interpretation," 1489–90; and Klein et al., *Introduction*, 5–6.

5. The identification of the rhetorical structure of Romans has been debated in Pauline scholarship. For example, Wuellner, "Paul's Rhetoric," 133–46, identified the *exordium* as Rom 1:1–15, and Rom 1:16–17 as the *transitus*. Johann D. Kim, *God*, 62–64, identified the *exordium* as comprising of Rom 1:1–13 and v. 15 and connected Rom 1:14 with a new section that continues in Rom 1:16 through v. 21. He argued that v. 15 was a "parenthetical digression." The rhetorical structure of Romans argued by Jewett will be accepted for this research: the *exordium* (1:1–12); the *narratio* (1:13–15); the *propositio* (1:16–17); the *probatio* (1:18—15:13); and the *peroratio* (15:14—16:16 + 16:21–23). Jewett, *Romans*, 29–30.

have upon the meaning of the phrase ὑπακοὴν πίστεως in Rom 1:5? Given the connection between Paul's phrase ὑπακοὴν πίστεως and his description of obedience as "among all the Gentiles," the Gentile debate within first-century Christianity and Judaism is significant for understanding the meaning and rhetorical function of the phrase in Romans. Ancient Jewish and Christian literature attests to the various streams of particularism and inclusivism within the ongoing discussion concerning the relationship between Jews and Gentiles.[6] The historical context of the particularistic and inclusivistic discussion in which Paul coined the phrase also must be considered in order to delimit the likely range of meaning of the phrase ὑπακοὴν πίστεως in Rom 1:5.

Considering the contextual relationship between Paul and the first-century synagogue, targumic literature is of central importance to the investigation of the various particularistic and inclusivistic streams within the synagogue setting. As Aramaic paraphrases of the Jewish Scriptures used within the synagogue, the Targums present in part the Jewish exegetical traditions of the Scriptures current during the time of the writing of Romans.[7] As was noted earlier, Paul's prominent rhetorical use of Isaiah in Romans suggests that Paul's reading of Isaiah may figure prominently into his argument concerning the "obedience of faith among all the Gentiles." Therefore, understanding the relationship of Romans and the Isaiah Targum to the various first-century particularistic and inclusivistic streams would aid in establishing the meaning of the phrase ὑπακοὴν πίστεως in Rom 1:5 within its historical context.

---

6. Inclusivism is defined as the elevation of the Gentile nations to the status of Israel as co-partakers of the blessings once promised to Israel. Particularism is defined as the prominence of Israel over all other nations as sole beneficiary of God's blessings. The definitions for *inclusivism* and *particularism* offered here are adopted from the definitions offered by Aschalew Kebede for *universalism* and *nationalism*. His terms are reflected commonly in Isaian scholarship in reference to the various streams of tradition concerning the conversion of the Gentiles in Isaiah. The terms *inclusivism* and *particularism* are used in this research for the purpose of clarity for the benefit of a wider audience beyond that of Isaian scholarship. Kebede, *How Can the Concepts*, 4.

7. As targumic scholars often have noted, the Targums are one of the best windows into the historical world of exegetical traditions of the Jewish synagogue during the Tannaitic period. For discussion of the direct role that the synagogue played in the development and use of the Targumim, see Le Déaut, *Message*, 37–40; McNamara, *Targum and Testament*, 64–84; Bowker, *Targums and Rabbinic Literature*, 8–9; Chilton, *Judaic Approaches*, 308; Smolar and Aberbach, *Studies in Targum*, 61; and Stenger, "Rebuke Tradition," 51–52. For further discussion of the connection between the Targums and Jewish schools, see York, "Targum in the Synagogue," 74–86.

Introduction

The purpose of this research is to determine the meaning of the phrase ὑπακοὴν πίστεως in Rom 1:5 by examining the literary context of the phrase in Romans and the historical context of the phrase within the first-century Jewish milieu with a specific focus on the Isaiah Targum. The thesis is that a literary analysis of the context of Isaiah, the Isaiah Targum, and Romans will provide a sufficient basis for understanding the probable meaning of ὑπακοὴν πίστεως in Rom 1:5.

An analysis of the intertextual relationship between Isaiah, the Isaiah Targum, and Romans will clarify that Paul's coinage of ὑπακοὴν πίστεως was motivated by a first-century discussion concerning the Jewish Scriptures in relation to the Gentile debate.[8] The phrase ὑπακοὴν πίστεως in Rom 1:5 functions rhetorically as a polemic against a Jewish particularism, which includes a forced submission of the Gentiles as evidenced in the Isaiah Targum. The hypothesis is that the Pauline hermeneutic of ὑπακοὴν πίστεως is the articulation of the position of inclusivism in response to the targumic tradition of particularism concerning the nature of the conversion of the Gentiles.

Although the phrase ὑπακοὴν πίστεως also occurs in the doxology of Rom 16:26, the context of the doxology will not be included in the consideration of the meaning of the phrase in Romans. Though the authenticity of the doxology in Rom 16:25–27 has long been debated, a scholarly consensus for non-Pauline interpolation has developed.[9] The researcher deems this doxology to be a non-Pauline interpolation and

---

8. The state, and even acceptance, of the Scriptures in the first century can be described as one of pluriformity. The state of research concerning the textual sources for scriptural citations in the New Testament (NT) has demonstrated that multiple literary editions, revisions, and translations were accepted and cited as "Scripture" both within the NT and in extrabiblical Jewish literature as well. This view of the Scriptures in the first century also is accepted here as the referent for the Jewish Scriptures. For more detailed discussion on the debate concerning the nature of the Jewish Scriptures during the first century, and as understood by the NT writers, see McNamara, *Palestinian Judaism*; Evans, "Old Testament," 579–90; Campenhausen, *Formation*; Longenecker, *Biblical Exegesis*, 6–14; McLay, "Biblical Texts," 38–58; and Watson, *Paul*, 78–126.

9. For discussion of the historical development and the textual witness concerning the interpolation of Rom 16:25–27, see Gamble, *Textual History*, 108–26; Dunn, *Romans*, 2:912–17; Walker, *Interpolations*, 190–99; and Jewett, *Romans*, 997–1011. For arguments in favor of the Pauline authenticity of Rom 16:25–27, see Moo, *Epistle to the Romans*, 937–41; and Schreiner, *Romans*, 810–18.

Introduction

therefore will not be considered in determining the Pauline hermeneutic of ὑπακοὴν πίστεως in Romans.[10]

---

10. Though scholarly consensus that the doxology is an interpolation has formed, a consensus concerning the historical development and purpose of the interpolation is lacking. The doxology contains parallels with authentic Pauline vocabulary in Romans, but some scholars have argued that the rhetorical use of the vocabulary within the doxology differs from the parallel vocabulary in Romans. For example, Walker argued that the phrase ἀποκάλυψιν μυστηρίου in Rom 16:25 reflects a revelation scheme that appears only in pseudo-Pauline or other post-Pauline texts (*Interpolations*, 197). Likewise, Brendan Byrne further suggested that the use of μυστηρίου in Rom 16:25 differs from the use of μυστηρίου in Rom 11:25. Byrne, *Romans*. Jewett pointed to the change of preposition from ἐν πᾶσιν τοῖς ἔθεσιν in Rom 1:5 to εἰς πάντα τὰ ἔθνη in Rom 16:26 as another significant difference (*Romans*, 1006–9). Although Dunn likewise concluded that the doxology is an interpolation, he saw continuity between the doxology and Romans. He stated that the doxology "has summarized well the basic concerns of the letter" (*Romans*, 2:917). Whether the doxology is seen as a summary of or at odds with the letter of Romans, in either case as an interpolation the text is not helpful or at best subsidiary to this research.

1

Romans, Targums, and Intertextuality

The Phrase Ὑπακοὴν πίστεως in Romans

The phrase ὑπακοὴν πίστεως has been understood variously within modern New Testament (NT) scholarship. Much of the debate centers on the relationship of the genitive to the substantive. Charles E. B. Cranfield is one among many who has suggested three major interpretational possibilities for the genitive: subjective, objective, and apposition or definition. After examining seven ways to translate the phrase, Cranfield argued for the genitive of apposition or description based on the structure of Paul's thought in Romans. He further stated that true obedience for Paul is a response to the gospel message. He gave a number of examples supporting an epexegetical usage of the genitive, including a comparison between Rom 1:8 and 16:19, as well as between 10:16a and 16b.[1] Like Cranfield, Ernst Käsemann also argued for a genitive construction that is "explicative." Taking the same example as Cranfield of Rom 10:16, he described faith as obedience to the gospel. Käsemann further suggested that faith and obedience are interchangeable terms. He saw the phrase as not only ethical but also eschatological.[2]

For Dunn, explaining the importance of faith to the gospel was one of Paul's "chief objectives" in the letter, and therefore his use of the Greek word ὑπακοὴν in connection with his description of faith is significant. Paul's use

---

1. Cranfield, *Critical and Exegetical Commentary*, 1:66. Others also have concluded that these three are the major possibilities. Michel, *Brief*, 33. Dunn, *Romans*, 1:17. Jewett, *Romans*, 110. Fitzmyer further suggested genitive of source as a possibility, though he argued for an epexegetical usage (*Romans*, 237–38).

2. Käsemann, *Commentary on Romans*, 14–15.

of ὑπακοὴν suggests a parallel with the Septuagint (LXX) usage of ὑπακοὴν for שמע and in connection with "faith" suggests a "response to faith." In support of this understanding of ὑπακοὴν πίστεως, he noted the overlap in meaning with ἀκοῆς πίστεως in Gal 3:2, 5. Dunn opted for both subjective and appositional usages of the genitive and described the two senses of the genitives as "interchangeable."[3] Douglas Moo also accepted both subjective and appositional senses of the genitive as intended by Paul. He concluded that interpreting the genitive as simply subjective without any sense of appositional use or vice versa is too limiting on Paul's intent. He explained the meaning of ὑπακοὴν πίστεως as a submission to Christ as Lord that includes both a conversion and continuing commitment.[4]

Although both a subjective relationship and an appositional relationship between "obedience" and "faith" are present within the Pauline corpus, the two relational constructions have very different, though not antithetical, meanings. Stretching the genitive construction in Rom 1:5 to include both senses would seem to stretch the intended meaning too broadly for rhetorical purposes. Dunn's conclusion that the two senses are "interchangeable" is an oversimplification. While Dunn's conclusion concerning the use of the genitive may be oversimplified, his connection between ὑπακοὴν πίστεως and Paul's "chief objective" to explain the gospel is an important observation. The question he neglected to explore fully was how does the phrase rhetorically function as an explanation of the gospel? Although the discussions by Cranfield, Käsemann, Dunn, and Moo offered considerable insight and helped to clarify the viable options of meaning, a fuller understanding of ὑπακοὴν πίστεως requires more historical consideration.

Don Garlington offered an extensive treatment of the concept of ὑπακοὴν πίστεως in Romans by examining the phrase within Paul's larger historical context. Although he acknowledged that ὑπακοὴν πίστεως could be understood as an ethical principle within the Pauline literature, he also proposed that the immediate context suggests a more specific concern. Like Dunn, Garlington emphasized Paul's core concern in Romans as the explanation of his gospel and further emphasized Paul's explanation of the gospel as "for all the nations." In an effort to establish the historical context for Paul's phrase, Garlington explored the relationship between the concepts of obedience and faith in the Apocrypha and

---

3. Dunn, *Romans*, 1:17.
4. Moo, *Epistle to the Romans*, 51–52.

selected parallel sources. He concluded that the two concepts were closely related in the Second Temple period and described faith's obedience as "one's commitment to the whole Mosaic covenant and its laws."[5] Garlington argued that Paul's gospel was in opposition to this definition of faith's obedience and his rhetorical use of ὑπακοὴν πίστεως was a polemic against his contemporaries who disagreed with his gospel.

Robert Jewett rejected Garlington's view that the phrase ὑπακοὴν πίστεως was polemic. He argued that the phrase was coined for the purpose of creating unity between Jews and Gentiles. "The coordination of these two terms conveys an interest in finding common ground. There is no hint of polemic in the wording of 1:5 or its rhetorical echo of 15:18."[6] Although Jewett's conviction that the phrase was coined to fit the "rhetorical exigency" of the letter is well placed, his exclusion of a polemical purpose for the phrase based on the overall rhetorical purpose of unity in the letter is an overextrapolation. Paul's overall rhetorical goal in the letter to create unity among the Roman house and tenement churches does not necessarily exclude the use of polemical rhetoric as a part of the overall goal.

For Thomas Schreiner, the two most likely options are the subjective and appositional genitive constructions. He wrote, "In the former case the sense would be the obedience that springs from or flows from faith. In the later instance the phrase could have been translated as 'the obedience that is faith.'" He concluded that both senses were most likely intended and then followed with a discussion about the relationship between obedience and faith. After referencing the phrase "obedience of the Gentiles" in Rom 15:18, he discussed the close connection of obedience to faith as a description of a changed life. He rejected Garlington's position that the phrase is polemical and Jewett's argument that Paul coined the phrase to emphasize unity between Jews and Gentiles.[7] Although Schriener rejected the argument for a polemic in the coinage of ὑπακοὴν πίστεως, he offered no supporting argument for his rejection.

The scholarly discussion has developed along two lines of argument toward determining the meaning of ὑπακοὴν πίστεως, one literary and the

---

5. Garlington understood the polemic within the parameters of the "new perspective" on Paul, which is consistent with the conclusions of Sanders and Dunn concerning the relationship between "covenantal nomism" and Paul. He stated that Paul's dispute with Israel over the Law was not a reflection of legalism versus grace but ethnically inclusive restrictions (*Obedience of Faith*, 3, 254, 265).

6. Jewett, *Romans*, 110–11.

7. Schreiner, *Romans*, 35.

other historical. Both of these considerations have proven to be necessary and fruitful. Although Garlington and Jewett disagreed on the rhetorical function of the phrase, they correctly drove the conversation toward the consideration of a rhetorical purpose of the coinage of the phrase. Garlington emphasized the historical backdrop of the two terms and concluded that the rhetorical function was polemical. Jewett emphasized the rhetorical purpose of the letter and concluded that the rhetorical function was devoid of a polemic and was rather for the purpose of uniting two streams of thought.

Although both Garlington's historical emphasis and Jewett's literary emphasis are necessary, neither was explored fully. Jewett's analysis falls short of considering the full impact that the rhetorical structure of the letter may have on explaining the meaning and rhetorical function of the phrase. Given Jewett's recognition of the close connection between the exordium and the peroratio, the absence of consideration of the context in the peroratio and the implications for determining the meaning of the phrase in Rom 1:5 is puzzling. Paul closed the probatio with a catena from the Jewish Scriptures in Rom 15:9–12 and, as Jewett acknowledged, restated his world mission in the peroratio "with language strongly reminiscent of Rom 1:1–7."[8] Would a greater emphasis upon the rhetorical structure of the letter, namely an exploration of the catena and the peroratio, aid in the debate concerning Paul's hermeneutic of ὑπακοὴν πίστεως?

Garlington's conclusion concerning the polemic nature of the phrase fits well with the historical background he developed with his analysis, but his data pool is limited. The close literary proximity of the catena in Rom 15:9–12 to the peroratio would suggest that the Jewish Scriptures cited by Paul should be included within a historical exploration. Would a broader data pool confirm his conclusion of a polemic function and perhaps result in the discovery of a more direct influence on Paul's coinage of ὑπακοὴν πίστεως?

Johann D. Kim elucidated the significance of the relationship between the exordium and the peroratio within the rhetorical structure of the letter in his treatment of Rom 9–11. In an effort to establish the rhetorical situation of the letter, he first established the importance of the rhetorical framework with a special focus upon the exordium and the peroratio. He identified Rom 1:1–13, 15 as the exordium and Rom 15:14—16:27 as the peroratio. Based on the norms of classical rhetoric as explained by Quintilian, Cicero, and Aristotle, Kim proposed that as parts of a speech the

---

8. Jewett, *Romans*, 97, 108.

exordium and the peroratio are closely related. Subjects simply outlined in the exordium are given fuller treatment in the peroratio. "The ancient audience who was familiar with rhetorical practices would naturally expect the rhetor to come back to the matters the rhetor introduced briefly in the exordium." Kim argued that Romans is a good example of the practice of reiteration and expansion of the themes of the exordium in the peroratio. His analysis identified fifteen thematic and vocabulary parallels between the exordium and the peroratio of Romans.[9]

Daniel Chae in his work on Paul's apostolic self-awareness also argued for a close connection between the personal and thematic introduction in Rom 1:1–17 and the personal and thematic conclusion in Rom 15:7–21. He argued that a close thematic coherence exists between Rom 1:16–17 and Rom 15:7–13. He identified the main theme as "the inclusion of the Gentiles in God's salvation." For Chae, the central theme of Romans is ἔθνος, and Rom 15:14–21 is the interpretive key. Even more specifically, he suggested that the concept "obedience of the faith" is central to the theme of Romans. Based on Paul's reference to the "Holy Scriptures" in the exordium in Rom 1:2 and the significant position of the catena of Rom 15:9–12 as the closing summary of the probatio, Chae argued that Paul's use of Scripture was a crucial interpretative key to his argument in Romans.[10]

Chae has not been alone in arguing for the significance of Paul's use of Scripture in the rhetoric of Romans.[11] The rhetorical and thematic coherence between the exordium and the peroratio would suggest that the catena in Rom 15:9–12 may be key in the discussion concerning the meaning and rhetorical function of ὑπακοὴν πίστεως. In commenting on the catena's purpose in Romans, Dunn stated that Paul used the quotations not only to elaborate the theme of Rom 15:8–9a, but also to broaden the whole discussion from the particular issue in Rom 14:1—15:6 to the overall theme of the letter.[12] As others have noted, Paul cited each of the three divisions of the

---

9. Kim, *God*, 58–89. For further discussion of the structure of classical speech rhetoric and its application to Romans, see Jewett, *Romans*, 29–30; idem, "Following the Argument of Romans," 265–77; Aune, "Romans as a Logos," 278–96; and Wuellner, "Paul's Rhetoric," 128–46.

10. Chae, *Paul as Apostle*, 13, 20–21, 39, 58–59.

11. For further discussion concerning Paul's rhetorical use of Scripture, see Hays, *Echoes*; Mack, *Rhetoric*; Evans and Sanders, eds., *Paul and the Scriptures*; and Stanley, *Arguing*.

12. Dunn, *Romans*, 2:848.

Paul and the Synagogue

Jewish scriptures and closed the catena with a quotation of Isa 11:10.[13] Even if Garlington is correct in concluding that the phrase ὑπακοὴν πίστεως demonstrates a polemic within Paul's historical background, an expansion of the data pool to include the specific Scriptural references in the catena may prove insightful.

Of the scriptural citations in Romans, the book of Isaiah is represented prominently. Nearly 30 percent of Paul's scriptural references in Romans come from Isaiah alone.[14] As Shiu-Lun Shum pointed out, of all the Jewish Scriptures, the text of Isaiah is significant in Paul's thinking.[15] When Paul's choice to close the probatio with a quote from Isaiah is considered alongside the observation of his prominent use of Isaiah throughout Romans, an intertextual exploration of Isaiah and Romans seems warranted in the effort to establish Paul's hermeneutic of ὑπακοὴν πίστεως.

Although some consideration has been given to the impact of Isaiah upon Paul's argument in Romans, a more specific exploration of the possible impact of the Isaiah text upon the phrase ὑπακοὴν πίστεως is lacking. Furthermore, when conducting an intertextual analysis of Romans, the majority of scholars have tended to focus on the Septuagint and Hebrew texts to the exclusion of the Targums.[16] More recently a call for including the Targums in consideration of the intertextual relationship of the Jewish Scriptures and the NT has been championed by several NT scholars.[17] Would an inclusion of the Isaiah Targum in expansion beyond Garlington's data pool yield any more specific conclusions regarding Paul's hermeneutic of ὑπακοὴν πίστεως?

---

13. Paul cited Deut 32:43 from the Law, Pss 18:49 and 117:1 from the Writings, and Isa 11:10 from the Prophets. Recent scholars to note the significance of Paul's citation from the three divisions of the Jewish Scriptures include Hays, *Echoes*, 70–71; Käsemann, *Commentary on Romans*, 386; Stuhlmacher, *Paul's Letter*, 232; Moo, *Epistle to the Romans*, 878; and Jewett, *Romans*, 893.

14. The ratio concerning the occurrences of Isaiah in Romans is based on the index of quotations in Aland, et al., eds., *Greek New Testament*, 889. See also Longenecker, *Biblical Exegesis*, 92–93.

15. Shum, *Paul's Use*, 2.

16. Generally speaking, when the Targums are included in the discussion, many scholars tend to consider them as post-New Testament witnesses to possible variant readings. This conclusion has led to a premature dismissal of the Targums for consideration. For example, see Longenecker, *Biblical Exegesis*, 92–116.

17. Stevens, "Literary Background," 152–53; Chilton, *Galilean Rabbi*; Evans, "Aramaic Psalter," 44–91; Shepherd, "Targums," 43–58.

In summary, the meaning of the phrase ὑπακοὴν πίστεως is disputed among scholars. Chief among the issues involved is the syntactical force of the genitive. Although various meanings have been suggested, the most commonly argued meanings have been the subjective and appositional genitives. Two prominent aspects in reference to the phrase have arisen in the conversation, namely the literary context and the historical context. The rhetorical structure of Romans with a specific focus upon the exordium and peroratio must be analyzed when considering the literary context of the meaning of the phrase in Rom 1:5. Furthermore, the historical context in which Paul coined the phrase also must be considered. At least one lacuna that remains at this point in the scholarly conversation is a broader analysis of the intertextual relationship between Romans and Isaiah with a focus upon the possible connection the catena of Rom 15:9–12 might have with Paul's coinage of the phrase. With the close relationship between the exordium and the peroratio and the close literary proximity of the catena at the close of the probatio, addressing this lacuna is warranted.

The Targumic Context of the New Testament

Interest in the Targums and their relationship to the NT was rekindled in the mid-twentieth century as a result of the impact of three major events: the publication of the Cairo Geniza fragments by Paul Kahle, the discovery of the Qumran Targums, and the identification of a particular Targum manuscript (ms), *Tg. Neof.*, in the Vatican Library by Diez Macho.[18] In the wake of these events, work began concerning the possible relationship between the Targums and the NT and was conducted with great enthusiasm. The rise of the Palestinian Targum (PT) within the discussion and its comparison to the NT led to a number of developments. The ensuing scholarly conversation included a number of issues from the date and development of the Targums to their level of influence upon the NT. Over the course of the scholarly conversation, the pendulum of consensus concerning these issues has swung fully in opposite directions. Decades later, scholarly consensus seems to have settled on an open yet cautious approach to the study of the Targums and the NT, which is due mostly to a more precise understanding of the Targums as a whole.

18. For a more detailed discussion of these discoveries and other aspects of the state of research in the mid-twentieth century, see McNamara, *New Testament and the Palestinian*, 22–33.

Scholarly discussion of the Targums and their relationship to the NT may be described as having resulted in two major observations, and these observations have left NT scholarship with a pressing need for a methodology. The first observation can be described as a literary perspective. As McNamara and many others have observed, the Targums and NT do contain enough similarities to indicate some level of relationship.[19] The second observation can be described as a historical perspective. As Bruce D. Chilton, Robert Hayward, and others have observed, the extant Targums are the product of a "phasal development" which began in the Tannaitic period (70–200 CE) and continued through the Amoraic period (200–600 CE).[20]

Over against the earlier work of Gustav Dalman, Kahle argued, based mostly on his understanding of the development of the Aramaic, that the PT is older than the Babylonian Targums (BT). He further stated that some passages in the Targums go back to ancient or pre-Christian times, as attested in the Cairo Geniza fragments.[21] Kahle influenced the discussion to such an extent that the antiquity of the PT over the BT was widely accepted and can be seen in the work of what often is referred to as the "Kahle School."[22] Another of Kahle's arguments that was accepted widely was that anti-mishnaic material must be pre-mishnaic material.[23] These arguments led to a pre-Christian dating of the origin of the PT, which in turn led to a new exploration of the possible relationship between the PT and the NT.[24]

McNamara was among the first scholars to offer a broad study of the relationship between the Targums and the NT, and he took two major approaches. First, he approached the study by examining similarities in

---

19. For examples of similarities, see ibid.; and Chilton, "From Aramaic Paraphrase," 23–43.

20. Chilton described the Targum's development as a "phasal development" in *Judaic Approaches*, 255. For other examples of discussion and application of this phasal development in relation to the Targums, see Chilton, *Glory*; Hayward, *Targum of Jeremiah*; and Chilton, *The Isaiah Targum*.

21. For discussion of Dalman's view of the language of *Onkelos* by Paul Kahle, as well as his view of the date of the PT, see *Cairo Geniza*, 119, 129–31.

22. For example, the impact of Kahle's work can be seen in Black, *Aramaic*; McNamara, *New Testament and the Palestinian*; and Bowker, *Targums and Rabbinic*.

23. For discussion of this exegetical principle, see Kahle, *Cairo Geniza*, 122–23; and McNamara, *New Testament and the Palestinian*, 257.

24. The Kahle school has been accused of going too far in asserting the existence of an official PT against a multiplicity of Palestinian Targum texts, but Kahle himself did recognize that the PT was not an authorized version and further stated that the PT "had no fixed text" (Kahle, *Cairo Geniza*, 125).

which the NT referenced the Jewish Scriptures. His research resulted in the observations of shared vocabulary between the NT and PT, at times even against the Hebrew and LXX texts. For example, he discussed the similar exegesis of Deut 30:11–14 by Paul in Rom 10:6–8 and *Tg. Neof.* Second, he approached the study by examining shared themes and vocabulary between the Targums and NT. For example, he argued that the names Jannes and Jambres in 2 Tim 3:8 are matched in *Tg. Ps.-J. Exod* 7:11, and the divine name in Rev 1:4, 8, 4:8, 11:17, and 16:5 is matched in *Tg. Ps.-J. Exod* 3:14. He also pointed out that the statement in Matt 5:48 is paralleled in *Tg. Ps.-J. Lev* 22:28, and the traditions of Isaac in the PT are reflected in the phrase "Lamb of God" in the NT.[25] McNamara further analyzed the relationship between the NT and Targums by examining both in light of various subjects. For example, he pointed out similarities both through parallels in vocabulary related to the sin of Adam and through eschatology regarding phrases such as "the day of great judgment."[26]

Le Déaut also offered a number of similarities as an illustration of the importance of the study of targumic traditions to NT study. His examples included a reference to *Tg. Ps.* 68:18 in Eph 4:8 and similar vocabulary of Mark 3:22 and *Tg. Neof. Deut* 13:1.[27] Even more recently, Craig A. Evans offered a treatment of the Aramaic Psalter and possible parallels to the NT. His approach also focused on similar vocabulary and themes. For example, he pointed to Paul's use of the phrase "first Adam" as paralleled in the five uses of the phrase in *Tg. Ps.*, which, as he noted, is distinctly targumic.[28]

Even from this brief survey one can see that the possible parallels are plentiful. Present scholarship is indebted to the efforts of McNamara, Le Déaut, Evans, and others for bringing to the surface these numerous

---

25. McNamara, *New Testament and the Palestinian*, 70–164.

26. McNamara, *Targum and Testament*, 120–41. McNamara recently has published a revised edition of *Targum and Testament* under the title *Targum and Testament Revisited*. While much of the content remains the same, McNamara's second edition does include discussion of the considerable advancements made in the field of Targum research. In his more recent work, McNamara maintained his principle objective and his basic argument concerning the viability of the Palestinian Targums for NT research despite the growing doubt in modern scholarship of a so-called Palestinian Targum. The similarities between the NT and the Targums discussed in the first edition are repeated in the second edition. For his discussion of the similarities, see McNamara, *Targum and Testament Revisited*, 139–252. In conclusion, McNamara made no significant advancements or changes to his basic premise concerning the relationship between NT and the Palestinian Targums.

27. Le Déaut, *Message*, 28–48.

28. Evans, "The Aramaic Psalter," 90.

parallels. Consensus has continued to hold that the similarities indicate some level of relationship. Often missing from many of these treatments are any significant analysis and conclusion regarding the nature of the relationship that these parallels may suggest. For example, Evans's observation of the parallel between "first Adam" in Paul and the distinctly targumic uses is intriguing, but nothing of the possible relationship or impact of the targumic use upon the NT has been determined.

Although some scholars have attempted to extrapolate the nature of the relationship, they most often based their conclusions on similarity alone. For example, in his discussion of the phrase "second death," McNamara pointed out a number of interesting parallels between Rev 20:14 and *Tg. Isa.* 65:15, and then concluded that the Targum passages contain "the presence of pre-Christian paraphrases which have influenced the thought and terminology of the Apocalypse."[29] Recognizing the parallel is only the first step and is inadequate for drawing any significant conclusions concerning the nature of the relationship. Should one conclude direct contact between the Targum and Revelation in this last example based solely on a parallel phrase? How much of the material within the context of the Targum text pre-dates the NT? Furthermore, how can one then conclude the direction of influence based on a recognized parallel alone? Indeed, the drawing of conclusions concerning the date of the Targum or the level of relationship to the NT simply from recognized parallels or similarities triggered much of the criticism toward the latter part of the twentieth century.

Some scholars later criticized earlier efforts to date the Targums as a whole by means of the similarities as flawed due to the historical perspective regarding the date and development of the Targums. In the latter part of the twentieth century, criticism began to emerge against the conclusions that were drawn concerning the preeminence of the PT as the oldest Targum and the implications of its relationship to the NT. With the work of Anthony York, Lester Grabbe, Stephen Kauffman, Bruce D. Chilton, and others, the pendulum has swung back toward a deeper appreciation of the antiquity of the BT and its significance for NT studies. As a result, a more nuanced view of the Targums as a whole has developed among scholars.

Anthony York challenged Kahle's view of the pre-NT date of the PT as flawed due to its underlying argument that anti-mishnaic equals pre-mishnaic. He further critiqued Diez Macho's nine reasons for the greater antiquity of the PT and argued that a methodology must include a way

---

29. McNamara, *New Testament and the Palestinian*, 124.

to distinguish between sources and oral traditions that may precede the sources. York's basic argument was built on an observation admitted by Kahle, McNamara, and others, namely that the extant Targums contain a significant amount of later material, not to mention of course the manuscripts themselves all post-date the NT. York acknowledged the literary similarities of the Targums and NT pointed out by others but stated that the principle "similarities prove borrowing" is uncertain at best. He concluded that a methodology for establishing the text of the extant Targum as that which corresponds to the text of the NT times still was needed.[30]

Kaufman also brought the lack of consensus concerning a methodological approach to Targum studies to the attention of the scholarly community. His thesis was that certain aspects of the methodological approaches within targumic studies, especially concerning chronology, must be agreed upon in order to move forward as a field of research. He argued that some of the conclusions of scholars desiring to identify parallels between the NT and the Targums were faulty due to a circular methodology. He suggested the acceptance of the philosophical basis that the PT contains material from the "pre-Tannaitic, Tannaitic, and post-Tannaitic periods, thus the antiquity of any given midrashic element can only be determined by reference to other literature."[31]

Kaufman's objection to the lack of consensus concerning methodology within targumic studies was pertinent to the targumic field. A simple survey of the published material concerning the Targums illustrates the many different conclusions concerning the chronology of the Palestinian and Babylonian Targums. The acceptance of the "pre-Tannaitic, Tannaitic, and post-Tannaitic" nature of the material in the Targums as a basis within the research field demanded more specific methodological approaches. Because of such criticism, a more reserved position was taken concerning the possible implications of similarities, and this reserved position limited the direct application of the Targums as a whole to the NT era.

Bruce D. Chilton has offered a methodological solution to the challenge that had arisen in the field. He argued that any study of the relationship between the NT and the Targums must take into account the interpretative framework of the Targum being studied. Through his study of the theology and provenience of the Isaiah Targum, he elaborated a phasal understanding to the development. Chilton attempted to reconstruct the exegetical

---

30. York, "Dating," 49–62.
31. Kaufman, "On Methodology," 117–24.

framework of the Isaiah Targum through a methodology containing two specific steps. The first step was to describe the theology of the Isaiah Targum by analyzing characteristic terms and phrases within its exegetical framework. The second step was to compare the exegetical framework to intertestamental literature, LXX, Rabbinic, and NT literature in order to fix the historical context of the exegetical framework. As a result of his attempt to reconstruct the exegetical framework of the Isaiah Targum, Chilton discovered that the final framework contained two different frameworks and was the product of two separate interpreters. The first framework was the result of interpretation of the Tannaitic period, and the second was the result of interpretation during the Amoraic period. He further discovered that the Tannaitic framework included two strata from before and after the fall of the temple in 70 CE[32]

Chilton's method of examining the uses of various characteristic terms and phrases throughout the Targum as a whole allowed him to construct the overall frameworks and differentiate between the different interpretive approaches of each meturgeman. His methodology has functioned as an answer to the challenges of York and Kaufman in their call for a method in determining the dates of various Targum readings. The method helps to create better parameters for comparison to the NT but is not designed for carrying out specific comparisons. In many ways the clarity concerning the phasal development of the Targums that resulted from Chilton's work calls for a more stringent method concerning studies of the Targums and the NT. As stated earlier, the conjunction between the literary perspective (similarities) and the historical perspective (phasal development of the Targums) has resulted in a problem of methodology.

Therefore, Chilton suggested approaching the study by identifying the comparisons as one of four types of affinities between the NT and the Targums. Comparisons of the first type include "comparable material with cognate wording, associated with the same text of scripture." Comparisons of the second type do not involve "the sharing of explicit wording" but do include a comparable understanding of the same text of Scripture. Comparisons of the third type include the appearance of characteristic Targum phrases in the NT. Finally, comparisons of the fourth type include shared thematic emphases between the NT and the Targums.[33]

---

32. The complete application of the method can be seen in Chilton, *Glory*, and see esp. 102–3 for a summary of his conclusions.

33. Chilton, "From Aramaic Paraphrase," 28–29. Chilton also earlier provided eight

Basically, these types of comparisons facilitate discussion concerning the degree of literary parallels by focusing upon the content of the affinity. As Chilton pointed out, the nature of the historical relationship between the texts cannot be determined from literary parallels alone. He argued that the similarities observed within the four types of comparisons suggest only that a type of "analogy" exists between the two texts. The question of historical relationship is a different question from that of literary relationship. The nature of the relationship cannot sufficiently be addressed through a comparison of types alone. Therefore, he also suggested the possibility of three types of historical analogies: common reference, shared context, and systemic.[34] His three types of historical analogies are a step closer to discovering the nature of the relationship between two given texts.

Chilton's method of comparison types and historical analogies attempt to deal with both the literary perspective and historical perspective outlined above between the two texts.[35] As a result of this description, his proposed method can be described best as an intertextual approach. As an intertextual approach his method still lacks the criterion for establishing a more determinative or detailed description of the historical relationship and level of impact of one text upon the other. His three types of historical analogies only describe the possible relationships in terms of broad categories without the means for exploring those relationships in more detail. Therefore, would any more specific applications of the advances made in the field of intertextuality be helpful in augmenting Chilton's method? How is one to deal productively with the similarities in light of the historical development of the Targums?

The nature of the problem concerning Targums and NT studies is essentially an intertextual one. Therefore, the solution is to be found in the development and application of an intertextual methodology. Can the application of advances made in the field of intertextuality add to the

---

theses for the use of the Targums in the NT. His eight theses have been taken into account here even though not addressed directly, because the theses are more guidelines than a constructed methodology. See Chilton, *Judaic Approaches*, 305–15.

34. Chilton, "From Aramaic Paraphrase," 41–42. For an example of his most recent treatment of the comparison types and historical analogies, see his co-authored work with Flesher, *The Targums: A Critical Introduction*, 385–408.

35. As Flesher and Chilton have recently argued, this approach to New Testament and Targum studies is more critical than previous suggestions and "has worked to chart a path between the two untenable extremes" of the dogmatic assertions of the pre-Christian exsistence of a Palestinian Targum and the total rejection of the Targums as a viable source for New Testament study (Flesher and Chilton, *The Targums*, 405–6).

ongoing discussion in Targums and NT studies? The absence of advances in the field of intertextuality within the discussion concerning the Targums and the NT suggests so.

Intertextuality as a Methodological Advance

Apart from the historical perspective of the Targums, Samuel Sandmel warned of the danger of drawing a conclusion concerning intertextual relationships between texts based on parallels alone. In his presidential address delivered at the annual meeting of the Society of Biblical Literature on December 27, 1961, he chided the scholarly community for their extravagance in approaching the intertextual relationship between the NT and Jewish literature. He described this extravagance as an overextrapolation from similarities concerning the source and derivation "as if implying literary connection flowing in an inevitable or predetermined direction." He referred to this phenomenon in scholarship as "parallelomania."[36] Sandmel was calling scholars beyond simple comparisons of texts based on excerpts to a consideration of the contexts of the texts. Since Sandmel's challenge, the field of intertextuality has matured significantly, especially in reference to the use of the Jewish Scriptures in the NT.

The term intertextuality has been used to refer to a variety of approaches to reading texts in relation to other texts. As Timothy K. Beal noted, intertextuality has been described broadly as a "total and limitless fabric, which constitutes our linguistic universe." His broad definition was built upon Julia Kristeva's original theory of intertextuality. Beal argued that intertextuality is an intersection of a surplus of textual surfaces and cultural readings. His theory of intertextuality creates an intersection that includes a wide array of possible "texts" or influences. For practical purposes, Beal suggested that the practice of intertextual reading would have to settle somewhere between "the closed structure of a single text and the uncontainable surplus fabric of language."[37] Beal's appeal to a medium approach is, in a way, an acknowledgment of the impact of both historical and literary factors involved in the production of meaning that comes with a given text. The intersection between two texts involves more than the shared vocabulary or themes, but rather is part of a larger historical conversation. Understanding this dynamic of an intertextual relationship between

---

36. Sandmel, "Parallelomania," 1.
37. Beal, "Ideology," 27–31.

two texts necessitates a reading approach that moves beyond the simple recognition of similarities toward an ability to reconstruct, even if only in Part, the larger discussion. The larger intertextual discussion is referred to here as the intertextual field.[38]

Scholars who have used intertextuality as a methodological approach to the use of the Jewish Scriptures in the NT have wrestled with a number of subjects throughout the twentieth century, including issues of intrabiblical or extrabiblical exegesis, identifying citations and allusions, and the exegetical methods and the sources of the NT writers.[39] As Dennis Stamps pointed out, the use of the Jewish Scriptures in the NT is a "broad and multifaceted issue."[40] Issues of historical context of the various texts, theological perspective of the writers, and questions of hermeneutics are all intersecting. The application of the broader discussion of intertextuality concerning the nature of the intertextual field, as witnessed to by Kristeva and Beal, to the Jewish Scriptures in the NT has resulted in considerable insights.

Perhaps one of the more productive advancements made concerning the intertextual nature of the Jewish Scriptures in the NT has been Richard B. Hays's treatment of the use of Scripture in the letters of Paul. Hays recognized the value of the intertextual advances made by literary critics to the study of the NT. He largely adopted Kristeva's theory of intertextuality as a matrix of discourse. Hays sought to analyze Paul's use of Scripture within the larger intertextual field in a limited sense by focusing on Paul's citations and allusions.

---

38. The phrase *intertextual field* is offered in this research as a summary of Beal's medium approach to intertextuality. According to Julia Kristeva's original theory, "intertextual," a term coined by her, denotes the "transposition of one sign system(s) into another." Kristeva rejected the narrow or minimalist view of the nature of a "text" as a self-contained unit, and "intertextuality" as an approach aimed at establishing a correct interpretation of a text. She described this more narrow approach as a "banal sense of source study" (*Revolution*, 59–60). Although the nature of "texts" and "intertextuality" continues to be debated in philosophical contexts, the work of post-structuralist and semiotic theorists will not be directly addressed in this research. As noted by Hays, the pursuit of meaning effects created by Paul's use of Jewish literature is "in principle neutral with regard to metatheories about language and truth" (*Echoes*, 227n60). For further discussion of the theory and practice of intertextuality and its relationship to larger issues concerning theories of language and texts, see Hays et al., eds., *Reading the Bible*; Thiselton, *New Horizons*. For a general glossary of terms from within the field of intertextuality, see Beal, "Glossary," 21–24.

39. For a brief survey of these issues and more within the state of research, see Longenecker, *Biblical Exegesis*, xiii–xli.

40. Stamps, "Use of the Old Testament," 9.

Rather than interpreting the Apostle Paul strictly through a reconstruction of the historical situation, Hays also sought to interpret Paul's letters according to their intertextual relationships with other texts. He sought an interpretive methodology that focused on the rhetorical and semantic effects of a reference to other texts rather than a historical-critical approach established on presuppositions.

Hays built on the work of John Hollander, who proposed a literary critical approach to poetic texts that focused on the rhetorical and semantic effects of an intertextual allusion rather than the author himself. Hays assessed the intertextuality of Paul's letters in terms of Hollander's concept of a "metalepsis," which Hays described as a "diachronic trope." He further explained, "When a literary echo links the text in which it occurs to an earlier text, the figurative effect of the echo can lie in the unstated or suppressed points of resonance between the two texts."[41]

Two basic principles of Hays's intertextual approach are important for this proposed research. First, his adoption of Hollander's concept of "metalepsis" reflects the content of an intertextual reference. According to "metalepsis," a reference by one text to another reflects a much larger transfusion of material. Not only is a text referencing a specific explicitly stated text but also the entire original context. Second, Hays's use of the term echo reflects the nature of an intertextual relationship. Although Hays made no distinction in definition between an echo and an allusion, the term echo communicates the idea of a resonance of the original text within the larger "chamber" of the text making the reference. In other words, the nature of the textual relationship is such that the context of the original text is not being referenced only but also in part is shaped by the rhetorical context of the newer text. The older text is heard in a new setting as the new text interprets the older text. Hays's interpretational approach emphasizes the rhetorical function of the older text's "echo" in the newer text.

Stamps also recognized the significance of a rhetorical approach to intertextuality. He noted the relationship between two texts is complex because the use of one text in another involves more than a transfer of meaning. The relationship reflects a range of "voices" and responses within the larger intertextual field.[42] As a result, Stamps also proposed that the use of the Jewish Scriptures in the NT was by nature a rhetorical device and therefore should be explored through a rhetorical approach.

41. Hays, *Echoes*, 19–20.
42. Stamps, "Use of the Old Testament," 19.

Romans, Targums, and Intertextuality

Both Hays's intertextual approach and Stamps's emphasis upon the rhetorical device of the use of the Jewish Scriptures in the NT lend themselves to the consideration of the relationship of the NT and Targums as a part of a larger intertextual field. Hays's two principles of "metalepsis" and "echo," when understood within Kristeva's and Beal's theory of intertextuality, lead toward the consideration that a scriptural reference in a NT text may not reflect just a larger transfusion of material from the original scriptural text but very likely also includes transfusion of material from the larger textual field. When the NT writers reference the Jewish Scriptures, they often, though not exclusively, do so within the textual field of the synagogue discussion. Intertextual references are not made in a vacuum. They are going to carry "echoes" of the larger conversation as well. Sometimes these echoes may be shaped by the newer text by way of acceptance or commonly agreed propositions, and sometimes they may be shaped by a polemic to a commonly agreed proposition in the intertextual field.

A method with an emphasis upon the rhetoric of the newer texts involved is necessary for developing a deeper understanding of the nature of the relationship. The significance of determining the rhetorical structure and the function of a textual reference within that structure can be seen in the context of Burton Mack's observation concerning the integrated nature of rhetoric and human communication. He argued that rhetoric is the basic element of all discourse in the social sphere.[43]

A Proposed Method for Intertextual Studies

As discussed earlier, the conjunction of the literary issue and the historical issue concerning the Targums has resulted in a problem of methodology for Targum and NT studies. The methodology proposed here is designed to deal with the nature of the problem and include the advances made in the field of intertextuality. The overall purpose of the method is to establish the nature of the relationship and impact of the Targums upon the NT for the purpose of a better understanding of the NT text.[44] The method includes

43. Mack, *Rhetoric*, 15–16. Mack argued that rhetorical criticism offers an approach to the NT that can bridge the gap between literary criticism, social-science criticism, and historical criticism. Given the nature of the intertextual field between the Targums and the NT, Mack's argument concerning rhetorical criticism parallels Hays's and Stamps's inclusion of rhetorical consideration in their approaches. For Mack's conclusions concerning the promise of rhetorical criticism for NT studies, see ibid., 93–102.

44. The overall approach of the method is tailored to the needs of a NT student. This

five major steps for conducting an intertextual study of the relationship between the Targums and the NT. After each step has been presented and discussed in terms of its goal, the relationship of the augmentation of the method to Chilton's proposed approach will be considered. An outline of the method is as follows:

1. Identify the source and nature of citation concerning original text(s) (Jewish Scripture) within the newer text (NT).

2. Examine the larger context of the original text (Jewish Scripture).

3. Apply the nuanced intertextual approach (Hays) to both the Targums and the NT use of the original text (Jewish Scripture).

4. Identify and analyze the thematic and verbal similarities and differences among the three texts (Jewish Scripture, Targum, and NT).

5. Analyze the rhetorical use of the material common to the NT and the Targum, yet unique from the older text.

The first step is a basic intertextual step concerning the study of the Jewish Scripture in the NT. The goal of this step is to identify the Jewish scriptural reference, the textual source, and the type of citation within the newer text. What is the textual tradition of the scriptural reference? Can the reference be identified as referring to a Hebrew, Greek, or other version of the text? Is the reference a direct citation with or without an introductory formula, or a more vague allusion? Establishing the source of the scriptural reference and the level of resonance of the older text in the newer text as either a direct citation or allusion can aid in establishing the rhetorical function of the older text in the newer in step three.[45] With this step, the

---

approach is not to degrade starting with the Targums as that of a flawed or somehow lesser approach. The need for a workable method for a NT student studying the Targums, especially in the wake of the publication of the Aramaic Targums in English, has been recognized already. For example, see Chilton, *Judaic Approaches*, 305–6.

45. The textual source sometimes can prove to be illusive and debatable. For example, see the reference of Hab 2:4 in Rom 1:17 and Deut 32:43 in Heb 1:6. In both of these examples, the exact textual reference is debatable, and, in relation to Rom 1:17 unknown; yet both are introduced with an introductory formula. The presence of an explicit introductory formula can indicate a high level of rhetorical function for the argument being made by the NT writer. For discussion of the types of introductory formulas in the NT, see Longenecker, *Biblical Exegesis*, 97–98. For a discussion of the possible rhetorical function indicated by the introductory formula, see Watson, *Paul*, 40–53.

text(s) to be used for step two are identified, and the process toward understanding both the nature and content of the reference can begin.[46]

Step two involves an examination of the larger context of the allusion or citation identified in step one. The goal of this step is to understand the narrative or thematic development of the text within the larger context. With step two appropriate literary questions are applied to the older scriptural text. How does the referenced text fit into its original context? Can any key terms or themes within the context be identified? How does the scriptural text function rhetorically within the original context? Once the researcher is familiar with the original context of the scriptural text, recognizing the material that is transferred beyond the cited text will be easier in step three.

In step three, Hays's nuanced intertextual approach is applied to both the NT and the Targums in relation to the older scriptural text. The goal of this step is to establish the rhetorical use of the original text in the contextual argument of the newer text. Concerning the principle of metalepsis, one can ask whether any additional content, vocabulary, or theme beyond the cited verse itself from the original context of the scriptural text is reflected in the context of the newer text. Concerning the principle of echo, one can ask, How does the transferred content shape the rhetorical argument in the newer text? In relation to the Targum, one can ask, How did the meturgeman interpret or shape the original context of the scriptural text? Are various aspects of the original context emphasized or changed in the Targum? Are any of the key terms or themes emphasized or echoed in other places of the Targum?

Some consideration of the targumic context in relation to the historical phasal development of the Targums in general may prove helpful at this step as well. As Chilton's approach to the Targum Isaiah illustrated, an overall understanding of the interpretative framework within a specific Targum is important for understanding the rhetorical focus of the meturgeman concerning a given text and its surrounding context.[47] Likewise,

---

46. Sometimes a rhetorical appeal to the Scriptures by a NT writer can involve not just a single scriptural citation but also a conglomerate of scriptural citations. For an example, see the OT catena in Rom 3:9–20 and Jewett's discussion of the catena in Jewett, *Romans*, 253–55. Other times, a single rhetorical appeal to the Scriptures possibly may refer to more than one text. For example, see Rom 7:7 in reference to Exod 20:17 and Deut 5:21, and Gal 3:16 in reference to Gen 12:7; 13:15; 24:7 and possibly 22:18.

47. See the overall argument in Chilton, *Glory*.

the rhetorically focused questions can be asked of the NT text as well.[48] The key with this step is to analyze more than just parallels and focus also on any rhetorical uses of those parallels.

With step four, the thematic and verbal similarities and differences among the three texts are identified and analyzed. The goal of this step is to establish both the material that is common among the three texts and the material that is unique to each text. The texts may share similar content either through paralleled vocabulary and themes or rhetorical function of those vocabulary and themes. Likewise, each text may demonstrate significant distinctives. Key to step four is identifying the material and the rhetorical function of the material that is common between the NT and the Targum, yet unique from the older text.

With step five, the rhetorical use of the materials common to the NT and the Targum yet unique from the older text are analyzed. The goal with this step is to establish the nature of the relationship between the NT and Targum text. Does the rhetorical use of the common material indicate common understanding or a direct polemic? Is any aspect of the rhetorical argument or use of the common material of one text echoed in the other? Is the polemic by one text directed against the rhetorical use of the material in the other text? If one text offers any degree of relationship at the level of the rhetorical use of the material in the other text, then direct relationship may be determined.

The Method as an Augment of Chilton's Approach

As pointed out earlier with the literary issue, common material between a Targum text and the NT indicates some level of relationship, but not necessarily direct relationship or dependency. A recognized parallel between a given NT and Targum text simply may reflect dependency upon a common traditional source. Therefore, a simple comparison of parallels is not sufficient. On the other hand, when Hays's more nuanced intertextual approach is applied to the texts involved within the intertextual field, another level of

---

48. Although Hays's intertextual method was applied to the use of the Jewish Scriptures in the NT, the same basic principles still can be applied to the Targums, albeit in a more limited fashion. Since the Targum is a different genre than any of the NT writings, most often defined as paraphrases or translations, much of the overall context, vocabulary, and themes of the original text naturally will be present. Still, various aspects of the original context may be emphasized, minimized, or specifically interpreted throughout the Targum as a whole.

relationship can be established. The application of the principle of metalepsis allows the analysis of larger amounts of content to be compared beyond just the text cited in the NT and translated or interpreted in the Targum. The application of the principle of echo allows analysis of the transferred material in reference to the way its rhetorical function both was shaped by the newer text and also shapes the newer text. The application of rhetorical criticism to the process of intertextuality allows one to move beyond recognized parallels toward the intent of the author in the use of those parallels. The presence of parallels or polemic in the rhetorical function of common material, especially in larger blocks of content, as opposed to a parallel of material in isolated vocabulary or themes, establishes a more intricate or higher level of relationship, because rhetoric indicates a level of organized intent beyond the unconscious use of cultural terms and phrases.

Although Chilton's four types of comparisons and three types of historical analogies provide for a useful description of the possible relationships between a given NT and Targum text, the types of relationships are left rather broad. Furthermore, the conclusions to be drawn from the parallels seem limited. Whether a relationship is categorized as common reference, shared context, or systemic, the resulting application to a better interpretation of the NT text is basically the same. The content of the Targum text provides a more detailed background concerning first-century Judaism toward understanding the NT, and indeed his approach accomplishes just that. Along these lines the Targums can take their legitimate place among the other Jewish literature of the Second Temple period for the understanding of the cultural background of the NT. In conclusion, Chilton's methodological approach to the NT and Targums is understandably constrained by the reality of the historical issue described above, namely the phasal development of the Targums.

On the other hand, given the location of the Targums within the intertextual field of the first century, namely the discussion of the synagogue setting, and the placement of the NT writers in the same intertextual field, is not a more detailed exploration of the intertextual relationship warranted? If so, then is an establishment of some level of historical relationship even possible beyond the proposal of a general source tradition?

Understandably the historical issue of the Targums calls for a great deal of caution in order to avoid anachronistic applications of targumic material. As has been demonstrated in the field of Targum studies, much of the material in the extant Targums did post-date the NT, but much of the material also has been demonstrated to pre-date the NT. One might ask if such a direct relationship did exist between the two texts, then how might one determine the nature of that relationship beyond Chilton's historical analogy types? The intertextual method presented here provides just such an opportunity. The NT student should not set Chilton's comparisons and analogies aside because not all parallels are directly related. The intertextual method proposed here simply allows for further work in some cases beyond the categorization of Chilton's analogies. The focus on the rhetorical and semantic effects of a reference to other texts supplied by this intertextual method seeks to augment rather than replace Chilton's approach.

As an augment to Chilton's approach, the most fruitful possibility for establishing any more detailed conclusions of intertextual relationships may be within his comparisons type one and two due to their same common quality. What both comparisons have in common is that they deal with the intersection between the NT, the Targums, and the same text of Scripture. The major difference is that type one shares cognate wording, and type two shares only the presence of comparable understanding. Since both types contain relationships based on the same text of Scripture, the opportunity for discovering the rhetorical function within a larger context of Scripture in each is greater than in types three and four, which deal only with similar random phrases and themes. For this reason this intertextual method begins with a step in which a direct citation or allusion of the Jewish Scriptures in the NT is chosen as the starting point.

2

Inclusivism and Particularism in Isaiah

Introduction

A preliminary application of step one of the methodology will be necessary in order to determine which passages in Isaiah need analysis in the application of step two.[1] A survey reading of Romans reveals seventeen explicit citations of Isaiah with various introductory formulas and a number of less explicit allusions.[2] Furthermore, the citations encompass a wide range of material throughout the book of Isaiah and are not confined to any single section. The number of citations from Isa 1–39 is nearly even with the number of citations from Isa 40–66.[3] Although this intertextual

---

1. A more detailed discussion of the identity of the textual sources and citations of Isaiah in certain passages of Romans will be given later.

2. For purposes of this research, analysis will be limited to the explicit citations of Isaiah that are accompanied by a citation formula in Romans. The texts include Isa 52:5 in Rom 2:24; Isa 59:7-8 in Rom 3:15-17; Isa 10:22-23 in Rom 9:27-28; Isa 1:9 in Rom 9:29; Isa 8:14 and 28:16 in Rom 9:33; Isa 28:16 in Rom 10:11; Isa 52:7 and 53:1 in Rom 10:15-16; Isa 65:1-2 in Rom 10:20-21; Isa 29:10 in Rom 11:8, which is a conflation of Deut 29:3, Isa 29:10, and Ps 69:23-24; Isa 59:20-21 and Isa 27:9 in Rom 11:26-27; Isa 45:23 in Rom 14:11; Isa 11:10 in Rom 15:12; and Isa 52:15 in Rom 15:21. For further listings and discussion concerning the identification of the Isaiah citations and allusions in Romans, see Aland et al., *The Greek New Testament*, 889; Longenecker, *Biblical Exegesis*, 92–93; Shum, *Paul's Use*, 177–264; and Stanley, *Arguing*, 143–69.

3. While the scholarly debate concerning the connection between the literary divisions and authorship of Isaiah, as evidenced in the often-used phrases "First Isaiah," "Second Isaiah," and "Third Isaiah," is acknowledged, historical issues concerning authorship of Isaiah are delimited for this research. An intertextual study of Isaiah, the Isaiah Targum, and Romans need not require a theory of authorship for Isaiah. For the purposes of this intertextual study, the canonical text of Isaiah will be analyzed as a literary whole with recognition of a thematic tripartite divisional structure of Isa 1–39, Isa

study will include an overall examination of the attitude toward the Gentiles throughout Isaiah, special attention will be given to the specific literary units related to the explicit citations in Romans, which include the contexts of Isa 1, 8, 10–11, 27–29, 45, 52–53, 59, and 65.

Though scholarly discussion has lacked consensus concerning the level of authorial intent with some of the suggested allusions, Paul's intentional inclusion of the formulaic and explicit citations is beyond debate. Both the frequency of Isaiah citations and placement of the citations within the rhetorical structure of Romans indicate that Paul's reading of Isaiah significantly impacted his argument in Romans. As Shum wrote, "The apostle Paul was greatly indebted to the 'theology' of the Isaianic tradition in shaping and formulating his own teachings."[4]

As scholarly discussion of ὑπακοὴν πίστεως has pointed out, the focus upon the Jew and Gentile relationship in the letter of Romans along with Paul's explicit description of the "obedience of faith" as being "among the Gentiles" in Rom 1:5 strongly suggests that a debate concerning the relationship of the Gentiles to Israel is central to Paul's purpose in Romans. Therefore, the analysis of Isaiah in this intertextual study will focus on the relationship between Israel and the Gentiles.

Scholars have argued that one of the strongest messages of inclusivism concerning the Gentiles in the Jewish Scriptures can be found in the book of Isaiah. More recently, scholars also have begun to argue that a strong particularistic message concerning Israel also is evident in Isaiah. Scholars now recognize the complexity of Isaiah's presentation of Israel's relationship to the Gentile nations. As Kebede wrote, "These two opposing concepts create a tension that sustains the discussion between universalism and nationalism within the Book of Isaiah."[5]

A consensus among scholars concerning the dominant attitude toward the nations in Isaiah is still lacking. Scholars in the debate have acknowledged the presence of both the inclusive and the particularistic voices.[6] The major debate regarding the book of Isaiah concerns not the presence of the

---

40–55, and Isa 56–66. For further discussion concerning the authorship and divisions of Isaiah, see Gray, *Critical and Exegetical Commentary*, xxix–xxxii; Oswalt, *Book of Isaiah*, 1:17–31; Baltzer, *Deutero-Isaiah*, 1–2; Childs, *Isaiah*, 1–8.

4. Shum, *Paul's Use*, 259.

5. Kebede, "How Can the Concepts," 3.

6. The term *voice* is not used in the sense of a single authorial witness, but rather as a synonym for the message reflected in the characteristic elements of both particularism and inclusivism concerning the relationship of Israel, the Gentile nations, and the Lord.

voices, but rather the reconciliation or literary interpretation of the voices. A conclusion concerning the reconciliation of the tension is not necessary for this intertextual exploration between Isaiah and Romans. Instead, the significant goal will be the recognition and identification of the inclusive and particularistic voices within the various sections of Isaiah. The crucial point that will be developed later is that the presence of both voices in Isaiah lies at the root of the dialogue within the intertextual field of Isaiah, the Isaiah Targum, and Romans.

In his treatment of Isaiah's attitude toward the Gentiles, Kebede argued for the presence of both particularistic and inclusive messages. He demonstrated the presence of an inclusive message by analyzing Isa 2:1–5, 19:16–25, and 42:1–9. He noted that in Isa 2:1–5 inclusion of the nations is pictured in their coming to the house of Jacob for teaching under God's kingdom of peace. Kebede argued that the response of the nations to the teaching from the house of Jacob is portrayed as a willing obedience. The obedience of the nations pictured in Isa 2:3 is apparent even more when contrasted with the disobedience of Israel in the surrounding context of Isa 1:31 and 2:6–22. A Gentile subordination to a second-class status in service of Israel is entirely absent, even though the text is focused upon the exaltation of Judah and Jerusalem. In Isa 19:16–25, Egypt and Assyria are placed on the same relational level to the Lord as Israel. Rather than being forced to come to Zion and submit to Israel, the Egyptians will worship the Lord in the land of Egypt (Isa 19:18–19). Egypt is described as blessed alongside Israel in status and is portrayed even as bringing sacrifices and fulfilling vows, which are practices normally used to describe the covenant between the Lord and Israel. In Isa 42:1–9, the Lord will reach out to the nations through the servant. Kebede argued that Isa 42:6 makes clear that the servant is given the twofold task of restoring both Israel and the world to the Lord.[7] The passages selected by Kebede demonstrate a voice of inclusivism through the use of inclusive language as well as the application of covenant blessings to the nations, which normally are reserved for Israel.

Charles Torrey also argued for the centrality of inclusivism in Isa 40–55 and saw Isaiah's portrayal of inclusivism as new and unique among the ancient Near Eastern religions. In support of his argument, he pointed to examples in the Servant Songs and Isa 55. Torrey further acknowledged the presence of a particularistic message in Isa 40–55 and suggested that the nationalistic passages were an early interpolation in polemic against the

---

7. Kebede, "How Can the Concepts," 47–110.

inclusivism in Isaiah.⁸ John McKenzie argued that the dominant theme in Isa 40–66 is not salvation, but more the mission of Israel for which the nation was saved. He noted that the inclusivism in Isaiah is explicit and without antecedent in earlier books of the Jewish Scriptures.⁹ J. Alec Motyer furthered suggested that the messianic representation throughout Isaiah "embraces equally Israel and the Gentile world."¹⁰

After concluding his study of inclusivism in Isaiah, Kebede demonstrated the presence of a strong particularism as well. He argued that the message of particularism in Isaiah expresses a salvation of Israel that includes their dominance over the nations. For example, he pointed to the particularistic context in Isa 45:14–19, 49:22–26, and 60:1–16. In Isa 45:14 Isaiah proclaimed that the nations will be humiliated, placed in chains, brought to worship Israel, and even will belong to Israel. The shame that will come to the nations in Isa 49:16 is contrasted with the lack of shame in the exaltation that will come to Israel. This same service by the nations to Israel is pictured in Isa 49:22–26, where the nations are described as facilitating the return of Israel's children from exile even as they are made to "lick the dust" from Israel's feet. The coming of the nations to Zion is portrayed in Isa 60:1–16 as well, but the means of their coming is not the same as presented in the more inclusive passages. In Isa 60:1–16, the nations come for the sole purpose of exalting and serving Zion, rather than for the purpose of equal inclusion in worship and covenant.¹¹

R. N. Whybray argued that the dominant attitude toward the nations in Isa 40–55 is particularism. He further rejected the view that Israel is presented as a missionary nation to the Gentiles in Isa 40–55. He examined key texts used to demonstrate inclusivism and argued that the passages often are misinterpreted. For example, he pointed out that the interpretation of the servant's mission turns on the interpretation of several key phrases: מִשְׁפָּט ("judgment") in Isa 42:1 and 4, תּוֹרָה ("law") in Isa 42:4; לְאוֹר גּוֹיִם ("a light of the nations") in Isa 42:6; and יְשׁוּעָה ("salvation") in 49:6. For Whybray, none of these terms in the original Hebrew suggests a mission to convert the nations. He equated the term *judgment* to God's universal sovereignty and

---

8. Torrey, *Second Isaiah*, 111–21.
9. McKenzie, *Second Isaiah*, lvii–lxv.
10. Motyer, *Prophecy of Isaiah*, 13–14.
11. Kebede, "How Can the Concepts," 111–77.

Inclusivism and Particularism in Isaiah

the term *salvation* to the victory of Israel. He further dismissed an inclusive interpretation of "a light of the nations" due of the vagueness of the phrase.[12]

Whybray's observation concerning the presence of particularism in Isaiah parallels the observations made by other scholars. Regarding his rejection of the presence of inclusivism in the book of Isaiah, his conclusion is unwarranted given the evidence that he offered. As Kebede argued, the term משפט in Isaiah involves societal order and expresses the "true religion" that the servant is expected to bring to the nations.[13] In response to Whybray's argument that the phrase "light to the Gentiles" is vague, a missionary meaning of the phrase as the servant's task can be found in the immediate context of Isa 42:6–7. Furthermore, Whybray's discussion of Isa 42 and one term in 49, without any analysis of the other inclusivistic passages in Isaiah, is too limited a sample of data to draw overall conclusions. Johannes Lindblom, in his treatment of the Servant Songs, described the two voices as the "missionary revelation" and the "triumph revelation." He concluded that the presence of two opposing interpretational traditions concerning the Gentile nations is evidenced well in the book of Isaiah.[14]

Based on this brief survey of the scholarly discussion, both similarities and differences between the particularistic voice and the inclusive voice in Isaiah are observable. Concerning the similarities, both voices hold to the election of Israel, the Lord as the God of history, salvation and prophecy, Israel's exaltation, and the glorification of the Lord in the world. Concerning the differences, each voice has a distinct focus on the role of Israel and the nations in the Lord's restoration program. For example, a difference is evident in reference to the purpose for the gathering of the nations to Zion. In passages that reflect inclusivism, the nations are described as worshipping the Lord in equal status to Israel (cf. Isa 2:3; 19:18–19). In passages that reflect particularism, the nations are described as worshipping in subordination to Israel (cf. Isa 45:14; 49:23; 60:12–14). Another difference can be seen in the nature of the nation's obedience to God's law. In passages that reflect inclusivism, the nations demonstrate a willing obedience to God's law (cf. Isa 2:3). In passages that reflect particularism, a willing obedience to the law by the nations is absent, while a forced obedience and service of

---

12. Whybray, *Second Isaiah*, 62–65.

13. Kebede, "How Can the Concepts," 96–97.

14. For further discussion including a helpful list of passages that reflect elements of the missionary revelation and triumph revelation in Isaiah, see Lindblom, *Servant Songs*, 52–74.

the nations to Israel is present. Israel's missional task to convert the world stands at the forefront with the inclusive voice, while Israel's deliverance from and triumph over the nations stands at the forefront with the particularistic voice.

Both particularistic and inclusive voices have been observed in various passages throughout Isaiah, but what about the specific passages that intertextually intersect with Romans? As noted earlier, various texts from Isa 1, 8, 10–11, 27–29, 45, 52–53, 59, and 65 are all cited explicitly in Romans. Can any of the unique elements of either inclusivism or particularism be found within the context of Isa 1, 8, 10–11, 27–29, 45, 52–53, 59, and 65?

Analysis

Three goals will be accomplished through the contextual analysis offered below of the Isaiah texts cited by Paul in Romans. The first goal will be to establish the literary boundaries of the unit that contains the Isaiah text cited by Paul in Romans.[15] Attention to the thematic development of the texts will be the means for establishing the literary boundaries. The second goal will be to analyze each Isaiah citation within its literary unit in order to establish an exegetical interpretation. The analysis will focus on the key themes, vocabulary, and rhetorical purpose of the unit. The third goal will be to observe and identify the presence, if any, of either particularism or inclusivism within the unit.

---

15. Research of Isaiah has resulted in a variety of conclusions concerning the literary structure of Isaiah, which has demonstrated the complexities involved with identifying the literary structure. The identification and relation of the various units within Isaiah have been analyzed through the use of form, redaction, and literary criticisms. The early historical-critical approaches by scholars such as Claus Westermann and John D. W. Watts resulted in a fragmentation of the Isaiah text. More recently, the literary-critical approaches by scholars such as Oswalt, Moyter, and Childs resulted in a larger horizontal unity of the Isaiah text. Consideration of the historical origins of the various units within Isaiah is beyond the scope of this research due to the irrelevancy of the origins to the intertextual study of the possible relationship between Isaiah, the Isaiah Targum, and Romans. Both the meturgeman and Paul were reading a canonical form of Isaiah comprised of all sixty-six chapters. Therefore, the Isaiah text will be analyzed here in its final literary form. The historical perspective of the units will be considered, but the examination of a possible multilayered development of the final form will not be pursued.

Isaiah 1

Scholars routinely have recognized that Isa 1 functions within the literary structure of Isaiah as an introduction to the major Isaianic themes.[16] The superscript of Isa 1:1 establishes the context of Isa 1, if not the entire book of Isaiah, within the pre-exilic experience of Judah. Isaiah 1 details Judah's rebellious situation and God's call for them to return to him, which introduces the major themes of judgment, return, and restoration. The major focus of Isa 1 is not on Isaiah the prophet or on the people of Judah but rather on the Lord. As Childs rightly noted, Isa 1 is predominantly "theocentric" in its function.[17]

Isaiah 1 contains a divine accusation against the people of Judah and Jerusalem concerning their choice to forsake the Lord. Judah's broken and desolate condition is described in vv. 2–9, along with a sharp polemic against the people's cultic practice and lack of justice in vv. 10–17. A call for obedience is extended in vv. 18–20, and the Lord's response to Judah's rebellion is portrayed in vv. 21–31. Central to the Lord's response in vv. 21–31 is both his coming judgment of the wicked in Jerusalem and Judah as well as his coming redemption and restoration of Zion.[18]

The presence of Deuteronomic language in Isa 1 indicates that covenant is also a major theme. For example, the opening appeal in vv. 2–3 is reminiscent of Deut 32:1 and 30:19. Oswalt suggested that the use of the terms ישראל ("Israel") and ידע ("know") in v. 3 likely indicates a conscious reference to the covenant language of Deuteronomy by Isaiah.[19] John D. W. Watts noted that the term עזב ("abandon"), which occurs in v. 4 and v. 28, is also a term frequently used in covenant literature.[20] The description

---

16. A consensus among scholars concerning the literary function of Isa 1 as an introduction of Isaianic themes has developed, yet a consensus concerning the identity of the literary context referred to by the superscription of Isa 1:1 is still lacking. The most often suggested literary contexts include Isa 1–5, Isa 1–12, and all of Isa 1–66. The interpretation of Isa 1 functioning as an introduction to the literary context of Isa 1–66 as a whole is adopted for purposes of this research. For further discussion of the literary function of Isa 1 within the structure of Isaiah, see Oswalt, *Book of Isaiah*, 1:79–81; Motyer, *Prophecy of Isaiah*, 38–41; Childs, *Isaiah*, 16–17.

17. Childs, *Isaiah*, 17.

18. For further discussion on the structure of Isa 1, see Oswalt, *Book of Isaiah*, 1:84–85, 94–95, 103–4; Motyer, *Prophecy of Isaiah*, 42, 45, 48–49, 50–51; Childs, *Isaiah*, 16–17.

19. Oswalt, *Book of Isaiah*, 1:85.

20. The examples offered by Watts include Deut 31:19–20; Judg 10:6, 10, 13; 1 Sam 8:8; 12:10; and Jer 14:21. Watts, *Isaiah*, 1:18–19.

of Judah's condition in vv. 5–8 corresponds to the description of the curses that result from the breaking of the covenant in Deut 27–30.[21] Finally, the call for the rulers and people to listen to תּוֹרָה ("law") in v. 10 also indicates that Isa 1 should be interpreted within a covenantal context.

Alongside the Lord's declaration of judgment, Isaiah also records a glimmer of hope for the nation of Israel in Isa 1:9. The prophet returns his focus upon God and notes that Zion would have been completely destroyed like Sodom and Gomorrah without the Lord's intervention in leaving a remnant. The remnant theology is not elaborated fully in Isa 1. In subsequent chapters, the remnant theology will be developed more fully as a major theme of the Lord's programmatic restoration of Israel.[22]

While the nations are mentioned briefly in v. 7 in reference to their destruction of Israel's fields, no mention is made of their role within Israel's restoration. Neither the voice of inclusivism or particularism is explicitly present in Isa 1, though as Kebede noted the voice of inclusivism can be observed in the immediate context of Isa 2:1–5.[23] Likewise, the voice of particularism may be connected indirectly to the remnant introduced in Isa 1:9 within the larger literary context. For example, the next major development of the remnant occurs in Isa 10:11–34, where the restoration of the remnant is promised.[24] Alongside the promised restoration of the remnant in Zion, Isaiah also proclaimed the destruction of Israel's enemy, when the Lord's wrath turns from Israel to Assyria (Isa 10:24–25). Though the explicit voices of inclusivism and particularism are absent from Isa 1, they are not far from the context. The voice of inclusivism can be heard in the close literary proximity of Isa 2:1–5 and the voice of particularism within the remnant theology of Isa 10.

---

21. For example, the fruitless land, desolation of the country, fields stripped by foreigners, and burned cities are all covenantal curses as expressed in Lev 26:14–35 and Deut 28:15–42.

22. For example, see Isa 1:27; 2:2–4; 4:3; 6:13; 7:3; 8:11–20; 10:20–23; 11:11; 17:3.

23. See previous discussion of Kebede's treatment of Isa 2:1–5.

24. The שְׁאָר "remnant" is mentioned only briefly in Isa 4:3 and 7:3. A lengthier presentation of the Lord's plan in reference to the remnant and their enemy is contained in Isa 10:11–34. A more detailed discussion of the remnant in the context of Isa 10 will be offered below.

Inclusivism and Particularism in Isaiah

Isaiah 8

Isaiah presented the Lord as a stumbling stone in Isa 8:14 within the larger context of Isa 7:1—9:6, which includes the Immanuel motif and the motif's implications for Israel during the Syro-Ephraimitic crisis.[25] Isaiah 8 serves as an elaboration of the messianic hope of Isa 7 and begins to develop, though not fully, the remnant theme. In reference to Isa 8:11–23 (Eng. 9:1), Oswalt wrote that the unit constitutes "a reflection upon all which has preceded from 7:1 onwards."[26]

Isaiah developed the motif of Immanuel and its implications upon disobedient Israel in Isa 8. In vv. 1–4, Isaiah prophesied the Lord's use of the Assyrian Empire to destroy both the northern kingdom of Israel and Damascus. In vv. 5–8, Isaiah prophesied the Lord's use of Assyria to bring judgment upon the southern kingdom of Judah. In vv. 9–10, Isaiah prophesied a coming judgment upon the nations or peoples of "distant lands" who plan Israel's destruction. In vv. 11–15, the Lord's presence among his people (i.e., Immanuel) is described as a sanctuary for some and a stumbling stone for others. In vv. 16–23 (Eng. 9:1), Isaiah contrasted the dark and gloom of the Lord's judgment of Israel with the light and hope of his salvation of Israel. In 9:1–6 (Eng. 9:2–6), Isaiah reaches a climax with the promise of a coming Davidic king, who would bring about an ideal reign. Throughout Isa 8, the consequences of Immanuel are described as an experience of both judgment and salvation for the nation of Israel.[27]

The nations are mentioned explicitly within Isaiah's presentation of the Lord's plan of judgment and salvation for Israel in Isa 8. Though Israel is made to suffer at the hands of the Assyrians for a time, Isaiah assured them that the judgment is coming for their oppressors as well (Isa 8:9–10). The futility of international hostility toward the city where the Lord dwells

---

25. The Syro-Ephraimitic crisis is a reference to a historical situation concerning the alliance of Pekah of Israel (Ephraim) and Rezin of Damascus (Aram) and subsequent war with Jotham and his son Ahaz of Judah in the eighth century B.C. The alliance against Judah was in response to Judah's refusal to ally with Ephraim and Aram against the threat of Tiglath-pileser III of the Assyrian Empire. For further discussion of the historical particulars of the Syro-Ephraimite crisis, see Oswalt, *Book of Isaiah*, 1:5–9; Irvine, *Isaiah*; Smith, *Isaiah*, 27–29.

26. Oswalt, *Book of Isaiah*, 1:231.

27. For further discussion of the literary structure of Isa 7:1—9:6 and more specifically 8:11–21, see Oswalt, *Book of Isaiah*, 1:231, 194–95; Moyter, *Prophecy of Isaiah*, 62–63, 70–71.

in vv. 9–10 is a theme reminiscent of Pss 2 and 46–48.[28] If Ps 2 is echoed in Isa 8, then the dominance of the nations by the anointed one, as seen in Ps 2, may be present within the denunciation of the war cry of the nations in Isa 8. Though the destruction of the nations and the eventual salvation of the remnant of Israel are portrayed within the same context of Isa 8, the two are not necessarily linked. Isaiah's purpose in Isa 8:9–10 is not to promote the exaltation of Israel at the expense of the nations but rather to promote the Lord's sovereignty over everything, even a powerful nation like Assyria.

Isaiah also pronounced the removal of Israel's oppression in Isa 9:3 (Eng. Isa 9:4), which again reflects a more particularistic than inclusive attitude. The focus of Isa 9:3 (Eng. Isa 9:4) on the end of Israel's subjugation rather than on the destruction of the nations does suggest caution toward interpreting Isa 9:3 as necessarily particularistic. Though the seeds of particularism may be identified in Isa 8:9–10 and Isa 9:3 (Eng. Isa 9:4), an explicit presence of inclusivism or particularism is absent from the context of Isa 7:1–9:6.

Isaiah 10–11

Unlike the contexts of Isa 1 and 8, the context of Isa 10 contains explicit treatment of the relation of Israel's salvation to the nations, especially Assyria. Though the proclamation of judgment in Isa 10:1–4 may be directed toward Judah alone, the following oracle in Isa 10:5–34 quickly extends that judgment toward the Assyrians. Indeed, most scholars divide Isa 10:5–34 from Isa 10:1–4 as a separate oracle.[29]

---

28. Moyter and Childs both suggested a connection between Ps 2 and the language in Isa 8:9–10 concerning the tradition of the futility of international hostility toward the Lord's anointed. Moyter further stated that the uproar of the nations is "a part of the cultic representation of the international hostility" (Moyter, *Prophecy of Isaiah*, 93–94). Childs, *Isaiah*, 73–74.

29. While some scholars have argued that the judgment oracle of Isa 10:1–4 is directed exclusively toward Judah, others have suggested that nothing in the contexts demands that view and that the explicit focus upon Assyria in Isa 10:5–34 suggests that the judgment oracle of Isa 10:1–4 is directed at all the nations. For support of Judah as the primary object of the judgment oracle in Isa 10:1–4, see Childs, *Isaiah*, 86–87. For support of Assyria as the primary object of the judgment oracle in Isa 10:1–4, see Oswalt, *Book of Isaiah*, 1:258–59. In reference to the structure of Isa 10, Watts argued that the repetition of the refrain "In all this his anger has not turned, His hand is still outstretched" in 10:4b suggests that 10:1–4 is part of the Isa 9:7—10:4 unit and functions as a pivot to the oracle in Isa 10:5–34. Watts, *Isaiah*, 1:143–44. For further discussion of the structure of Isa 10, see Oswalt, *Book of Isaiah*, 1:250–51; Childs, *Isaiah*, 90–91.

Inclusivism and Particularism in Isaiah

In Isa 10:5–34, Isaiah assured the remnant that though the Assyrians will come against them as a rod, they are still only a rod in the hand of the sovereign Lord. In Isa 10:5–19, Assyria's judgment will come because the nation's actions have exceeded its divine mandate as a tool for punishment concerning Israel. Furthermore, the condition of Assyria's "heart" is presented as proud and boastful (vv. 10:7, 12–15) and its intentions misguided (vv. 10:8–11). Therefore, Assyria's future judgment is pronounced as certain.

Alongside the judgment of Assyria, Isaiah presented the return of "the remnant of Jacob" (Isa 10:21). The return of the remnant, which suffered under God's judgment as a part of Israel, was portrayed in Isa 10 as a repentance due to divine correction.[30] The future deliverance of the remnant from Assyrian rule was compared to Israel's past deliverance from both the Midians and the Egyptians (Isa 10:24–26) and presented as a fulfillment of the Abrahamic covenant promise (10:22–23). The context of Isa 10 contains a close connection between the destruction of Israel's enemy, namely Assyria; and the deliverance of the remnant can be observed.[31] Though the role of the nations is not central to the oracle of Isa 10:5–34, the context is more inclined toward particularism.

The literary context of the prophecy of Isa 11 is significant in that the prophecy serves as a summary of the major division of Isa 7–12.[32] Watts wrote that Isa 11 is "from the stock of literature belonging to the lore of the

---

30. The term שׁוב is ambiguous and can be translated as "turn," "return," or "repent," and scholars have debated whether Isa 10 portrays a return from exile (i.e., return) or a turning away from a misplaced trust in Egypt for deliverance to a trust in God (i.e., repent). The interpretation of שׁוב as "repentance" in Isa 10 is justified for several reasons. First, the remnant is presented as a recipient of God's judgment in Isa 10. As Childs noted, the remnant in Isaiah "are not exempt from the destruction of Israel, but share fully in the nation's judgment" (*Isaiah*, 94). Second, Israel's restoration in conjunction with their repentance is presented both in Isa 10 and elsewhere in Isaiah (Isa 1:27, 10:25).

31. Childs noted that the passage concerning the deliverance of the remnant and subsequent judgment of Assyria (Isa 10:20–23) is introduced as an eschatological vision. He further suggested that the remnant would return to the prophesied messianic ruler portrayed in Isa 9:5 (*Isaiah*, 94–95). If the oracle of Isa 10:5–34 is to be identified as an eschatological vision of the coming reversal, then the explicit discussion of the remnant in Isa 10 could prove to be a central concept of Isaiah's vision of Israel's destiny. While discussing the significance of the remnant concept in Isaiah, Oswalt likewise suggested that the remnant concept may be "the most apt summary of the entire book, since it captures the interwoven themes of redemption and judgment that prevail from beginning to end" (*Book of Isaiah*, 1:269).

32. For further discussions and outlines of the divisions of the book of Isaiah, see Young, *Book of Isaiah*, 23–24; Oswalt, *Book of Isaiah*, 1:54–60; Childs, *Isaiah*, 1–2.

Davidic monarchy."³³ The exaltation of a Davidic king and the subsequent implications upon both the earth and the people of Israel are the central focus of the passage. The Davidic king is described as a "shoot from the root of Jesse" in Isa 11:1 and a "root of Jesse" in Isa 11:10. The Davidic figure is described as one in which a right relationship between the Lord and the king will be established, which will result in the king's ruling with sound judgment, righteousness, and wisdom (Isa 11:2–5). The effects of the Davidic figure's rule upon God's creation will be a universal peace (Isa 11:6–9), and his programmatic rule will include the gathering of the exiles of Israel (Isa 11:10–16).

A consideration of the relationship between the nations and the programmatic rule of the Davidic figure is present within Isa 11. For example, the "knowledge of the Lord" is predicted to fill the earth (Isa 11:9), and the nations will דרש ("seek") the "root of Jesse" (Isa 11:10). Twice the Davidic figure is described as a נס ("banner") to the nations (Isa 11:10, 12). His function as a banner is described more fully in Isa 11:12–16 for the purpose of drawing the remnant back from exile. As scholars have noted, one of the major themes in Isa 11 is the remnant.³⁴

Although the prediction in Isa 11:10 that the nations will "seek" after the Davidic figure reflects an element of inclusivism, the context of Isa 11:11–16 suggests that the nations will be subjected to the remnant of Israel. When Isa 11:11–16 is read in isolation from the surrounding literary context, the voice of particularism is observed. Otto Kaiser reconciled these two messages concerning the nations by dividing Isa 11 into two sections (Isa 11:1–9 and 11:10–16) and argued for a later post-exilic composition of Isa 11:10–16. For Kaiser, the post-exilic editor sought to link his own prophecy, which centers around the return of the remnant who "remained conscious of its distinctive" while in exile, to the more inclusive portrayal of peace in Isaiah's original prophecy in Isa 11:1–9. He further argued that the phrase בכל־הר קדשי ("on my holy mountain") in v. 9 was an intentional interpolation by the later editor meant to limit the scope of peace brought by God.³⁵ In opposition to the argument concerning the presence of par-

---

33. Watts, *Isaiah*, 1:173.

34. For further discussion of the overall background including the subjects of the remnant and the programmatic presentation of the Davidic figure in Isa 11, see Oswalt, *Book of Isaiah*, 1:276–89; Childs, *Isaiah*, 157–66.

35. Kaiser, *Isaiah*, 163–66. Herntrich, *Prophet Jesaia*, 217, suggested that v. 10 be viewed separately from vv. 1–9 and vv. 11–16 because the messianic witness in v. 10 differs from vv. 1–9 and v. 12. Wildberger, *Isaiah*, 463, 482, similarly recognized the different messianic

ticularism in Isa 11, Childs argued that when the redactional move concerning the combination of the phrase "root of Jesse" with "banner" in v. 10 is understood fully, a better resolution to the tension becomes apparent. For Childs, the redactional effect joins the Messiah and his community to the flowing of the nations to Zion pictured in Isa 2:1–4.[36]

Apart from trying to resolve the tension concerning the role of the nations in the programmatic rule of the Davidic figure in Isa 11, several observations can be made. First, Isa 11 is significant in that the prophecy brings to a culmination the themes presented in Isa 6–10, which include the coming Davidic ruler, as well as the relation of his reign to both Israel and the nations. Second, the role of the nations in relation to the programmatic rule of the Davidic figure is not the main focus of the text, though elements of the voices of both particularism and inclusivism can be found within the text. As the scholarly discussion reflected by Kaiser and Childs demonstrates, the portrayal of the nations in the passage can be read with an emphasis upon inclusivism or particularism.[37]

Isaiah 27–29

Some of the same elements of particularism and inclusivism present in Isa 11 can be recognized in Isa 27–29 as well. While debate concerning the major divisions of Isa 13–39 has occurred in scholarly discussion, a considerable consensus concerning the divisions of Isa 24–27 and Isa 28–33 as smaller units within Isa 13–39 also can be noted. Isa 24–27 has been called the "apocalypse of Isaiah" due to its abundance of eschatological language and apocalyptic imagery.[38] The Lord's judgment expressed in Isa 13–23,

---

expectations between vv. 1–9 and vv. 11–16, and concluded that Isa 11:10 reflects the hand of a later redactor. He further concluded that the redactor inserted v. 10 as a parallel with the more universal messianic expectation witness in Isa 2:2–4. While vv. 1–9 and 12–16 do focus more on the remnant of Israel and v. 10 focuses on the role of the nations, the two are not necessarily dichotomous.

36. Childs, *Isaiah*, 105–6.

37. For example, Gray argued in reference to Isa 11:10 that the exaltation of the capitol of the monarchy of the restored Jewish community will result in the nations coming and consulting with the king "as an organ of the revelation of the one true God. cf. 2:2–4" (*Critical and Exegetical Commentary*, 224). Reflecting a more particularistic interpretation, Watts wrote, "The claim is put forward (v10) that the king should be the rallying point of the nations, i.e., that his 'glory' will be in military leadership. This accords with the monarchy theory. God will rule through the Davidic king" (*Isaiah*, 1:175).

38. Oswalt, *Book of Isaiah*, 1:440.

specifically in reference to a list of particular nations, is expanded into a broader expression of his lordship over the whole earth in Isa 24–27. Isaiah 28–29 then begins a series of woe oracles that continues through Isa 33. The woe oracles of Isa 28–29 are directed at Judah and the nation's leaders.

Isaiah 27 closes the eschatological presentation of the Lord's sovereignty in Isa 24–27 and illustrates his sovereignty with respect to Israel and the nations. The sovereignty of the Lord over Israel is described with a vineyard analogy in Isa 27:2–6. Israel was prophesied to take root and fill the earth with fruit. The sovereignty of the Lord over the nations is portrayed as the destruction of Israel's oppressors in Isa 27:7–11. The Lord's sovereignty over Israel then is illustrated in the anticipated return of the exiles from among the nations in Isa 27:12–13. The exiles in Egypt and Assyria again will experience worship in Jerusalem.

As Childs noted, the most controversial section of Isa 27 is vv. 7–11.[39] The central focus upon Israel's return from exile and the atonement of her sins seems beyond debate. What can be debated is the role of the nations in relation to Israel's atonement and return. Does the atoning of Jacob's sin, mentioned in Isa 27:9, demonstrate the destruction of the nations or just the removal of idolatry from Jerusalem? The harsh accusation toward Israel's oppressors in Isa 27:7 and the possible identification of the city made desolate and the people of the city who receive no compassion or favor from God in Isa 27:10–11 suggest that the destruction of the nations is in view. The conclusion hinges on the interpretation of two crucial elements, namely the referent of "this" in Isa 27:9 and the identity of the city and its people in Isa 27:10–11.

The phrase בזאת ("by this") in Isa 27:9 can be understood within the context of Isa 27 to refer to the exile of Israel. The punishment of Israel is contrasted with the punishment of their oppressors in Isa 27:7, and as a result the message to Israel is that their punishment was for a different purpose. Israel's punishment was for discipline, whereas the punishment upon the nations resulted in their complete destruction. The description of exile as a tool for the Lord to bring about the atonement of Israel is the focus of Isa 27:7–9. As a result, the city made desolate in Isa 27:10 can be understood as a reference to Jerusalem during the time of the exile. If the city made desolate in Isa 27:10 is Jerusalem, then the annihilation of the

---

39. Childs stated that the interpretation of Isa 27:7–11 is made difficult due to the uncertainty of the Hebrew text. Gray likewise noted that the "unintelligibility" of the Hebrew text in Isa 27 makes the interpretation difficult. For further discussion, see Gray, *Critical and Exegetical Commentary*, 453; Childs, *Isaiah*, 194.

nations as a part of Israel's return, which is an element of particularism, is absent from the context. On the other hand, the mention of a complete lack of compassion and favor upon the people of the city would seem to contradict the message of God's sovereignty over Israel reflected in the context of Isa 27:1–9. This description of God's attitude toward the people of the city would suggest that the city refers to the nations. The destruction of the nations as a part of Israel's restoration would indicate the presence of particularism in Isa 27.[40]

In conclusion, God's sovereignty over Israel as expressed in their return from exile is the central focus of Isa 27. Israel's exile was a temporary measure for the Lord to bring about Israel's atonement, and as a result the future return from exile is proclaimed confidently. The implications of God's sovereignty for his relationship to the nations are more difficult to ascertain. Both elements of particularism and inclusivism can be read from the text depending upon one's interpretation of "this" in v. 9 and the identity of the people of the city in vv. 10–11.

The tone concerning Israel changes from the positive message in Isa 27 to a negative and critical message in Isa 28–29.[41] The prophetic messages of Isa 28 and 29 both begin with a distinct term of lament, הוֹי ("woe"), signaling a series of woe oracles. The situation concerning the people of Israel and their leaders is depicted as deplorable. In Isa 28:1–13, the northern kingdom is denounced and predicted to fall. With the explicit turn in criticism toward Jerusalem and the leaders of Judah in Isa 28:14—29:24, the messages of Isa 28–29 are directed entirely toward Judah and Jerusalem. The denouncement of Ephraim's drunkenness and lack of insight serves as an example of comparison to the Israelites in Judah and Jerusalem. As Oswalt noted, Isaiah's indictment of the northern kingdom in Isa 28:1–13 warned the people of Judah that they were not to rejoice over the fall of

---

40. Oswalt disagreed and saw the city as a symbol of Judah's oppressors (*Book of Isaiah*, 1:499). Gray also interpreted the identity of the people without understanding in v. 11 as the nations and argued that this identity reflects a later Jewish thought that the nations must be instructed in the ways of the Lord if they are to keep from perishing (*Critical and Exegetical Commentary*, 459).

41. Childs noted that four distinct units in Isa 28 could be identified (vv. 1–6; 7–13; 14–22; 23–29). He further argued that these units were linked together through a "lengthy historical development." He stated that the "major exegetical task turns on determining the thematic coherence of this passage as a whole" because the earlier Isaianic texts were taken up and reworked within the new composition. He also offered a similar conclusion of Isa 29, which he divided into three units (vv. 1–8; 9–14; 15–24). Childs, *Isaiah*, 204, 214.

Paul and the Synagogue

Samaria, but to learn from Samaria's demise lest they fall as well.[42] The essential point of the woe oracles of Isa 28–33 is that trusting in foreign powers, as Judah was doing with Egypt, instead of the Lord was a fatal mistake.

The polemic against Jerusalem and the people of Judah is especially strong in Isa 28–29. The Lord is described as laying siege to Jerusalem (Isa 28:2–4), silencing the people's speech (Isa 28:5), and bringing about a spirit of stupor and blindness to the people of Jerusalem (Isa 29:9–10). The Lord's action against Jerusalem will be in spite of the people's religious activities (Isa 29:1, 13).

The woe oracles in Isa 28–29 include not only warnings of judgment toward Israel but also promises of restoration to the remnant. For example, the prophet promised in Isa 28:5–6 that "in that day" the Lord would restore "glory" and "beauty" to the remnant. This promise of restoration to the remnant is reflected again in Isa 28:16–17a. As Childs pointed out, the unit of Isa 28:14–22 is one of the most complex in the oracle.[43] The focus has shifted explicitly toward Jerusalem, and the city's fate is predicted to be the same as that of Samaria. The passage portrays a future עשׂה ("work") of the Lord against his enemy and compares the future work to the work the Lord did when he rose up against the Philistines at Mount Perazim and against the Canaanites fleeing from Gideon (Isa 28:21). The Lord's future work will be זר ("strange") and נכרי ("alien"; Isa 28:21) because this time he will come against his people as their enemy.

The future work of the Lord is described also in Isa 28:6–17 as the laying of a stone in Zion. The summary given in the prophecy of Isa 28:16–17 reflects both the message of judgment to the enemy and restoration to the remnant.[44] The laying of the stone within the larger context is described as a "work" that brings about judgment for unbelief and salvation for belief. The same dual function exists in Isa 8:14–15, where the presence of the

---

42. Oswalt, *Book of Isaiah*, 1.515.

43. Childs argued that form-critical analysis has identified the elements of promise in the oracle of Isa 28:5–6 and 16–17a as a separate oracle entirely distinctive from the "invective-threat" oracle in the context. He suggested that the larger editorial shaping combined the two oracles into an "organic unit" (*Isaiah*, 207–10).

44. The suggestions concerning the exact identity of the stone have been many. For purposes of this intertextual study, a more general observation concerning the function of the laying of the stone in the prophecy will suffice. For a summary of the scholarly discussion and a list of the various suggestions, see Oswalt, *Book of Isaiah*, 1:517–19. For discussion of the major interpretational difficulties regarding the stone in Zion, see Childs, *Isaiah*, 208–10.

Lord is described as a stone that both causes some to stumble and serves as a sanctuary for others.

The term גוים ("nations") occurs only twice in the oracles of Isa 28–29 in Isa 29:7–8, where the tone shifts suddenly to describe the destruction of Jerusalem's enemies in Isa 28:5–8. The attackers of Jerusalem eventually will become frustrated, and destruction will come upon them. The focus of the destruction is specifically upon Jerusalem's attackers as opposed to the nations in general. The specific focus upon Jerusalem's attackers emphasizes the main point of the oracle, which was to highlight the failure of trusting in the nations as opposed to the Lord. While the eventual restoration of the remnant expressed in Isa 28–29 can coincide with either particularism or inclusivism, an explicit expression of either particularism or inclusivism is absent from the context of Isa 28–29.

Isaiah 45

The text of Isa 45 consists of two related oracles, namely 45:1–8 and 45:9–25. The oracle of Isa 45:1–8 continues Isaiah's discussion from ch. 44 of the Lord's use of Cyrus to deliver Israel from Babylonian captivity. The oracle of Isa 45:9–25, which comprises of two units, addresses questions raised by the Lord's use of Cyrus in vv. 9–13.[45] Finally, the disputation between the God of Israel and the nations concerning his sovereignty is continued in vv. 14–25.[46] In the disputation of Isa 45:9–25, the God of Israel is compared to the false deities and idols of the nations. The Lord's identity as creator establishes the futility of trusting in false idols and the superiority of trusting in the God of Israel. As creator, the Lord is justified in doing what he wills with Israel, Cyrus, and the nations. The declaration of v. 23 that "before me

---

45. For further discussion of the structure of Isa 45 and its immediate context, see Watts, *Isaiah*, 2:153–54, 159–60; Moyter, *Prophecy of Isaiah*, 352–53; Oswalt, *Book of Isaiah*, 2:212–14; Childs, *Isaiah*, 354.

46. The nature of the disputation and audience of the Isa 45:9–25 oracle has been debated. For example, Oswalt suggested that the disputation was evoked by Israel's objection to the Lord's unusual plan to use Cyrus, a pagan king, to deliver his people. He suggested that all three units in Isa 45 (i.e., vv. 1–8; 9–13; 14–25) were directed toward Israel as the main audience and serve to substantiate the Lord's right to use Cyrus (*Book of Isaiah*, 2:212–13). Childs, on the other hand, suggested that Isa 45:9–13 comprises a single unit and is not addressed to Israel but the nations (*Isaiah*, 354–55). Though the oracle of Isa 45:14–25 is addressed directly to the nations, Israel still may be the primary audience, as seen in the oracles to the nations in Isa 13–23. For discussion in support of Israel as the intended audience of Isa 13–23, see Childs, *Isaiah*, 114–16.

every knee will bow; and by me every tongue swear" reflects Isaiah's focus upon God's unmatched sovereignty. Not only will Israel acknowledge the exclusivity of the God of Israel but so also will the nations.

In the disputation of Isa 45, Israel's captivity does little to prove the superiority of the false gods of the nations over the God of Israel. To the contrary, Israel's captivity serves as an opportunity for the God of Israel to demonstrate his superiority as the creator and Lord of all the nations. As Oswalt noted in reference to Israel's captivity, "in this way Israel's extremity has become God's opportunity."[47]

Most probably the mention of exiles in Isa 45:13 is a reference to Israel and the oracles are a prophetic promise to Israel concerning the nations, though the characteristics of the nations' role within the prophetic promise of Israel's return and deliverance are debatable. For example, the wealth of Egypt and Cush is predicted to become the property of Israel and the Ethiopians are described as coming to Israel "in chains" (v. 14), both of which reflect a more particularistic perspective. On the other hand, the nations are described as proclaiming that "there is no other god" in reference to the God of Israel (v. 14). Furthermore, the nations are extended an explicit invitation to abandon their false idols and join in the salvation of Israel (vv. 22–24). The salvation of the people in the world who turn to the God of Israel portrayed in vv. 22–24 is a clear expression of the inclusive view. As a result, elements of both particularism and inclusivism can be observed within the oracles of Isa 45.[48]

---

47. Oswalt, *Book of Isaiah*, 2:221.

48. Some scholars have argued the possibility that the context of Isa 45 supports the interpretation that the language of Isa 45:14 does not necessarily refer to a forced captivity of the nations by Israel. For example, Oswalt suggested that the references to the nations may serve simply as a representation "of such things as the ends of the earth, great wealth, physical beauty, and so on." He concluded that consideration of the overall context of Isa 45 should result in the interpretation that the chains of v. 14 do not reflect a forced submission but rather a voluntary submission by the nations (*Book of Isaiah*, 2:214–15). Childs likewise concluded that the reference to chains in v. 14 should be viewed as a "voluntary enslavement" to Israel that results from their acknowledgment of Israel's role in their liberation (*Isaiah*, 354–55). Moyter also interpreted the submission as voluntary submission to Israel as a part of their conversion to the Lord, and so is the result of a "religious motivation" (*Prophecy of Isaiah*, 361–62). The context of Isa 45 does suggest the possible interpretation of a voluntary submission of the nations. The observation made here is that a submission to Israel, especially when described as captivity (i.e., "in chains"), reflects particularism. The salvation extended to the nations in Isa 45 is not on equal terms with Israel but rather in subservience to Israel.

Inclusivism and Particularism in Isaiah

Isaiah 52–53

Isaiah 52–53 most often is divided into two major sections (Isa 52:1–12 and 52:13–53:12).[49] In context of Isa 52:1–12, Isaiah is focused entirely on the future salvation of Zion, the city of Jerusalem. Zion's future restoration is described as a proclamation that Zion's God reigns (Isa 52:7). The reign of God in Zion will bring שלום ("peace"), טוב ("good"), and ישועה ("salvation"). The context indicates that the salvation of Jerusalem is expressed as a deliverance from bondage in exile. Jerusalem is described as שבי "captive" and in מוסרי ("bonds"; Isa 52:2). The prophet placed the salvation of Zion with the covenant history of the Lord and Israel by connecting the Babylonian exile with the exodus of Egypt and the oppression of Assyria. As Beltzer noted, the references to עמי ("my people") in Isa 52:5 and עמו ("his people") are covenant language.[50] The proclamation in Isa 52:1–12 is that the Lord, as king of Israel, has remained faithful to his covenant people and acted to redeem and restore Zion from the consequences of exile.

The role of the nations figures prominently in Isa 52:1–12, and explicit mention of them is made several times. For example, Isaiah proclaimed in v. 1 that the ערל ("uncircumcised") will not enter the city again. He further stated in v. 5 that the foreign rulers of Israel blaspheme the Lord. Finally, Isaiah described the nations in v. 10 as witnessing the holy arm of the Lord, and the ends of the earth will witness the salvation of Israel's God.

At first glance, the attitude toward the nations seems to reflect particularism, though a closer look may indicate otherwise. The refusal to allow the uncircumcised to enter in Isa 52:1 suggests a rejection of the nations. On the other hand, the contextual focus upon the holiness of the city for the purpose of honoring the Lord's name suggests a different conclusion. The Lord redeems Zion and ends the oppression of the people of Israel in exile because the oppressors mock God's name (Isa 52:5). The nations are presented negatively due to their blasphemy but the real focus is on the reason for the Lord's salvation, namely his own honor. Although the nations' witness of Israel's salvation in Isa 52:10 is devoid of any language regarding their inclusion, the text does not demonstrate explicitly their destruction either.[51] The overall focus of the passage is upon the Lord's honor as the

---

49. For further discussion of the divisional structure of Isa 52–53, see Torrey, *Second Isaiah*, 409–14; Whybray, *Isaiah*, 169; Oswalt, *Book of Isaiah*, 2:15; Baltzer, *Deutero-Isaiah*, 15–21; Childs, *Isaiah*, 401.

50. Baltzer, *Deutero-Isaiah*, 381.

51. Baltzer argued that the phrase "bears his holy arm" in Isa 52:10 reflects the idea "to

purpose of Israel's salvation. The presence of the seeds of particularism in Isa 52 does not necessarily imply a particularistic attitude on the part of Isaiah, because a fully developed and explicit exclusion or destruction of the nations is absent. Coupled with the lack of distinct elements of inclusivism, Isaiah's attitude toward the nations in Isa 52 is left open for debate.

Isaiah 52:13—53:12 often is described as a servant song.[52] The servant is described first as exalted and lifted up (Isa 52:13), which is followed immediately by a description of his suffering (Isa 52:14–15). The servant's identity is unclear, but some aspects of his function can be ascertained.[53] Isaiah described one of the servant's functions as suffering for the iniquities of others (Isa 53:6). Still, the scope of the servant's sacrificial suffering is unclear. Who are the "many" who are appalled at his appearance in Isa 52:14? Whose iniquity does the servant bear in Isa 53:6? The servant is exalted, yet his suffering will cause him to be rejected (Isa 53:3). Who are the "many" who are appalled at and reject the servant? Are they the same as the lamenters who confess the servant's role in bearing their iniquities in Isa 53:1? Ambiguity in the text concerning the identity of each group has led to various interpretations of the scope of the servant's suffering.[54]

---

help" (*Deutero-Isaiah*, 384). Watts claimed that the "bearing of his holy arm" was a reference to the rebuilding of the temple (*Isaiah*, 2:217). Both of these suggestions support the idea that the main focus is on Israel's salvation as opposed to the destruction of the nations.

52. For further discussion of the identity of Isa 52:13–53:12 as a servant song, see Lindblom, *Servant Songs*, 37–38; Oswalt, *Book of Isaiah*, 2:375; Baltzer, *Deutero-Isaiah*, 393–94; Childs, *Isaiah*, 441.

53. As Oswalt noted, a survey of scholarly research concerning Isa 52:13–53:12 yields two observations: the amount of scholarly work done on the passage is considerable, and surprisingly little consensus has emerged (*Book of Isaiah*, 2:377). The identity of the servant is one of the major issues debated. The identification of the servant is beyond the scope of this research and therefore will not be addressed. For further discussion of the major issues of interpretation, especially in relation to the identity of the servant, see Baltzer, *Deutero-Isaiah*, 394–95; Childs, *Isaiah*, 410–11; Watts, *Isaiah*, 2:228–29. Lindblom likewise argued that one's identification of the "we" is dependent upon one's identification of the servant. He concluded that the servant is Israel personified, particularly Israel in captivity. As a result, he also concluded that Israel's suffering was for the benefit of the Gentiles (*Servant Songs*, 42– 51).

54. For example, Childs rejected identifying the confessing "we" in Isa 53 as the nations. Instead, he argued that a change in speaker takes place in Isa 52:15b. The people astonished and appalled in Isa 52 are the nations, and the people who recognize and confess the suffering of the servant are the people of Israel (*Isaiah*, 412–13). Oswalt argued that the identity of the confessing "we" in Isa 53 centers on the identity of the servant. If the servant is collective Israel, then the "we" is the nations of Isa 52:14–15. If the servant is not Israel, which is the position Oswalt argued, then the "we" is Israel (*Book of Isaiah*, 2:381–82).

Inclusivism and Particularism in Isaiah

Furthermore, the exact attitude toward the nations in Isa 52:13—53:12 is debatable. Are the nations included within the "all" whose iniquities are carried by the servant? Does the scope of the servant's intercession include or exclude the nations? The astonishment of the nations at the appearance of the servant is apparent in Isa 52:14-15. If the servant is interpreted as Israel, then the "all" who are benefited by the vicarious suffering of the servant could include the nations. The inclusion of the nations within the scope of the servant's mission would reflect an attitude of inclusivism. If the servant were interpreted as an individual apart from Israel, then Israel would be the "all" who are benefited by the vicarious suffering of the servant. The combination of the astonishment of the nations in Isa 52:14-15 and the omission of an explicit inclusion of them within the mission of the servant in Isa 53 would reflect an attitude of particularism. The ambiguity within the text itself can lead to either a particularistic or an inclusive interpretation.

Isaiah 59

Isaiah 59 concludes the first unit in Isa 56-66. Several of the themes, such as righteousness, covenant, and sin, occurring in Isa 56-58 are repeated and addressed more fully in Isa 59. Isaiah 59 consists of the three closely related units of vv. 1-8, 9-15a, and 15b-21.[55] The charge against Israel's wickedness in Isa 59:1-8, which summarizes the accusation of rebellion and sin given in Isa 58:1-14, then is followed by a confession of guilt and helplessness by the people of Israel in Isa 59:9-15a. The Lord's silence toward Israel introduced in Isa 58:2-3 is revisited and defended against false claims concerning the Lord's inability to hear and save in Isa 59:1-2. Isaiah

---

55. Isaiah 59 contains several interpretive difficulties, such as the shifts in literary style, alterations of the speaker and audience, and change in tenses from perfect to imperfect at v. 15b. Still, wide consensus exists on the divisional structure of the chapter. For further discussion in support of this three-part structural division of Isa 59, see Moyter, *Prophecy of Isaiah*, 484, 489-90; Oswalt, *Book of Isaiah*, 2:512, 530-32; Childs, *Isaiah*, 484-86. Watts offered a slightly different structural division of Isa 59 into two sections, vv. 1-15a and vv. 15b-21. His combining of vv. 1-8 and vv. 9-15 into one unit was based on his perception of a chiastic structure in vv. 1-15a, which has little to commend (*Isaiah*, 2:280-82). Perhaps the most debated issue in reference to the structural division of the chapter is the relation of v. 21 to its surrounding context. Some scholars have thought v. 21 to be a prose addition. Even if v. 21 is taken to be a prose addition, the literary function of v. 21 as a summary of Isa 59 argues for its close literary connection to vv. 15b-20 and its interpretation within that unit.

43

then gave a description of Israel's failure to demonstrate social justice in Isa 59:3–8.[56] Faced with the accusation of wickedness expressed throughout Isa 56:1—59:8, the repentant among Israel confessed their sin without offering any excuses in Isa 59:9–15a. The Lord's response to Israel's confession is given in Isa 59:15b–21, which serves as an introduction to the eschatological context of Isa 60–66. The Lord is a righteous warrior who acts to bring justice and salvation to Israel by himself.

The main focus throughout Isa 59 is upon the concept of righteousness in its relation to the covenant.[57] The Lord emphatically described Israel's lack of righteousness (vv. 4, 9, 14) and his subsequent restoration of righteousness (vv. 16, 17) as related to "my covenant" (v. 21).[58] The Lord himself will intervene in judgment to answer the demand for righteousness given in Isa 56–58 (59:15–20). The Lord will come as a redeemer "to Zion and to those who have turned from rebellion in Jacob" (v. 20).[59]

As a part of the Lord's intervention, he is described as repaying anger to his adversaries and retribution to his enemies (v. 18). Notably, the identity of his enemies as the foreign nations is not stated explicitly in Isa 59. Isaiah 59 contains no reference to Assyria, Babylon, Persia, or any of Israel's other neighbors. The enemy that plagues Israel in Isa 56–66 no longer is

56. As Oswalt noted, the sin of social injustice and the sin of idolatry are the two key accusations against Israel throughout Isaiah, and the two sins sum up Isaiah's understanding of sin as a rebellion against God (*Book of Isaiah*, 2:512). Childs also noted the expression of Israel's sin as social injustice in Isa 59, and further suggested that the focus of Isa 59 is the larger "ontological question of the nature of evil within the nation of Israel." He wrote, "The issue of Israel's separating itself from God through sin is not developed as a rebuttal of one specific incident of rebellion, but dealt with on the broader plane of its theological significance to the essential righteousness of God" (*Isaiah*, 486–87).

57. The repeated occurrence of צדק "righteousness" in the immediate context (Isa 59:4, 9, 14, 16, 17), the literary function of v. 21 as a summary of Isa 56–59, and the literary function of Isa 59:15b–21 as an introduction to Isa 60–66 suggest that righteousness in relation to covenant is not only the major focus of Isa 59 but probably of Isa 56–66 as a whole. As Childs noted, the term ברית "covenant" occurs often throughout Isa 56–66, and its occurrence in v. 21 "seems obviously linked to its programmatic occurrence in 56:5–6, addressed to those who join themselves with him." Concerning v. 21, he concluded, "The effect is to summarize and to interpret the whole section comprising chapters 56–59" (*Isaiah*, 490).

58. The presence of the formula "As for me" at the beginning of v. 21 and the repetition of "says the Lord" at the beginning and the end of v. 21 serve to emphasize the Lord's full commitment to the covenant.

59. LXX contains an active verb and reads ἀποστρέψει ἀσεβείας ἀπὸ Ἰακώβ ("he will turn ungodliness from Jacob"), but MT ולשבי פשע ביעקב contains a genitive object of the participle construction and literally reads "those who return of rebellion"; Dead Sea Scrolls and Targum agree.

Inclusivism and Particularism in Isaiah

pictured as Babylon, but Israel's own inability to do justice and righteousness. In short, the enemy is Israel's own sin.[60] Furthermore, the judgment of the Lord is pictured as being worldwide (vv. 18–19) and likely includes the wicked of both the Gentile nations as well as Israel. Though the effect of the Lord's intercession is presented as worldwide, explicit discussion of the relation of the nations to the Lord's covenant with Israel is absent in Isa 59. The role of the nations in relation to Israel's salvation is not addressed explicitly in Isa 59, though the role of the nations surfaces throughout Isa 56–66, as will be observed below.

Isaiah 65

The final Isaiah text explicitly cited in Romans to be analyzed is Isa 65:1–2. The message of Isa 65 is connected closely to the overall message developed in Isa 56–66, which focuses on the issue of the true identity of the people of God.[61] The identity of the true people of God is elaborated in contrast to the misguided piety of individuals who mistakenly consider themselves the people of God. As Isa 56:1–8 indicates, not all who identify themselves as the people of God actually are the people of God. Furthermore, according to Isa 56:3, the people of the God can include also the foreigner who is outside of ethnic Israel.

The same thematic discussion concerning the identity of the people of God is continued also through the rest of Isa 65, in which the primary focus is on the issue of salvation and judgment. Childs noted that the function of Isa 65 as an answer to the people's lament in Isa 63:7—64:11 is arguable.[62] If Isa 65 does function as an answer to the people's lament, then the Lord's response concerning their situation is that he has not been silent. God reveals himself continuously to a people that are not looking. Israel's problem was not inaccessibility to the Lord, but rather their own failure to listen to

---

60. Oswalt suggested that the interpretation of the Lord's enemy as sin in Isa 59 is supported by the structure of Isa 56–59. For example, he noted the repetition of the call to righteousness (56:18; 58:1–14), the description of Israel's inability to do righteousness (56:9–57; 59:1–15a), and the climactic description of God's delivering power described as God's bringing of righteousness (57:14–21; 59:15b–21). Oswalt, *Book of Isaiah*, 2:527.

61. Some debate does exist over the divisional structure within Isa 56–66 and its literary connection to the rest of Isaiah. Still, a considerable consensus concerning the unity of Isa 56–66 and the developed themes in the text has emerged. For further discussion, see Whybray, *Second Isaiah*, 196; Oswalt, *Book of Isaiah*, 2:634–35; Childs, *Isaiah*, 439–49.

62. Childs, *Isaiah*, 535. Oswalt also agreed with this view (*Book of Isaiah*, 2:644).

and obey the Lord's call. The Lord's response that he has not been silent is precisely the point of Isa 65:1–2, which echoes the same defense given in Isa 59. The Lord has revealed himself to a sufficient enough degree to be found by a people who were not even looking (v.1). The rhetoric of Isa 65:1 clearly implies that if a people who were not looking found God, then a people who were seeking certainly could have found him. The people accused in Isa 65:1–2 are identified in the context of Isa 65:1–16 as the obstinate in Israel who refuse to seek God. In relation to the Lord's revelation, two groups are portrayed clearly in Isa 65, namely the faithful within Israel (v. 9) and the disobedient within Israel (v. 11). The two groups are contrasted explicitly in relation to the Lord in Isa 65:13–16, where the faithful are described as "servants."

While explicit expressions of inclusivism and particularism are not present in Isa 65, they are present in the larger context of Isa 56–66. For example, the nations were described as serving Israel with their wealth in the proclamation of the year of the Lord's favor (Isa 61:6–9) and trampled by the Lord in the day of vengeance and redemption (Isa 63:1–6). In contrast, the nations also were described as seeing the Lord's glory (Isa 66:18) and invited to join the people of the Lord (Isa 56:1–8). As has been observed throughout Isaiah, the tension between inclusivism and particularism is evidence in the immediate context of Isa 65 as well.

Conclusion

In conclusion of the exegetical analysis of the contexts of Isa 1, 8, 10–11, 27–29, 45, 52–53, 59, and 65, several observations can be made. First, the analysis identifies the emphasis of several key Isaian themes and the repetition of key Isaian vocabulary throughout the chapters. The major themes of judgment, return, and restoration, as seen in the introductory chapter of Isa 1, are maintained as the major focus of Isaiah's overall prophetic message. Furthermore, Isaiah's focus upon the judgment, return, and restoration of Israel is presented within the context of the covenant and is discussed often in conjunction with covenant language. The Deuteronomic language in Isa 1, the focus upon the Abrahamic covenant in Isa 10, and the presence of covenant terminology in Isa 52 and 59 are all examples of the sustained covenant-oriented context throughout Isaiah.

The prophecy of Isaiah is concerned with the uncertainty of Israel's destiny in the midst of such flagrant violation of their covenant with the

Lord, as given in the Law of Moses and specifically expressed in Deuteronomy. How will the Lord fulfill the Abrahamic covenant to Israel, given their violation of the Law of God? Central to Isaiah's prophetic answer to this question is the remnant. As was observed in the analysis above (q.v. discussion of Isa 1, 8, 10, 11, 28–29), the remnant concept surfaces throughout Isaiah as God's programmatic means of restoring Israel and maintaining his faithfulness to the covenant for the sake of his own glory.

Second, the analysis identified an eschatological element to the themes of judgment, return, and restoration in Isaiah. For example, Israel's destiny portrayed in the restoration of the remnant was connected to the eschatological coming of a Davidic ruler in Isa 11. Also, the judgment and restoration of Israel in Isa 27 and the woe oracles of Isa 28–29 are presented in conjunction with the apocalyptic imagery of Isa 24–27. Finally, the focus upon the Lord's righteousness in relation to his covenant with Israel in Isa 59 is within the eschatological context of Isa 56–66.

Third, the analysis further supports Kebede's thesis that the voices of both inclusivism and particularism are present throughout Isaiah. Explicit expressions of either inclusivism or particularism were found in the contexts (i.e., Isa 8, 10) of several of the Isaiah texts cited by Paul in Romans. Other contexts (i.e., Isa 1, 11, 27–29, 45, 52–53, 59, 65) contain an ambiguity in that elements within those various contexts created the potential of reading the voice of either inclusivism or particularism.

As stated above, the reconciliation of the voices of inclusivism and particularism in Isaiah has occupied much of Isaian scholarship. The purpose of this analysis was not to reconcile the voices or to offer a historical development of the presence of the voices within Isaiah. Rather, the purpose of this analysis was to identify any occurrences of the voices within the specific literary units of Isaiah cited by Paul in Romans and to analyze the contexts of those literary units in order to establish a basic exegetical interpretation for comparison to the Isaiah Targum and Romans. Most significant for purposes of this intertextual research is that the two voices are indeed present and creating tension throughout Isaiah's prophecy concerning the eschatological judgment, return, and restoration of the remnant of Israel; and their presence and tension were observed within many of the literary units cited by Paul in Romans.

3

Particularism in Isaiah Targum

Introduction

As D. E. Hollenberg summarized, "There appears to be a serious conflict between nationalism and universalism in Isaiah xl-lv. There are passages which express the narrowest national self-interest and hatred for Israel's enemies; and there are passages with an exalted vision of world-wide salvation for 'the nations.'"[1] As the analysis of Isaiah demonstrated, the tension created by the presence of the voices of both particularism and inclusivism in the book of Isaiah subsequently has created a debate concerning the interpretation of Isaiah's attitude toward the nations. Various methods of reconciliation of the two voices in Isaiah have been attempted. If the tension was noticed by modern scholarship, did ancient interpreters notice the tension as well? What is the treatment of the tension witnessed in the Isaiah Targum? The intertextual analysis offered here will explore the treatment of the tension in the Isaiah Targum by identifying any unique elements of the two voices in the text. The analysis will focus on the passages that are cited explicitly in Romans. When applicable for interpreting the passage, the analysis also will include elements of the voices found throughout the Isaiah Targum.

Analysis

As noted previously, Chilton identified two major exegetical frameworks controlling the interpretation of Isaiah within the Isaiah Targum: both a

---

1. Hollenberg, "Nationalism and 'The Nations,'" 23–36.

two-level Tannaitic framework and an Amoraic framework, which reflects the historical conjunction between the development of early rabbinic theology and the synagogue context. The presence of the two frameworks reveals an interpretative continuum in which the later Amoraic meturgeman adopted the earlier Tannaitic framework and then added his own framework with its distinct interpretational nuances. A preliminary discussion of the theological similarities and differences of the exegetical frameworks will aid as a backdrop for the analysis of the Isaiah Targum.

Common to both frameworks is an expectation of messianic involvement and restoration of the people of God. Within both frameworks, Israel is a chosen people who possess the divine promise to Abraham and at the same time are rebellious to the Law, which is the central manifestation of that divine election. The contradiction between Israel's divine election and its rebellion to that election, which is its sin, creates a reality in need of a divine intervention. In the Isaiah Targum, the messianic program is the solution to the paradox in Israel.

Distinct to the frameworks are the application of the paradox and a nuanced understanding of the messianic program to the specific historical situation of each meturgeman. The distinctions in the theological frameworks of both the Tannaitic and the Amoraic meturgemanin are observed most clearly with each meturgeman's contextual understanding of key terms and phrases. Chilton identified a number of terms and phrases that evoke the theology of each meturgeman, including "the house of Israel," "Abraham," "the law," "the sanctuary," "the righteous," "Jerusalem," "exile," "Holy Spirit," "repentance," "memra," "Shekinah," "glory," and "Messiah."[2] Both the Tannaitic and the Amoraic meturgemanin contextualized these terms and phrases within their historical circumstances. As a result, they shaped the Isaiah Targum with their own distinct understandings of Israel's situation of rebellion as well as their future restoration in the Lord's messianic program.

For the Tannaitic meturgeman, Israel's sin was a cultic abuse against the Shekinah, which was closely associated with the temple; and Israel's sin manifested due to a lack of teaching of the Law (*Tg. Isa.* 1:3; 2:3; 6:8; 28:12, 24; 33:22; 43:22; 54:13).[3] As a result, the Shekinah was removed temporarily

2. For more detailed discussion of Chilton's identification of these terms and phrases as significant to the identification of the theology of the Isaiah Targum, see Chilton, *The Isaiah Targum*, xiv–xv; and *Glory*, 102–9.

3. As noted by Chilton, the association of teaching and Law in the Isaiah Targum reflects the meturgeman's view of the Law as a living tradition. The meturgeman's

to heaven and was expected to return soon (*Tg. Isa.* 6:1, 6).[4] The threat of removal of the Shekinah due to cultic abuse suggests a pre-70 CE level (*Tg. Isa.* 1:15; 5:1–5; 8:17–18; 28:10), and a return of the Shekinah alongside a literal restoration of the temple suggests a 70–135 CE level (*Tg. Isa.* 53:3–5; 54:8, 10; 60:1–2). The Tannaitic meturgeman portrayed an imminent expectation of the Messiah's intervention throughout the Isaiah Targum and placed his hope in a literal and practical vindication (*Tg. Isa.* 4:2–3; 11:1–10; 28:5–6; 52:11–13; 53:5, 10). For the Tannaitic meturgeman, Israel was communal; and he described them with the more nationalistic phrase "the house of Israel" (*Tg. Isa.* 1:2; 5:3; 42:7; 52:14). The Messiah was expected both to bring and to keep the teaching of the Law (*Tg. Isa.* 9:5–6; 53:5), remove the subjugation of Gentile oppressors (*Tg. Isa.* 10:27; 11:10–14; 33:23; 53:7–12), restore the exiles to the land of Israel (*Tg. Isa.* 42:7; 52:12–13; 53:8), and rebuild the city of Jerusalem and the sanctuary (*Tg. Isa.* 53:5).

For the Amoraic meturgeman, Israel's sin was defined more generally; the individual's responsibility concerning sin was more the focus (*Tg. Isa.* 21:12; 43:14). The urgent call to repentance indicative of the Tannaitic meturgeman was moderated by the Amoraic meturgeman, who saw some in Israel as already repentant (*Tg. Isa.* 33:13; 57:18–19). Israel was described in the Amoraic framework as a "congregation," which suggests a synagogue-oriented community as opposed to the national entity more indicative of the Tannaitic framework (*Tg. Isa.* 12:6, 40:3, 57:14). Furthermore, the Tannaitic expectation of the Messiah's imminent arrival, vindication, and literal deliverance of Israel from exile fades in the Amoraic framework and is overlaid with an acceptance of the exile as the status quo. For the Amoraic meturgeman, the Messiah, the Shekinah, and the temple are already realities before God in heaven and at times are symbolically with Israel in exile (*Tg. Isa.* 12:1–6; 43:10–14).[5]

The interpretative continuum of the two theological frameworks of the Isaiah Targum is understandable within the historical context of and subsequent to Second-Temple Judaism. The historical context of Judea

---

association of teaching with the Law and his emphasis upon the teaching of the Law as central to the messianic program correspond more to the milieu of the early Tannaitic period in conjunction with the Bar Kokhba revolt rather than the later Amoraic period (*Glory*, 15–18).

4. At times, the meturgeman located the Shekinah in Zion, which most likely reflects a pre-70 provenience of the exegetical tradition. For example, see *Tg. Isa.* 17:11 and 18:7.

5. For a more detailed discussion of the theology of the Isaiah Targum, see Chilton, *The Isaiah Targum*, xiv–xv; and *Glory*, 97–102.

in 66–135 CE, which was characterized by the Roman occupation, Jewish tensions concerning temple and priestly impurity, and the first Jewish war and subsequent destruction of the temple, produced the fervent nationalistic expectations witnessed in the Tannaitic framework. A national repentance to the teaching of the Law was expected to prompt the arrival of the Messiah, who would deliver Israel from the dominance of Rome and restore the nation to prominence. Following the disappointment of the Bar Kokhba revolt in 135 CE for Israel and the subsequent deflation of literal messianic hopes, the rabbis reconsidered their interpretation of Israel's paradoxical situation. While repentance to the Law of God as an expression of their divine election remained central, the application and nature of that repentance adjusted to meet the new circumstances. A more theoretical understanding of the relationship between Israel, the Shekinah, and the sanctuary was adopted. The national call to repentance to the Law and to military revolution was replaced with an individual call to endurance in exile and personal obedience to the Law. The messianic program became less eschatological and literal and more conceptual and realized.

Isaiah Targum 1

Considerable overlap in the content and rhetoric between Isaiah and the Isaiah Targum is to be expected, given the Targum's genre as an Aramaic translation of the Hebrew text. Perhaps more surprising is the extensive amount of innovation demonstrated by the meturgeman. Although the same major thematic elements discussed in the analysis of Isa 1 are present also in *Tg. Isa.* 1, so are also some key distinct targumic interpretations.

For example, the meturgeman shaped the divine accusation against the Israelites in Judah and Jerusalem to reflect his interpretation of his own historical context. The meturgeman described Isaiah's original accusation against Israel as a failure to "*teach to* know *the fear of me*" and an ignorance concerning their need "*to return to the law*" (*Tg. Isa.* 1:3).[6] With Isaiah's original call for obedience specifically described as repentance to the Law in the four insertions of "law" into the Isaiah text, the meturgeman

---

6. Additional material and changed vocabulary will be italicized in the English translations of the Targums. Translations of Targum texts are the author's own unless otherwise noted. All Targum texts are from *Targum Johnathan to the Prophets*.

explicitly articulated the significance of the Law as the primary means of Israel's repentance (*Tg. Isa.* 1:3, 16, 18, 27).[7]

The meturgeman further expanded Isaiah's charge that Israel had forsaken the Lord with the addition of cultic terminology. According to the meturgeman, Israel was said to "have forsaken *the service of* the Lord" (*Tg. Isa.* 1:4). He further wrote that "when the *priests* spread *their* hands *to pray*," the Lord declared that he would "*take up the face of my Shekinah*" (*Tg. Isa.* 1:15). For the meturgeman, Israel's abandonment of the Lord was interpreted specifically as a temple cultic abandonment, and he closely associated the cultic temple abuse and the removal of the Shekinah.

As in Isaiah, Israel's covenant with God remained a central focus for the meturgeman. Distinct to the Isaiah Targum is not only an emphasis of Israel's elect status among the nations but also an apparent recognition by the meturgeman of the tension between Israel's elect status and the nation's sinful abandonment of the very God who elected them. The meturgeman wrote, "Woe *because they were called a holy* people, *but* sin*ned*; *a chosen congregation, they have multiplied sins; they were named as a beloved* seed but *they acted* wicked*ly, and it was said of them, 'Cherished sons', but they* corrupt*ed* their ways" (*Tg. Isa.* 1:4).[8] The accusation against Israel's sin in Isaiah became an opportunity for the meturgeman to wrestle with the paradox of Israel's sin in conjunction with the nation's particular status as articulated in the covenant. The meturgeman's angst over the paradox also is observed with his inclusion of a refusal motif into the Isaiah text. According to the meturgeman's interpretation of the current situation, Israel "does not understand, *to return to my law*" (*Tg. Isa.* 1:3); and they "*do* not *desire* repentance" (*Tg. Isa.* 1:6).[9]

---

7. The significance for the meturgeman of the giving of the Law to Israel is observed also in his declaration that even the heavens shook at the revelation of the Law. "Hear, O heavens *which trembled when I gave my law to my people*" (*Tg. Isa.* 1:2).

8. The meturgeman's addition of the ד as a causal conjunction is an innovative syntactical shift, which further demonstrates his concern for and focus upon the paradox. In the Targum, the "woe!" cry does not concern just a nation who sins, as in the Hebrew text, but concerns the paradox itself. For the meturgeman, the real angst is not just that the people have sinned, but that a chosen, holy, beloved, and cherished people who are in possession of the covenant and the Law have sinned.

9. As Chilton noted, the refusal motif is consistent with the call to repentance and highlights both urgency for Israel to repent and the cause of their destruction should they continue to refuse. For further discussion of the refusal motif in the Isaiah Targum, see Chilton, *The Glory of Israel*, 41–42. The further assertion made here is that the conjunction of the motif with the emphasis of the covenant status of Israel also highlights

Particularism in Isaiah Targum

Though the people of Israel hold an elect position among the nations through the covenant, they ironically persist in a refusal to repent. As a result, the meturgeman declared, "*They have no righteousness to protect them*" (*Tg. Isa.* 1:6). How can an elect people, who posses the Law, demonstrate such a persistent refusal to repent? Furthermore, how will God respond? Despite Israel's refusal to repent, God in his "*abounding goodness*" and "*in his mercies*" has left a remnant. Israel declared that if not for God's intervention, "*our sins would have been with us*"; and they would have been destroyed as Sodom and Gomorrah (*Tg. Isa.* 1:9). For the meturgeman, the remnant is evidence of God's faithfulness to the covenant, which establishes Israel's particular status among the nations. In spite of Israel's refusal to repent to the Law, God has extended an opportunity to the remnant.

Elements for both the Tannaitic and Amoraic interpretative frameworks are evidenced in *Tg. Isa.* 1, but the interpretational innovations discussed above derive from the Tannaitic level. The cultic context of Israel's sin (vv. 4, 15), Israel's present state of refusal to repent (vv. 3, 6), the threat of removal of the Lord's Shekinah (v. 15), the nationalistic reference to the people as "*the house of Israel*" (v. 2), and the expected imminent consolation of Jerusalem (v. 24) all witness to the Tannaitic milieu.[10]

Alongside the absence of any elements of the inclusive attitude, the context of *Tg. Isa.* 1 does contain elements of the particularistic attitude within its targumic additions. The Tannaitic meturgeman's nationalistic hope and concern for a literal rebuilding of Jerusalem produced a very innovative rendering of Isa 1:24, where he wrote, "Therefore the Lord *of the world* says, the Lord Almighty, the strong one of Israel, '*The city of Jerusalem I myself am about to comfort*, but *woe to the wicked, when I am revealed to take just payment* from the enemies *of the people*, and I will *return* vengeance to *the enemy*.'" Without warrant in the Hebrew text of Isa 1:24, the meturgeman inserted a consolation of Jerusalem motif. As Chilton noted,

---

the meturgeman's observation of and perhaps his struggle with the paradox itself. Furthermore, the meturgeman's use of קבל ("accept") in the place of the Hebrew שׁמע ("hear") in *Tg. Isa.* 1:10 also may reflect the refusal motif. Chilton acknowledged the more literal rendering of קבל as "accept" but argued that context favored the rendering "listen to" (*The Isaiah Targum*, 2–3). On the other hand, the context of *Tg. Isa.* 1 suggests that קבל as an imperative in contrast to Israel's present state of refusal to repent is better translated to reflect that contrast with "accept" or even "obey." The same meaning of קבל as "accept" in contrast to the refusal motif can be seen elsewhere in the Isaiah Targum. For example, see *Tg. Isa.* 1:19, 20; 9:5; 12:3.

10. An Amoraic influence can be observed with the insertion of "congregation" in *Tg. Isa.* 1:8.

Paul and the Synagogue

the consolation of Jerusalem is inserted into several places throughout the Isaiah Targum, even within contexts that are focused entirely upon retribution and judgment.[11] The pronouncement of judgment upon Israel as the enemy of God in Isa 1:24 has become in the Isaiah Targum a pronouncement of judgment upon the nations who oppress Jerusalem as the enemies of God. A particularistic attitude toward the nations is closely related to the expression of the consolation of Jerusalem in *Tg. Isa.* 1.

Isaiah Targum 8

The same Immanuel theme, which expressed both the judgment and salvation that accompany the Lord's presence with Israel observed in the analysis of Isa 8, was maintained as a central theme in the Isaiah Targum. As was observed in the analysis of *Tg. Isa.* 1, *Tg. Isa.* 8 likewise contains a number of targumic interpretations added to the text. For example, the consolation motif present in *Tg. Isa.* 1 also was inserted into *Tg. Isa.* 8:2. Immediately following a declaration of the coming curses, the meturgeman added, "*Even so all the consolations which I promised to bring . . . I am about to bring back*" (*Tg. Isa.* 8:2). The meturgeman gave greater specification to the Lord's use of Assyria to judge Judah in Isa 8:5–8 with the addition that he would bring against them "*the armies of the Gentiles*" (*Tg. Isa.* 8:7). He further specified Isaiah's description of the judgment of Assyria as an overflowing river sweeping into Judah as reaching to the city of "*Jerusalem*" (*Tg. Isa.* 8:8). As Chilton noted, the meturgeman portrayed the judgment of Isaiah's text in military terms.[12]

---

11. Though Chilton did observe the presence of the consolation motif in the Isaiah Targum, he refrained from including the motif as a theologoumenon. He noted the presence of the consolation motif in *Tg. Isa.* 1:24; 25:2; 54:15; 56:9; 66:6 and observed the connection of the motif to the city of Jerusalem. For further discussion of the consolation of Jerusalem motif within the Isaiah Targum, see Chilton, *The Glory of Israel*, 25–26. The exaltation and restoration of Jerusalem also is witnessed in 4:3; 8:8; 25:2; 45:14; 54:10; 56:9; 60:1, 4, 12, 17. A further observation that could be added is the meturgeman's insertion of נחמה ("consolation") in conjunction with the motif (cf. *Tg. Isa.* 4:3; 8:2; 18:4; 33:2; 40:2; 41:27; 62:1, 10). While the concept and vocabulary of "comfort" are present in the Isaiah text (e.g., Isa 40:1; 66:11), the meturgeman evokes the term consistently in conjunction with literal restoration of Jerusalem or national Israel. The meturgeman's consistent insertion of the consolation motif with the term נחמה and the close association of the motif with the Tannaitic expectation of the restoration of Jerusalem suggest that the occurrence of the motif may be useful as a targumic theologoumenon.

12. Chilton, *The Isaiah Targum*, 19.

Particularism in Isaiah Targum

The concept of exile, also identified by Chilton as a key theologoumenon in the interpretative framework of the Isaiah Targum, figures prominently in *Tg. Isa.* 8. Although the meturgeman described the Shekinah as present on Mount Zion (v. 18), he also presented the exile as a reality in *Tg. Isa.* 8:19—19:1. The meturgeman inserted the same refusal motif observed in *Tg. Isa.* 1 in *Tg. Isa.* 8:16 as the reason for the exile.[13] Despite Israel's lack of desire to learn from the Law (v. 16), the offer for a return from exile and a return of the Shekinah was extended on the condition that Israel repent (v. 18). As might be expected, the meturgeman explicitly identified the coming Davidic king in Isa 9:1-6 (Eng. 9:2-6) as the Messiah. According to the meturgeman's messianic program, the Messiah will remove Israel's oppression (*Tg. Isa.* 9:4), accept and obey the Law (*Tg. Isa.* 9:5), and bring peace to Israel (*Tg. Isa.* 9:6). The presence of the refusal motif, the urgent call to repentance, the removal and expectation of the return of the Shekinah, the focus upon the city of Jerusalem, and the expectation of an imminent restoration brought by the Messiah are all elements that point toward the Tannaitic framework as the dominant interpretational framework of *Tg. Isa.* 7:1-9:7.

As in the Hebrew text of Isa 8:14, the meturgeman presented the Lord as a potential stumbling block in *Tg. Isa.* 8:14 but with a few significant interpretational changes. In Isaiah, the Lord will serve as a מקדש ("sanctuary") for both houses of Israel. In the Isaiah Targum, the מימר ("memra") will be פורען ("an avenger") among Israel. God's promised presence, resulting in safety for Israel in Isa 8:14, becomes a warning in the Targum concerning the coming judgment upon Israel's sin.[14] Furthermore, the stumbling block warning, which is addressed to both houses of Israel in Isaiah, is addressed to the "two houses *of the leaders of* Israel," who "*have been divided against those of the house of Judah*" in the Targum (v. 14).

In reference to the meturgeman's attitude toward the nations, an element of particularism is present in Isa 8:9-10 with a declaration of judgment against Israel's oppressors. Furthermore, the meturgeman's messianic program explicitly includes the removal of Israel's oppression (*Tg. Isa.* 9:4). The seed of particularism present in the context of *Tg. Isa.* 8-9 already was

---

13. The refusal motif is demonstrated with the targumic additions of *"for they do not accept"* and *"they do not wish to learn from it"* as the reason for the Lord's command to Isaiah to seal and hide the law.

14. As noted by Leivy Smolar and Moses Aberbach, the meturgeman's focus in *Tg. Isa.* 8:14 reflects the divine judgment of wrath to come upon Israel for their sin. Smolar and Aberbach, *Studies in Targum*, 199.

observed in the Hebrew text of Isaiah. So, although the destruction of Israel's oppressors (Isa 8:9–10) and removal of Israel's oppression (*Tg. Isa.* 9:4) are included within the meturgeman's messianic program in the context of *Tg. Isa.* 8–9, these elements of particularism are not an innovative insertion into the text by the meturgeman. When the meturgeman innovatively discussed nations in *Tg. Isa.* 7:1—9:6, the nations served as instruments of God's wrath upon Israel (*Tg. Isa.* 9:5).

Two significant observations can be made concerning the role of the nations pictured in the context of *Tg. Isa.* 7:1—9:6. First, the meturgeman accepted the particularism present in the Isaiah Hebrew text without adding any innovative enhancements or alterations. Second, the meturgeman made no attempt to include inclusivism into the messianic program. These two observations suggest that while the voice of particularism was not inserted overtly, the lack of any elements of inclusivism and the acceptance of the particularism already present in the Isaiah Hebrew text reflects a more particularistic attitude on the part of the meturgeman.

Isaiah Targum 10–11

The meturgeman clarified the ambiguity of the addressee observed in Isa 10:1–4 with his additions identifying Israel as the recipient of the pronounced judgment. In *Tg. Isa.* 10:4, the meturgeman portrayed the exile motif in distinctive terms, "*outside of your land*" and "*outside of your cities.*" He also repeated the refusal motif seen in *Tg. Isa.* 9:12, 17, 21 with the same innovative language, "For all this *they did not repent of their sin that his anger might turn from them* and *still now they continue to strengthen their rebellion and* still *his stroke is about to take retribution from them.*" The same themes of Israel's refusal to repent and God's resulting judgment upon Israel seen in *Tg. Isa.* 8–9 are carried over into *Tg. Isa.* 10:1–4.

Likewise, *Tg. Isa.* 10:5–34 contains many innovative expansions by the meturgeman. For example, the meturgeman more distinctively portrayed the conquest of Assyria than in the MT with militaristic terms in *Tg. Isa.* 10:13, 14.[15] The meturgeman continued to portray the exile of Israel (*Tg.*

---

15. Chilton observed the presence of a detailed military triumph in *Tg. Isa.* 10. He suggested that the rendering might have derived from the meturgeman's knowledge of the Roman destruction of Jerusalem (*The Isaiah Targum*, 25). Smolar and Aberbach further suggested that the innovative rendering in *Tg. Isa.* 10:32 may be a midrashic addition reflecting the Roman advancement against Jerusalem under Titus (*Studies in Targum*, 76–77).

Particularism in Isaiah Targum

Isa. 10:13) as the result of Israel's sin, which he described as a transgression of the Law (*Tg. Isa.* 10:6). The same judgment brought upon Assyria for the nation's pride and arrogance seen in Isaiah was made even more precise by the meturgeman in the Targum.[16]

The meturgeman also further developed the remnant motif observed in Isa 10:21–24. He wrote in v. 21, "A remnant *that have not sinned, and that have repented from sin,* the remnant *of the house of Jacob* will return to serve before the mighty God." The remnant was defined specifically as those who repent from sin and by implication turn to the Law of God. For the meturgeman, the result will be a return to the cultic service of the temple by the remnant. Furthermore, the meturgeman described the remnant's return with language echoing the exodus narrative of Israel's liberation from Eygpt (v. 22).[17]

Within Isaiah's prophecy of the return of the remnant, the meturgeman found occasion to invoke the Messiah and explicate the messianic program (*Tg. Isa.* 10:26–27). Even more significant is that central to the meturgeman's messianic program as rendered in *Tg. Isa.* 10 is the simultaneous destruction of the nations. For example, the meturgeman's expansion of Assyria's destruction witnessed in *Tg. Isa.* 10:17–19 illustrates an acute interest in the destruction of Jerusalem's enemies. Likewise, the messianic program includes the destruction of *"the wicked"* (v. 23) for the benefit of those who are of *"the house of Jacob"* (v. 25). Lastly, the meturgeman boldly proclaimed in *Tg. Isa.* 10:27 that *"the Gentiles will be shattered before the Messiah."* With the innovative additions to *Tg. Isa.* 10, the meturgeman displayed an overt attitude of particularism.

The Isaiah Targum also contains a number of interesting interpretational glosses in the text of Isa 11. For example, the "son of Jesse" in Isa 11:1 was described as משיחא (*"the Messiah"*) in the Targum. The interpretation of the son of Jesse as the Messiah is significant in that *Tg. Isa.* 11 offers a

---

16. For example, the meturgeman rendered the MT phrase "Therefore the Lord, the Lord Almighty" in Isa 10:16 with *"Because the king of Assyria has magnified himself, therefore the master of the world, the Lord of hosts"* in *Tg. Isa.* 10:16. Also, the destruction of "his thorns" and "his briers" in Isa 10:17 was rendered as the destruction of "his rulers" and "his tyrants" in *Tg. Isa.* 10:17.

17. For example, the MT's בו כליון חרוץ שוטף צדקה ("with it the decreed destruction overflowing with righteousness") was rendered in the Targum דמתגברן ומידברן בזכו יתעבדן להון גבורן ("for them powerful deeds will be made which are mighty deeds bringing righteousness"). The close proximity of this inventive rendering with the recurrence of גבר ("mighty deeds") in the clear analogy of the exodus event in *Tg. Isa.* 10:26 strongly suggests the presence of the exodus narrative echo in *Tg. Isa.* 10:22.

composite view of the messianic program expected by the meturgeman, who described the Messiah as a מלך ("*king*") who will be רבי ("*exalted*"; *Tg. Isa.* 11:1). The meturgeman also made a close connection between the exaltation of the Messiah and the gathering of צדיקיא ("the righteous"; *Tg. Isa.* 11:5). He also used the opportunity presented by the more general connection between righteousness and the son of Jesse in the Hebrew text to insert an eschatological expectation concerning the gathering of the exiles. As the context of *Tg. Isa.* 11:10–12 also indicates, the return of the exiles to the land was central to the meturgeman's expectation of the messianic rule. The meturgeman contextualized the return of the remnant presented in the Hebrew text to fit his historical context by inserting "India," "Babylon," and "the islands of the sea" into the list of geographic location from which the remnant will be drawn (*Tg. Isa.* 11:11).[18]

Several aspects within view of the messianic program in Isa 11 point to an earlier Tannaitic meturgeman. For example, the actualization of peace during the messianic reign (v. 6) and a literal return of the exiles to the land (v. 6) both suggest an earlier Tannaitic meturgeman. Furthermore, the imminent expectation of the start of the messianic program seen with the insertion of the description of the Messiah as one "who is about to" stand as a sign is another indication of a Tannaitic meturgeman (v. 10).

The meturgeman's view of the role of the nations in relation to the messianic rule also is witnessed in the interpretational glosses. As Chilton noted, an element of military triumph over the nations is present in *Tg. Isa.* 11:10.[19] The meturgeman stated that מלכון ישתמעון ("*the kingdoms will be obedient*") to the Messiah (*Tg. Isa.* 11:10). Although the obedience in *Tg. Isa.* 11:10 is in reference to the Messiah's gathering of the exiles, a forced obedience due to a military conquest of the nations is present also within the context, as seen in *Tg. Isa.* 11:14. An intentional effort to emphasize the particularistic attitude and deemphasize the inclusive attitude in Isa 11 also can be observed with the meturgeman's addition of "*in the land*" in reference to the peace brought by the Messiah (*Tg. Isa.* 11:6). The meturgeman interpreted the universal peace in Isa 11:6–8 as taking place within the land of Israel.[20] Furthermore, as Chilton noted, the description in *Tg. Isa.* 10:27

---

18. The shift in the geographic reference in *Tg. Isa.* 11:11 to the east (i.e., "India" instead of Ethiopia, "Babylon" instead of Shinar, and "islands" instead of coastlands) may reflect the meturgeman's focus on the Romans. For further discussion, see Chilton, *The Isaiah Targum*, 29.

19. Chilton, *The Isaiah Targum*, 29.

20. A similar intentional effort to emphasize the particularistic attitude and

concerning the shattering of the Gentiles by the Messiah "provides the governing context for the messianic teaching in chapter 11."[21] The righteous remnant of Israel is the sole beneficiary of the messianic rule.

The particular treatment of the relationship between the Messiah and the destruction of the nations in *Tg. Isa.* 10–11 seems to have influenced the meturgeman's translation of other parts of the book of Isaiah. For example, the parallel occurrences of the term נס ("signal") from Isa 11:10, 12 in Isa 18:3 and 49:22 offered the meturgeman opportunity to insert his understanding of the messianic rule into Isa 18 and 49 as well. In *Tg. Isa.* 18:2–4, the "signal" is toward the nations and announces the deliverance of Israel, "whose land *the Gentiles plundered*." Furthermore, the deliverance of the exiles includes the destruction of the nations (*Tg. Isa.* 18:5–6). The connection between the Messiah and the subjugation of the Gentiles also is present in *Tg. Isa.* 49, where the meturgeman described the signal raised over the nations as a disclosure of God's might resulting in the nations bowing before and ministering to Israel (vv. 22–25). The meturgeman even proclaimed that those who oppressed Israel would go into exile themselves (*Tg. Isa.* 49:17).

How did the meturgeman resolve the tension concerning the role of the nations in the programmatic rule of the Davidic figure as seen in Isa 11? In short, he emphasized the particularistic voice and deemphasized the inclusive voice. The meturgeman gave no hint in *Tg. Isa.* 11 or the corresponding contexts of *Tg. Isa.* 18 or 49 of a Gentile salvation within the messianic program. The meturgeman presented the obedience of the nations (*Tg. Isa.* 11:10) to be the result of a military dominance by the Messiah.

Isaiah Targum 27–29

The same particularistic voice heard faintly in *Tg. Isa.* 1, 8 and loudly in *Tg. Isa.* 10–11 can be heard also in *Tg. Isa.* 27–29. An attitude of particularism is present in the heightened rhetoric against the oppressors of Jerusalem and in Israel's complete military domination over their enemies at their return. For example, the meturgeman offered a nuanced interpretation of Isa 27 concerning the purpose of the exile as well as the identity of the city

---

deemphasize the inclusive attitude in reference to the scope of the peace of the messianic rule can be seen also in the meturgeman's translation of Isaiah 9:2, 6, where the Messiah's peace was limited to those of *"the house of Israel"* (*Tg. Isa.* 9:2, 6).

21. Chilton, *The Isaiah Targum*, 29.

and those in the city who are denied compassion. The meturgeman saw the exile as a tool used by God to forgive the sins of the house of Israel (*Tg. Isa.* 27:9). The question in Isa 27:7, which reflects on the promise to restore Israel in Isa 27:6, becomes a rhetorical accusation in the Targum against the oppressors of Israel through the shift from הכמכת מכהו ("has he smitten") in the Hebrew text to הכמחתא דהוה ("have *they* smitten") in the Targum text. The meturgeman skillfully maintained the identity of the city as Jerusalem in Isa 27:10 without attributing the Lord's lack of compassion and favor in Isa 27:11 to Israel. He accomplished this nuanced interpretation by contextualizing the city as an occupied Jerusalem. With this exegetical move the meturgeman interpreted the judgment and lack of compassion toward the city of Jerusalem in the Hebrew text to be toward the occupying Romans in the city of Jerusalem. For the meturgeman, the Lord's judgment and lack of favor will be directed toward the Roman occupiers of Jerusalem who have dealt harshly with Israel. As Chilton wrote, "the complete, military (v. 10) and religious (v. 11) domination of the enemy by those who return from exile is the final image of the chapter (vv. 9–13)."[22]

The meturgeman's rhetoric against Roman authority was continued in his translation of Isa 28–29. In *Tg. Isa.* 28, God has exiled Israel (v. 13) for their failure to respect the temple (vv. 10–12), their disobedience to the Law (v. 10, 13), and their misplaced trust in idols (v. 10).[23] The meturgeman interpreted the stone laid in Zion (v. 16) as the terrible king who exiles Israel.[24] As Chilton noted, the Roman authorities, as well as the royal and priestly authorities, who rely on Roman power are in view in *Tg. Isa.* 28:1–4.[25]

Despite Israel's present predicament of exile and punishment, the meturgeman did maintain a robust attitude of messianic deliverance. In the place of the Lord himself serving as the crown of the remnant (Isa 28:5), the meturgeman placed the Messiah as the crown of the remnant (*Tg. Isa.* 28:5).[26] The meturgeman placed the promised restoration of Israel in Isa

22. Chilton, *The Isaiah Targum*, 53.

23. The meturgeman rendered the people of Israel's mocking of the prophets in Isa 28:10 with a lengthy expansion in which he presented the accusation against Israel. For the meturgeman, the accusation is that Israel did not perform the Law. Their failure to perform the Law resulted in their falsely placed trust in idols and lack of regard for the temple. Chilton described this failure as "Israel's failure to meet its vocation" (*The Isaiah Targum*, 55).

24. Chilton identified the "terrible king" of *Tg. Isa.* 28:16 as the Roman Emperor Vespasian (*The Isaiah Targum*, 57).

25. Chilton, *The Isaiah Targum*, 55.

26. Chilton described the messianic insertion in *Tg. Isa.* 28:5 as a realistic expectation and not an idealistic expectation (*The Glory of Israel*, 89).

Particularism in Isaiah Targum

28:5–6 in the context of messianic rule, which will result in the destruction of Roman authority. The meturgeman's rendering of Isa 28:6 incorporates a call to the righteous to understand God's use of the terrible king as corrective judgment upon Israel and to obey the Law. According to the meturgeman, the Israelites who listen to the prophets and perform the Law will not be shaken in the midst of the distress of exile.[27] The meturgeman's translation of *Tg. Isa.* 28–29 portrays a messianic expectation of the return of the righteous of Israel from exile and the destruction of Roman authority.

As Chilton noted, chapter 28 of the Isaiah Targum exhibits an overall Tannaitic framework with elements of a pre-70 context. The Tannaitic framework can be seen in elements such as the focus on the temple and priestly service, the emphasis on the perversion of the temple cult as opposed to the loss of the temple, the close association of the Shekinah with the sanctuary, the focus upon national repentance as opposed to individual repentance, and the literal expectation of return to the land.[28] In *Tg. Isa.* 28–29, the meturgeman expected the messianic reign to do away with the corruption of Israel and establish a literal renewed Zion. Both the expectation of a messianic rule, which involves the end of Roman authority, and the absence inclusivism in the *Tg. Isa.* 28–29 correspond with the attitude of particularism observed in *Tg. Isa.* 1, 8, 10–11, 27.

Isaiah Targum 45

As in Isa 45, God appointed Cyrus to the task of liberating Israel from exile in the Targum (*Tg. Isa.* 45 1–4, 13). In addition, the meturgeman acknowledged Cyrus's ignorance of God with the statement "you do not know *to serve before* me" (*Tg. Isa.* 45:4, 5). The disputation between God and the

27. The interpretation of *Tg. Isa.* 28:16 as a call to return and obey the Law is predicated upon the interpretation of אלין ("these things") as a reference to an understanding of God's reason for the appointing of the stone in Zion (i.e., the terrible king). The meturgeman's insertion of the declaration of Isa 28:16 into the mouth of the prophet and his insertion of "the righteous" as the identification of the believers in *Tg. Isa.* 28:16 both allude to the larger context of the prophet's call to obedience to the Law. Note the meturgeman's expansion in *Tg. Isa.* 28:23–25 in which the prophet calls the house of Israel to perform the Law. The prophet's call then is followed immediately by a targumic insertion that closely parallels *Tg. Isa.* 28:16b, which results in a more detailed explanation of "these things." The meturgeman's declaration in *Tg. Isa.* 28:16 is paralleled also in *Tg. Isa.* 30:18, where the righteous are described as Israelites who hope for God's deliverance in the midst of the judgment of exile.

28. Chilton, *The Glory of Israel*, 20, 29–30, 89.

nations concerning his sovereignty is reflected further in the meturgeman's insertion of an attack on idolatry in v. 9. Not surprisingly, the Lord's sovereignty and the corresponding certainty of his salvation remained the central issue for the meturgeman in *Tg. Isa.* 45.

As was observed in the analysis of Isa 45, elements of both voices of particularism and inclusivism are present within the oracles. How did the meturgeman deal with the tension of the two voices in Isa 45? Surprisingly, the rendering of *Tg. Isa.* 45 seems to lean more toward inclusivism as opposed to the consistent pattern of particularism seen in the previous analysis of the Targum. Though the particularistic elements witnessed in Isa 45:13 remain in Targum, the meturgeman tempered the subjugation of the nations to Israel by rendering the Hebrew text "to you they will bow down, and to you they will pray" with "*from* you they will *seek and give thanks*" in v. 14. Again, in *Tg. Isa.* 45:24 the meturgeman rendered the Hebrew text "and all who are angry with him will come and be ashamed" with "all *the Gentiles* who were *provoked* against *his people* will *give thanks* and be ashamed *of their idols*." In both examples, the meturgeman reflects a more inclusive attitude. Israel's dominance and captivity of the nations (vv. 13–14) result in the nations' recognition of Israel's God (v. 14), their voluntary turn from idols (v. 24), and their expression of thanks (vv. 14, 24).

Assigning the interpretational material of *Tg. Isa.* 45 into either the Tannaitic or Amoraic exegetical framework is difficult due to the lack of identifiable characteristics of the frameworks in *Tg. Isa.* 45. Perhaps the most significant clues to the exegetical milieu of *Tg. Isa.* 45 are the meturgeman's mention of the Shekinah dwelling "*in the strength of the height*" (v. 15), his use of the term "*serve*" in reference to Cyrus's lack of knowledge of the Lord (vv. 4, 5), and the insertion of "*the house of*" in reference to Jacob (vv. 19)—all of which point toward a Tannaitic milieu. On the other hand, the lack of other dominant Tannaitic characteristics, such as the expectation of the imminent return from exile, the rebuilding of Jerusalem, and the arrival of the messiah is puzzling. The return from exile already present in the context of Isa 45 would seem a prime opportunity for a Tannaitic meturgeman to include seamlessly the characteristics of his exegetical framework. Furthermore, the removal of the Shekinah seems more definitively eliminated with no hint of an expected return. These characteristics of *Tg. Isa.* 45 suggest the hand of the Amoraic meturgeman. In conclusion, the context of *Tg.*

Isa. 45 clearly leans toward inclusivism and seems to reflect the exegetical frameworks of both the Tannaitic and Amoraic meturgemanin.[29]

Isaiah Targum 52–53

The meturgeman explicitly inserted his messianic expectation in *Tg. Isa.* 52–53 with his identification of the servant as the Messiah in *Tg. Isa.* 52:13 and 53:10. The good news heralded to *"the congregation of Zion"* in *Tg. Isa.* 52:7 is that *"the kingdom of your God is revealed."* Furthermore, the meturgeman interpreted the future salvation of Zion portrayed in the Hebrew text of Isa 52:1–12 with an increased emphasis upon the scope of the restoration as being confined to the land of Israel. For example, the phrase ארעא דישראל (*"of the land of Israel"*) was added to clarify the identity of the mountains where the proclamation is made (*Tg. Isa.* 52:7). The nature of the salvation of Zion was described within a similar exilic context as seen in the previous Isaiah Targum passages. For example, the exodus motif present in Isa 52:11 was translated with the insertion of a return from exile motif in the Targum. Like the Hebrew text, the Targum also maintains that the restoration of Zion is for the purpose of honoring God's name.

The role of the Gentile nations in relation to the messianic program anticipated by the meturgeman clearly is present in *Tg. Isa.* 52–53. Although the exaltation of God's name בעממיא (*"among the peoples"*) in *Tg. Isa.* 52:6 could be understood as a benefit to the nations, the context of *Tg. Isa.* 52:7–15 indicates otherwise. The disfigurement attributed to the servant in the Hebrew text is attributed to an exiled Israel in the Targum, and the eventual exaltation of Zion will cause the nations to become like their captives (*Tg. Isa.* 53:3). The Messiah's restoration of Israel will בדר (*"scatter"*) the nations and cause kings to be שתק (*"silent"*; *Tg. Isa.* 52:15). The Gentile nations were described further as being handed over to Israel in *Tg. Isa.* 53:7 and plundered by Israel in *Tg. Isa.* 53:11. According to the meturgeman, the exaltation of Zion will take place at the expense of the nations.

Just as in the contexts of *Tg. Isa.* 10–11 and 27–28, the messianic expectation witnessed in *Tg. Isa.* 52–53 reflects more of a Tannaitic than an

---

29. The presence of the depiction of the Shekinah in the heavens and the terms "serve" and "the house of" also could have been adopted by the later Amoraic meturgeman. The same terms also occur in the Amoraic exegetical material of *Isa Tg. Neb.* 57:11, 17; 59:13. If so, then the dominant framework of *Tg. Isa.* 45 could be that of the Amoraic meturgeman despite the presence of Tannaitic characteristics.

Amoraic milieu. The eminent expectation of the Messiah's appearance (*Tg. Isa.* 52:12), the literal expectation of a return from exile to the land (*Tg. Isa.* 52:8), and the literal removal of the Gentiles from the land of Israel (*Tg. Isa.* 53:8) all indicate a Tannaitic date of the exegetical material. Furthermore, the removal of the Shekinah (*Tg. Isa.* 53:3) and the promise to rebuild the temple (*Tg. Isa.* 53:5) point toward a post-70 date for the exegetical material. Chilton argued that the meturgeman's messianic understanding of the servant in Isaiah attests to a "primitive exegesis common to Judaism and Christianity." He suggested a date of 70–135 CE for the exegetical framework witnessed in *Tg. Isa.* 52–53.[30]

Isaiah Targum 59

The meturgeman portrayed the present state of Israel in *Tg. Isa.* 59 as one of desperate moral depravity (vv. 4–6, 13) and suppression before their enemies (v. 11). The result of Israel's sins, as seen in Isa 59:2, "your sins have hidden his face from you," offered occasion for the meturgeman to invoke the removal of the Shekinah: "Your sins *caused* the face *of the Shekinah to be taken up* from you" (*Tg. Isa.* 59:2). The meturgeman's interpretation concurs with the original message observed in the analysis of Isa 59. The implication is that Israel's sin is the cause of their present state and not God's lack of ability to hear or to save. In *Tg. Isa.* 59:7–9, the meturgeman identified the people who rush to do evil by shedding blood as the wicked of Israel. As in Isa 59:20–21, the meturgeman declared that the Lord himself would come as a redeemer to Zion and uphold his covenant with them. But how would God accomplish uphold the covenant and resolve this paradox? The meturgeman offered an innovative rendering of Isa 59:20 that resolves the paradox between Israel's sinful state and the covenant. The meturgeman rendered the Hebrew text "He will come as redeemer to Zion and to those who have turned from rebellion in Jacob" with "He will come as a redeemer to Zion and to *return the rebels of the house of* Jacob *to the law*" (v. 20). For the meturgeman, Israel's return to the Law is the programmatic solution to the tension between the promises of their Abrahamic covenant and their sinful state.

As Chilton noted, the Lord's response of salvation to Israel's confessed state is absent any hint of messianic vindication. Alongside this observation,

30. Chilton, *The Glory of Israel*, 94–96.

Particularism in Isaiah Targum

Chilton pointed to several more features of *Tg. Isa.* 59 that suggest the milieu of the Amoraic meturgeman, including the perspective of the Shekinah's removal, the uselessness of prayer, the presence of moral wickedness, and the presence of the Euphrates River simile.[31] Witness to the Amoraic meturgeman's adoption of elements of the Tannaitic framework also can be added to Chilton's observations. For example, the sin of Israel was described as a turning away "from following *the service of* our God" (v. 13), which reflects a cultic context. Also, the Lord was prophesied to return "*the house of* Jacob" (v. 20), which reflects a communal understanding of Israel. Finally, the words placed in the mouth of the people were described as prophecy as opposed to teaching (v. 21), which also reflects a Tannaitic milieu.

Interestingly, the meturgeman innovatively emphasized the connection of God's salvation of Israel to the retribution God would take "*from the enemies of his people*" (v. 17). With this subtle shift, the meturgeman has identified God's enemies as the enemies of his people as opposed to sinful Israel. While much of the exegetical material in *Tg. Isa.* 59 reflects the Amoraic meturgeman, the context is devoid of any hint of inclusivism. Instead, *Tg. Isa.* 59 demonstrates a particularistic interpretation with retribution to the enemies of Israel in conjunction with Israel's salvation.

Isaiah Targum 65

The final literary unit to be analyzed is *Tg. Isa.* 65. The Messiah is not mentioned explicitly in *Tg. Isa.* 65, nevertheless elements of the Tannaitic meturgeman's expectation of the messianic intercession are present. The focus upon the identity of true Israel observed in Isa 56–66 is maintained in the Targum. The meturgeman's central lament in *Tg. Isa.* 65 is Israel's rejection of the Law and abandonment of the service of the Lord (*Tg. Isa.* 65:1, 11). The unrepentant and disobedient within Israel were identified as רשיעיא ("the wicked"), and the servants who are faithful to the Law were identified as צדיקיא ("the righteous"; *Tg. Isa.* 65:13–15). The close connection between the righteous and the Messiah found elsewhere in the Isaiah Targum suggests that the promised intercession for the righteous pictured in *Tg. Isa.* 65 is reflective of the meturgeman's messianic expectations (cf. *Tg. Isa.* 11:1–6; 28:5, 16; 52:13—53:2). As in the context of Isa 65, the meturgeman identified the accused in Isa 65:1–2 as obstinate Israel.[32]

---

31. Chilton, *The Isaiah Targum*, 115.
32. The meturgeman inserted language most applicable to Israel throughout Isa

Interestingly, the meturgeman rendered Isa 65:1 with an innovative interpretation in *Tg. Isa.* 65:1, "I was *asked by my* memra by those who did not ask *before* me. I sought *teaching of my law* from those who did not seek *my fear*. I said, 'Here I am,' *while being asked continually all the day*, by a *people* not *praying* in my name." With his rendering, the meturgeman heightened the polemic against obstinate Israel and removed any trace of the rhetorical force of God's implication that he has been found by those who were not seeking. Israel's problem was that they did not ask sincerely or pray properly.[33] The meturgeman argued that Israel was under the threat of judgment because they have rejected the teaching of the Law.[34]

Several characteristics of *Tg. Isa.* 65 suggest a Tannaitic milieu. The reference to *"the house of Israel"* and their forsaking of *"the service of"* the Lord both reflect the communal and cultic emphasis of the Tannaitic meturgeman (v. 15). Likewise, the urgent call to belong to the righteous coincides with the urgent Tannaitic call to repentance. Finally, the expectation of the return of the Shekinah within the immediate context (*Tg. Isa.* 63:17; 64:7; 66:1, 20) corresponds to the Tannaitic expectation observed elsewhere in the Isaiah Targum.

Although explicit elements of particularism are absent in *Tg. Isa.* 65, an explicit expression of particularism is present in the immediate context. For example, a clear distinction between the people of God and the Gentiles is drawn in *Tg. Isa.* 63:17–19, where the Gentiles are described as having no portion in the teaching of God's Law. The contrast between Israel and the Gentiles then is carried into *Tg. Isa.* 64:1, where the Gentiles are excluded from the benefit of the Lord's revelation. The meturgeman then described the Lord's revelation (*Tg. Isa.* 64:1–2) to be on behalf of *"the righteous"* (*Tg. Isa.* 64:4). A particularistic attitude toward the nations was inserted in the context surrounding the text of *Tg. Isa.* 65.

65:1–2, such as "I *sought teaching of my law* from those who did not seek *my fear*" and "I *sent* my *prophets.*" The same language was repeated in *Tg. Isa.* 65:10–12 in conjunction with an explicit identification of "the *house of Israel.*"

33. Chilton added the word "truly" in parentheses as an adverb modifying "ask" in his translation of *Tg. Isa.* 65:1 (*The Isaiah Targum*, 122–23). While he offered no explanation in the apparatus for his addition, Chilton's translation coincides with the interpretation that the accusation against Israel in *Tg. Isa.* 65:1 is an insincere or dishonest asking. This interpretation also contextually fits well with Israel's complaint immediately preceding in *Tg. Isa.* 64:12, "You *are giving reprieve to the wicked, even those who subjugate* us *severely.*"

34. The judgment of obstinate Israel is portrayed in an eschatological context in *Tg. Isa.* 65 with the targumic additions of the threat of *"Gehenna"* (v. 5) and *"second death"* (v. 6) as *"the retribution of their sins"* (v. 6).

Particularism in Isaiah Targum

Other Isaiah Targum Texts

The analysis above has demonstrated that particularism has been the dominant voice in reference to the Targum texts that correspond to the key Isaiah texts explicitly cited in Romans (i.e., chs. 1, 8, 10–11, 27–29, 52–53, 59, and 65). The one exception was *Tg. Isa.* 45 where the inclusive voice was more dominant. What about the other inclusive texts of Isaiah, and, more specifically, the three major inclusive texts cited by Kebede (i.e., Isa 2:1–5; 19:16–25; 42:1–9)? How did the meturgeman render these inclusive texts in the Targum?

Explicit shifts from inclusivism to particularism in the Targum are present even in Kebede's three key texts. For example, a particularistic interpretation can be seen in the meturgeman's rendering of Isa 2:6–22, which follows the inclusive passage of Isa 2:1–5. The judgment upon Israel portrayed in the Hebrew text is turned against the *"kings of the Gentiles," "tyrants of the provinces,"* and *"all those who dwell in the islands of the sea"* in the Targum (*Tg. Isa.* 2:13–16). The meturgeman's focus is upon the judgment and destruction of Rome as opposed to the judgment of Israel witnessed in the Hebrew text.

Again, an intentional shift from inclusivism to particularism is witnessed in *Tg. Isa.* 19. The Hebrew text of Isa 19 exalts Egypt and Assyria to equal status with Israel, while the interpretive emphasis in the Targum is on the Jewish Egyptians. The shift is seen most clearly in *Tg. Isa.* 19:25 where the meturgeman interpreted the blessing of Egypt and Assyria in the Hebrew text as a blessing of the Jewish exiles in Egypt and Assyria.[35]

Finally, the meturgeman also inserted a particularistic interpretation in *Tg. Isa.* 42 as well. In Isa 42:6, the exaltation and return of the exiles is said to serve as לניהור עממין ("a light to the peoples"), but in what sense? The meturgeman clarified any possible ambiguity in the Hebrew text regarding the nature of the servant's mission in Isa 42 as "a light to the peoples." The people who receive the light are defined clearly in *Tg. Isa.* 42:6–7 as *"the house of Israel"* who are prisoners of and exiled among the nations.[36] The inclusivism aspects of the Hebrew text were interpreted in the Targum to coincide with particularism.

---

35. Chilton likewise noted the emphasis upon the Jewish Egyptians in *Tg. Isa.* 19 (*The Isaiah Targum*, 39).

36. See *Tg. Isa.* 49:9, where Israel was described as "bonded *among the Gentiles*" and "imprisoned *among the kingdoms*."

67

The particularistic pattern of interpretation observed in the analysis above also seems to be the dominant voice throughout the Isaiah Targum. Another originally inclusive message in Isa 56:2–3 also is displayed with a particularistic attitude in the Targum. According to the Hebrew text, the Lord proclaimed that even the בן־הנכר ("son of a foreigner") who keeps the Sabbath will be included in restored Israel (Isa 56:2–3). Alongside the inclusive language concerning the foreigner, which is maintained in the Targum, the meturgeman added that the restoration of the exiles would be at the expense of the Gentile kings (*Tg. Isa.* 56:9). Interestingly, the term used to describe the יסף ("addition") of the sons of foreigners in *Tg. Isa.* 56:3, 6 also was used in *Tg. Isa.* 14:1 within a heavily particularistic context. In the Hebrew text of Isa 14:1, the גור ("alien") is joined and added to Israel. The addition of the alien is expressed in particularistic terms concerning the relationship between the Gentiles and Israel in both the Hebrew and Targum texts of Isa 14. The overall understanding of the relationship of the Gentiles to Israel is one of Israel's subjugation and ownership of the nations (*Tg. Isa.* 14:2). Furthermore, the meturgeman connected the retribution brought on the Gentile nations in *Tg. Isa.* 14 to the deeds of the Messiah in *Tg. Isa.* 14:29–32. In both Isa 14 and 56, the explicit inclusivism of the Hebrew text is overshadowed in the Targum text by the particularistic connection made between the return of the exiles and the subsequent judgment upon and subjugation of the Gentile nations.

Conclusion

The analysis offered above suggests at least three observations. First, the Isaiah Targum witnesses an extensive particularism. Regarding the tension observed in the book of Isaiah, the analysis demonstrates that the meturgeman emphasized the particularistic voice over the inclusive voice. An attitude of particularism was observed either in the passage itself or in close literary proximity (i.e., *Tg. Isa.* 1, 8, 10–11, 27–29, 52–53, 59, 65). The meturgeman even inserted an attitude of particularism into other originally inclusive Isaiah passages (i.e., Isa 2, 19, 42, 56). Of the passages analyzed, the only exception to the constant particularistic interpretation was *Tg. Isa.* 45.

Second, the particularistic interpretation occurred most often in conjunction with the Tannaitic framework. Analysis of key terms and phrases of the exegetical frameworks identified by Chilton in the specific passages analyzed above (i.e., *Tg. Isa.* 1, 8, 10–11, 27–29, 52–53, 59, 65) resulted in the observation of a predominance of the Tannaitic framework. The only exception to the predominance of the Tannaitic framework was *Tg. Isa.* 45, 59.

Third, the Tannaitic meturgeman consistently inserted the particularistic interpretation in conjunction with textual expansions reflecting his messianic expectations (i.e., *Tg. Isa.* 8:9–9:6; 10:17–27; 11:1–14; 52:7—53:11).[37] The conjunction of particularism and the Tannaitic meturgeman's messianic expectation is not surprising. A military dominance of Israel resulting in the destruction of the oppressing nations and subjugation of the Gentiles seemed far more possible prior to the failure of the Bar Kokhba revolt in 135 CE. Particularism was much more compatible with the eschatological and literal expectation of the Tannaitic meturgeman rather than the more conceptual and realized understanding of the Amoraic meturgeman. The Tannaitic meturgeman of the Isaiah Targum seems unable to envision a messianic intervention without the removal and destruction of Israel's Gentile oppressors. For the Tannaitic meturgeman, God's eschatological intervention through the Messiah means salvation and deliverance for the righteous of Israel and retribution and subjugation for the nations.

More significant is the implication of the above observations for this research concerning the intertextual relationship between Isaiah, the Isaiah Targum, and Romans and the role the key text of Isa 11:10 plays in that relationship. In reference to the meturgeman's interpretation of the phrase "to him will *kingdoms be obedient*" in *Tg. Isa.* 11:10, the analysis of *Tg. Isa.* 11:10 demonstrated the presence of both the Tannaitic messianic expectation and particularism. Furthermore, the wider analysis of the Targum also demonstrated that the particularistic interpretation in *Tg. Isa.* 11:10 is consistent with the Tannaitic framework. In each Targum passage corresponding to the Isaiah passages cited in Romans, apart from the Amoraic context of *Tg. Isa.* 45, the analysis revealed the presence of meturgeman's particularistic interpretation. When faced with the presence of inclusivism or any ambiguity in the Isaiah text concerning the role of the nations within the messianic program of the restoration of Israel, the Tannaitic meturgeman displayed a particularistic interpretation with his targumic rendering.[38]

---

37. Alongside the Targum passages analyzed here, the Isaiah Targum offers further witness to the meturgeman's exegetical connection between the exaltation of Israel during the messianic rule and the subsequent subjugation of the nations. For example, see *Tg. Isa.* 14, 16, 28.

38. The same presence of particularism within a messianic expectation in reference to Isa 11:10 also is witnessed in other Tannaitic and pre-Tannaitic literature. For example, an influence of a messianic interpretation of Isa 11 along with a particularistic

4

Inclusivism in Romans

Introduction

The presence of both particularism and inclusivism in the book of Isaiah and Paul's frequent use of Isaiah within his argument in Romans concerning the gospel to the Gentiles raises the question of Paul's reading of the tension in Isaiah. Was Paul aware of the tension in Isaiah? If so, how did he reconcile the tension between particularism and inclusivism in the Isaiah text? Was Paul's use of the phrase ὑπακοὴν πίστεως in Rom 1:5 a reflection of his solution to the tension in his reading of Isaiah?

Analysis

Isaiah 52 in Romans 2

Paul's first explicit citation of Isaiah is Isa 52:5 in Rom 2:24 and occurs in the midst of a diatribe with a Jewish interlocutor in Rom 2:17–29.[1] The citation

---

interpretation is witnessed in *Pss. Sol.* 17:23–24, where the arrival of Israel's king was described as resulting in the purging of Jerusalem "from nations that trample down to destruction." The king was described further as destroying "the godless nations with the word of his mouth." A similar influence of the messianic interpretation of Isa 11 along with a particularistic interpretation is witnessed in *1 En.* 62:1–16. The exaltation of the "Elect One" of Isa 11 was described as resulting in the salvation of the righteous elect of Israel (*1 En.* 62:13) and destruction and punishment on the kings and nations of the earth for their oppression of Israel (*1 En.* 62:11–12).

1. Stanley K. Stowers argued that the diatribe in 2:17–29 is part of a longer discussion in Rom 2:17—14:22 between Paul and a Jewish teacher who had taken upon himself the teaching of Gentiles to keep the Law. Stowers, *Rereading*, 37–38, 143–58. For further

serves as a conclusion to the first of two units comprising the diatribe (i.e., vv. 17–24 and 25–29). The first part of the diatribe functions rhetorically as a harsh accusation against the Jew, who would count his Jewish identity, which is defined by his covenant with God as demonstrated in his possession of the Law (vv. 17–18), as a means of exceptionalism (vv. 19–20).[2] In the voice of the interlocutor, Paul offered five Jewish boasts of superiority over the Gentiles.[3] Paul then responded to the interlocutor with five rhetorical questions, which function as a condemnation directly upon the interlocutor and indirectly upon the audience (vv. 21–22).[4] The questions condemn by demonstrating the interlocutor's failure to keep the Law while he trusts in his possession of the Law as a symbol of higher status. According to Paul, the Jews who boast in their possession of the Law ironically dishonor God by their disobedience to the same Law (v. 23).

Paul's citation of Isa 52:5, τὸ γὰρ ὄνομα τοῦ θεοῦ δι' ὑμᾶς βλασφημεῖται ἐν τοῖς ἔθνεσιν ("For the name of God is blasphemed among the Gentiles because of you") is accompanied by the introductory formula καθὼς γέγραπται ("as it is written"). The various introductory formulas used by Paul with his direct citations of Isaiah in Romans demonstrate a rhetorical purpose for the formulas within their immediate contexts. While the formula used for Isa 52:5 in Rom 2:24 is more standard in comparison to some of his other introductory formulas, the placement of the formula after the citation is unique. The postponement of the formula serves to connect the citation as an answer to the proceeding question. The citation matches the LXX except for a few changes.[5] As noted by Jewett, Paul's postponed place-

---

discussion of the literary structure of Rom 2:17–29 and the identification of Rom 2:17–29 as a diatribe, see Dunn, *Romans*, 1:108–9; Fitzmyer, *Romans*, 315; Jewett, *Romans*, 219–20.

2. As noted by Stowers, Paul's criticism in Rom 2:17–29 is not against Judaism in general but rather a specific imaginary kind of Jew (*Rereading*, 144).

3. The five Jewish boasts raised by Paul are a guide to the blind (v. 19), a light to those in darkness (v. 19), an instructor of the ignorant (v. 20), a teacher of infants (v. 20), a possessor of knowledge and truth through the Law (v. 20).

4. As Jewett noted, the formulation of the rhetorical question in conjunction with the second person address forced the audience to condemn itself even as they condemn the hypocritical interlocutor (*Romans*, 227).

5. The changes include the substitution of ὁ ὄνομα τοῦ θεοῦ for τὸ ὄνομα μου and the shift of ὁ ὄνομα τοῦ θεοῦ into an emphatic position at the beginning. The LXX also differs slightly from the Hebrew with the LXX's additions of δι' ὑμᾶς and ἐν τοῖς ἔθνεσιν. Jewett argued that the shift of "the Lord's name to the beginning was to emphasize God's honor and the rhetorical argument that Jewish unbelief cast aspersions" (*Romans*, 230).

ment of the introductory formula, substitution of "my" with "the name of God," and deletion of "continually" all serve to connect the citation more tightly to the concluding rhetorical question in v. 23.[6] The linguistic parallels between v. 23 and v. 24 suggest that Paul's polemic accusation against Jewish boasting in the Law is driven directly from his reading of Isaiah.[7]

In the immediate context of Isa 52:1–12, Israel's salvation and restoration were promised because the captivity of Israel had caused the Lord's name to be blasphemed by the Gentiles. As noted in the analysis of Isa 52, the Lord's honor is the central focus of Isa 52:1–12 and serves as the reason for Israel's salvation. In Romans, the citation serves as an accusation against Israel's transgression against the Law. Although Paul's rhetorical use of Isa 52:5 may seem at first glance to be out of context with Isa 52:1–12, consideration of the larger context of Isaiah indicates otherwise.[8] As Schreiner noted, according to Isaiah the people were in exile because of their transgression (cf. Isa 40:2; 42:24–25; 43:22–28; 50:1).[9] Although the salvific context of Isa 52:1–12 is concealed entirely in Romans 2, Paul's other uses of Isa 52 (i.e., Rom 10:15; 15:21) indicate that Paul has not overlooked the salvific implications of Isa 52.[10]

The addition of δι' ὑμᾶς in the LXX serves Paul's reading of Isaiah's larger argument concerning the real cause of the blasphemy of God's name among the nations. In the context of Isa 52:1–12, the exile and subjugation

---

6. Jewett, *Romans*, 230.

7. In discussing the intertextual relationship between a citation and antecedent, Watson, *Paul*, 43–53, argued that a scriptural citation often generates its antecedent. He based his conclusion on several factors, including the citation formula, lexical correspondence between the antecedent and the citation, and the format of the citation and the antecedent text.

8. Hays likewise acknowledged the potential for misunderstanding Paul's Isa 52:5 citation apart from the recognition of Paul's awareness of the larger context of Isaiah. Hays suggested that Paul's Isa 52:5 citation appears to be "a stunning misread of the text" only when the larger context of Isaiah and the larger context of Paul's rhetoric in Romans are ignored. For Hays, Paul turned "Isaiah's oracle of promise into a word of reproach" but only temporarily. The later citations of Isa 52:7 in Rom 10:15 and Isa 59:20 in Rom 11:26–27 demonstrate that God's promise of salvation to Israel present in Isa 56–66 is not absent in Paul's citation of Isa 52:5 (*Echoes*, 45–46).

9. Schreiner, *Romans*, 134–35. Shum also argued that the underlying theology of Isaiah concerning the people's failure to keep the covenant as the cause of their exile remains intact in Paul's citation (*Paul's Use*, 179).

10. Shum suggested that Paul's usage of Isa 52:5 is compatible with the context of Isaiah 52, and that Paul's use probably was based on his "deep reflection on the history of rebellious Israel" (*Paul's Use*, 179–80).

of Israel resulted in the blasphemy of God's name, but in the larger context of Isaiah, the exile and subjugation of Israel were caused by Israel's disobedience to the Law. Paul's rhetorical use of Isa 52:5 and his accusation against the interlocutor are in concord with Isaiah's accusation against Israel as witnessed in the larger context of Isaiah.

In conclusion, Paul's citation of Isa 52:5 indicates that the blasphemy of God's name among the Gentiles was a central concern for Paul. Both the direction against Israel of the polemic citation and the context of Rom 2 indicate that Paul placed the blame for the blasphemy not upon the Gentiles but upon the Jews. According to Paul, boasting in the Law as a marker of superiority over the Gentiles only results in a disobedience to the Law and a dishonoring of God. Though Paul's rhetorical use of Isa 52:5 does not directly demonstrate an inclusive reading of Isa 52, his rhetorical use conforms more to inclusivism than particularism. In the midst of discussing the Jews' responsibility to the Law and covenantal relationship to God, Paul cited an Isaiah text focusing on the salvation of Israel and left no room for an attitude of ethnic or national exceptionalism.

Isaiah 59 in Romans 3

Paul's citation of Isa 59:7–8 in Rom 3:15–17 occurs as part of a catena (Rom 3:10–18) within the final dialogue between Paul and the interlocutor (Rom 3:1–20). The overall context of the dialogue of Rom 3 concerns objections against Paul's argument that all people are under sin. The interlocutor assumes that Paul is correct, then raises the objection that Paul's argument nullifies God's covenant promises to Israel (Rom 3:1, 3). In view of Paul's argument, the interlocutor questions the status of the Jews in comparison to the Gentiles. Are the Jews advantaged or disadvantaged in reference to God's salvation? Paul utilized the conversation to highlight both God's continued faithfulness to the covenant of Israel (vv. 2, 4) and his impartiality regarding the judgment of sin (vv. 9, 19–20).[11] Paul closed his dialogue with

11. Scholars continue to debate Paul's logic and argument within the diatribe of Rom 3. For example, Dunn suggested that the diatribe functions as a "bridge between earlier and later parts of the letter." As a result, Paul is unable to give a proper response to the objections and the "dialogue loses momentum and direction" (*Romans*, 1:129–30). In contrast Fitzmyer concluded that the diatribe in Rom 3:1–9 formed an "integral development" in Paul's argument and should not be understood as digressive or incoherent (*Romans*, 325). Jewett stated that Paul utilized the diatribe as a means for "inducing an arrogant, self-righteous interlocutor to acknowledge that his evasive behavior places him in the class

the interlocutor with the literary unit of Rom 3:9–20, where he restated his argument (v. 9) and concluded with the catena (vv. 10–18). The catena functions rhetorically as a support and summarization of Paul's argument that all people are under sin, both Jew and Gentile alike.[12]

The catena as a whole is preceded by Paul's more common citation formula "as it is written." Paul's citation of Isa 59:7–8 matches closely to the LXX with some changes.[13] As in Isaiah, the citation in Rom 3:15–17 serves as a condemnation of social injustice. The difference between the two contexts is that whereas the accusation is solely against Israel in Isaiah, the accusation is aimed explicitly at both Jew and Gentile in Romans (Rom 3:9). The paradox between Israel's sinful state and the covenant observed in Isaiah is also a central issue, albeit implicit, in the diatribe between Paul and the interlocutor. The interlocutor's central question concerning God's faithfulness to Israel's covenant (Rom 3:3) echoes Israel's bewilderment concerning God's silence in their time of subjugation (cf. Isa 58:2–3, 59:1–2). Though for different reasons, both the interlocutor in Romans and Israel in Isaiah were asking the same question concerning God's faithfulness to covenant Israel. Both Isaiah and Paul responded by upholding God's faithfulness to Israel while also proclaiming God's judgment upon the sin.

In reference to inclusivism and particularism, Paul's Isa 59:7–8 citation in the catena does not address the issue directly. On the other hand, Paul's coupling of both Jew and Gentile in equal status in relation to sin and judgment concurs more with inclusivism than particularism. Despite Paul's consent to the interlocutor that Jews are advantaged in that they were entrusted with the words of God (Rom 3:2), he left no room for the national boasting of superiority in relation to salvation observed in particularism.

---

of 'sinner'" (*Romans*, 258). A detailed treatment of Paul's logic in the diatribe of Rom 3:1–9 is beyond the scope of this research. More significant for this research is the observation that the catena functions rhetorically as a concluding scriptural proof in support of Paul's argument that all people are under sin, that God will judge them without partiality, and that the overall focus of the diatribe concerns Jewish identity and status.

12. The original authorship of the catena is a matter of debate. Fitzmyer and Jewett suggested that Paul adopted an already existing list. Dunn acknowledged the possibility but suggested Pauline authorship based on the degree to which the verses fit Paul's argument. For further discussion of the literary structure of Rom 3:1–20 and the rhetorical function and authorship of the catena, see Dunn, *Romans*, 1.145; Fitzmyer, *Romans*, 333–34; Jewett, *Romans*, 254–55.

13. Paul replaced ἐπὶ πονηρίαν τρέχουσιν ταχινοί ("run quickly to wickedness") in the LXX with ὀξεῖς ("quickly") and changed the vocabulary of the verb "to know" from οἶδα in the LXX to γινώσκω.

Paul argued throughout the diatribe that Jews are not offered a special status based on their possession of the Law over Gentiles in reference to God's judgment of sin.

Isaiah 1 and 10 in Romans 9

Paul next cited Isa 10:22–23 in Rom 9:27–28 and Isa 1:9 in Rom 9:29 with explicit citation formulas that include references to Isaiah by name. The Isaiah citations occur in the catena of Rom 9:25–29. The catena functions as a scriptural proof for Paul's argument that God has chosen vessels of mercy (vv. 22–23), whom he called οὐ μόνον ἐξ Ἰουδαίων ἀλλα και᾽ ἐξ ἐθνῶν ("not only from out of the Jews but also out of the Gentiles"; v. 24).[14] In the context of Rom 9, Paul addressed the crisis of Israel's rejection of the messianic proclamation of his gospel. The central question raised by this crisis is expressed in v. 6 in reference to God's faithfulness to the covenant with Israel.[15] Paul then developed a midrashic discourse in Rom 9:7–29 as a refutation of the objection that his gospel of God's salvation to Gentiles implies God's unfaithfulness to Israel.[16] According to Paul in Rom 9:27–28, God has remained faithful to Israel by way of the remnant.

Paul's citation of Isa 10:22–23 in Rom 9:27–28, ἐὰν ᾖ ὁ ἀριθμὸς τῶν υἱῶν Ἰσραὴλ ὡς ἡ ἄμμος τῆς θαλάσσης, τὸ ὑπόλειμμα σωθήσεται … λόγον γὰρ συντελῶν καὶ συντέμνων ποιήσει κύριος ἐπὶ τῆς γῆς ("Though the number of the sons of Israel be as the sands of the sea, the remnant

---

14. As Dunn noted, ἐκ indicates a calling "out of" with the implication of separating from a larger body (*Romans*, 2:570).

15. The identification of Rom 9–11 as a unit and Paul's returning to the issue concerning God's faithfulness to Israel, first introduced in Rom 3, has been recognized widely among scholars. Paul's triumphant proclamations in Rom 6–8 raise the Jewish objection of doubt in God's faithfulness to Israel. Paul returned to the objection in Rom 9–11, which was first raised in Rom 3:1, 3, in order to address the issue more fully. Jewett identified Rom 9–11 in rhetorical terms as the third proof, which he described as "the triumph of divine righteousness in the gospel's mission to Israel and the Gentiles." He further described Rom 9:6 as the thesis of the third proof (*Romans*, 556–57, 573). Dunn noted that the problem had been exposed first in Paul's line of arguing in Rom 2, was addressed briefly in Rom 3, and was answered more fully in Rom 9–11 (*Romans*, 2:518–21, 529–30). For further discussion, see also Fitzmyer, *Romans*, 539–40; Mounce, *Romans*, 194–95.

16. Jewett argued that the midrashic discourse creates "a logical proof of the thesis in v. 6a by developing a disjunction in the paradoxical *sententia* of v. 6b between the elected true Israel and Israel as a whole" (*Romans*, 571). For further discussion of the midrash and diatribe of Rom 9:17–29, see Dunn, *Romans*, 2:536–37; Jewett, *Romans*, 570–72, 588–89.

Paul and the Synagogue

will be saved. ... For the Lord will accomplish the word with completion and promptness upon the earth"), is preceded by the introductory phrase Ἡσαΐας δὲ κράζει ὑπὲρ τοῦ Ἰσραήλ ("Yet Isaiah cries out on behalf of Israel"). Paul's citation of Isa 1:9 in Rom 9:29, εἰ μὴ κύριος σαβαὼθ ἐγκατέλιπεν ἡμῖν σπέρμα, ὡς Σόδομα ἂν ἐγενήθημεν καὶ ὡς Γόμορρα ἂν ὡμοιώθημεν ("If the Lord Almighty had not left for us a seed, we would have become as Sodom and we would have been made like Gomorrah"), is preceded by the introductory phrase καὶ καθὼς προείρηκεν Ἡσαΐας ("Just as Isaiah foretold"). His citations of the Isaiah passages are close to the LXX with some alterations.[17]

After utilizing the Hosea passages to support his claim of God's call to the Gentiles (vv. 24–26), Paul then cited Isaiah to deny that God's call to the Gentiles somehow nullifies his faithfulness to Israel (vv. 27–29). Paul's rhetorical use of Isaiah functions to evoke the remnant concept observed in the previous analysis of Isa 1, 10. Paul's citation and rhetorical use of Isaiah in Rom 9:27–29 concurs with Isaiah's presentation of the remnant as God's solution to the paradox in Israel.[18]

Several changes in Paul's citation of Isa 10:22–23 (LXX) reflect an effort to focus on the divine mercy of God's actions toward the remnant as opposed to the wrath and destruction of the earth.[19] The positive portrayal

---

17. In reference to Isa 10:22–23 (LXX), Paul replaced κατάλειμμα with ὑπόλειμμα, ὁ θεὸς with κύριος, and ἐν τῇ οἰκουμέν with ἐπὶ τῆς γῆς. He also omitted αὐτῶν, ἐν δικαιοσύνῃ, and ὅτι λόγον συντετμημένον. Paul's citation of Isa 10:22 in Rom 9:27 also is conflated with Hos 1:10a (2:1a in MT). For a more detailed discussion of the conflated citation of Isa 10:22 and Hos 1:10a as well as Paul's changes to both texts, see Jewett, *Romans*, 601-2.

18. Debate remains concerning the identity and extent of the remnant in Romans. Stowers rejected identifying the remnant as "Jewish Christians" and instead identified the remnant as "a trope for signs of Israel's salvation in times of doom." He further rejected the insertion of "only" in some English translations (e.g., RSV, NIV) of Paul's citation of Isa 10:22 and argued that the remnant is a guarantee for Paul that the Jews as a whole have a future with God (*Rereading*, 302). On the other hand, Dunn suggested that Paul's logic in reference to the remnant concept is that God's promises to Israel could be fulfilled, and yet only a small portion of Israel be saved. He further stated, "Here again then scripture gave clear warning against an exclusive presumption of final salvation based solely on God's original promises" (*Romans*, 2:575). The contrast between Stowers's and Dunn's interpretations also serves to illustrate the two uses of remnant language prior to and during Paul's time. As Dunn, *Romans*, 2:573, noted, the remnant concept was used negatively as a threat of judgment (Isa 14:22, 30; Ezek 5:10; 1QS 4.14; 1QM 1.6; 4.2; 14.5) and positively as a promise of salvation (Gen 45:7; Sir 44:17; 1 Macc 3:35; 1QM 13.8; 14.8–9).

19. As Jewett noted, the alteration of the prefix from κατάλειμμα to ὑπόλειμμα may indicate a softening of the judgmental quality of the remnant concept. Jewett noted also

of the mission to the Gentiles reflected in Paul's citations of Hosea in Rom 9:25–26 is balanced with a positive message to Israel in Paul's citations of Isaiah. Paul's positive interpretation of the remnant in Isaiah is demonstrated further in the introductory formula ὑπὲρ τοῦ Ἰσραήλ. The formula makes clear Paul's interpretation and rhetorical use of Isa 1:9 and 10:22–23. According to Paul, Isaiah "cries out" in the defense of and for the sake of Israel. God's faithfulness to Israel is witnessed in the survival of the remnant. Paul's citations of Hosea and Isaiah support his claim in Rom 9:24 that both the Jews and the Gentiles are called. As Jewett noted, Paul's rhetorical use of the Hosea passages along with the Isaiah passages serves to illustrate the inclusion of both the remnant of national Israel and the Gentile believers as those who are called λαόν μου ("my people").[20]

Paul's rhetorical use of Isa 10:22–23 and Isa 1:9 in Rom 9:27–29 clearly demonstrates an attitude of inclusivism. The particularistic expression observed in Isa 10:24–25 is entirely absent in the rhetoric of Rom 9. Paul did introduce Pharaoh as an object of wrath (vv. 17), but his reference to Pharaoh and the exodus event is primarily an example of God's sovereignty in showing mercy even to the undeserving.[21] Not only is any hint of the

---

that the ommission of ἐν δικαιοσύνῃ and Paul's choice to cite the LXX over the harsher judgmental language of the MT both further indicate a more positive presentation of the remnant by Paul (*Romans*, 602–3). Though God's judgment is present in the immediate context of the remnant concept in Isa 1:9, Paul's juxtaposition of Isa 1:9 to Isa 10:22–23 further suggests that Paul has a positive interpretation of the remnant in Romans.

20. Jewett, *Romans*, 599–600.

21. While Pharaoh at first seems to function as a foil to the vessels of mercy (vv. 16–18), by the end of Paul's midrash, Pharaoh serves as an exemplar of God's sovereignty in showing mercy to the undeserved. In Rom 9:15, Paul cited Exod 33:19, which, in the original context, is a statement made by God to Moses following Israel's rebellion in the golden calf incident. The juxtaposition of the Exod 33:19 citation and the Exod 9:16 citation in Rom 9:15–17 is a scriptural demonstration of Paul's argument in Rom 9:22–23 that God shows mercy to the undeserved based solely on his own divine character of mercy as opposed to human efforts or status (cf. Rom 9:16). Paul's major focus in the midrash of Rom 9:14–23 is on the conjunction of God's sovereignty and mercy. God's sovereign use of a rebellious Pharaoh and his mercy toward a rebellious Israel during the exodus event demonstrates God's sovereign use of rebellion as a means to show mercy. As God extended mercy to an undeserving Israel through the hardening of Pharaoh's heart, so also God will extend mercy to the undeserving Gentiles through the hardening of Israel's heart. Paul mentioned the commonly used Jewish example of Pharaoh as an object of God's wrath, which resulted in the salvation of Israel in the exodus, to make a shocking and ironic point. In Paul's treatment of the paradox in Israel in Rom 9–11 (i.e., the Jewish rejection of Paul's messianic gospel), Israel functions in the place of Pharaoh (cf. Rom 11:7, 25). According to Paul, the Scriptures witness to the sovereignty of God's mercy. Therefore, his application of

subjugation of the Gentile nations absent in conjunction with Israel's salvation in Rom 9–11, but Paul's central rhetorical point is the inclusion of the Gentiles into God's eschatological salvation.[22] In reference to Isaiah's observed paradox in Israel, Paul presented the salvation of Israel and the faithfulness of God to the covenant promises in conjunction with inclusive language. For Paul, the salvation of national Israel was compatible with, and perhaps even predicated by, the salvation of the Gentiles.[23]

Isaiah 8 and 28 in Romans 9 and 10

Paul's citations of Isaiah in Rom 9:27–29 were followed closely by a conflated citation of Isa 8:14 and 28:16 in Rom 9:33, ἰδοὺ τίθημι ἐν Σιὼν λίθον προσκόμματος καὶ πέτραν σκανδάλου, καὶ ὁ πιστεύων ἐπ' αὐτῷ οὐ καταισχυνθήσεται ("Behold, I lay in Zion a stone of stumbling and a rock of offense, and those who believe in him will not be ashamed"). The Isa 28:16 citation then was repeated in Rom 10:11 with the addition of πᾶς, along with the standard introductory formula "as it is written." The Isa 28:16 citations reflect the LXX more than the Hebrew but contain some changes. The

---

Hos 1:10, 2:23 to the Gentiles, a passage that originally referred to Israel, follows logically from his reading of the display of God's mercy to Israel in the exodus narrative. As God used Pharaoh to deliver Israel, so now God is using Israel to deliver the Gentiles (cf. Rom 9:5). The parallel between Pharaoh and Israel also is reflected in the close association of τρέχω (Rom 9:16) and διώκω (Rom 9:30–31). According to Paul's midrashic treatment of the Exodus passages in conjunction with Hosea and Isaiah, the acceptance of the Gentiles as "my people" is not a rejection of Israel. For further discussion of Paul's rhetorical use of Pharaoh and the exodus event in Rom 9, see Moo, *Epistle to the Romans*, 595; Dunn, *Romans*, 2:553–55; Jewett, *Romans*, 586.

22. A possible parallel in rhetoric also may exist between the destruction of Assyria in Isa 10:24–25 and the σκεύη ὀργῆς "objects of wrath" in Rom 9:16–22. In Isaiah, Assyria serves as God's instrument of divine judgment, which he used to bring about his purpose concerning the correction of Israel (cf. Isa 7:17–20; 8:4–7; 10:5–12). Similarly in Rom 9:16–22, Paul invoked the exodus narrative and God's use of Pharaoh as an instrument. The similarity between Isaiah's logic concerning Assyria and Paul's logic concerning Pharaoh may indicate that Paul has not ignored the particularistic voice of Isa 10:24–25 but rather contextualized that voice with the rest of Isaiah. Paul's logic in the midrash of Rom 9:15–29 may indicate his wider contextual consideration of Isaiah and his interpretation of the particularistic voice of Isa 10:24–25.

23. As Dunn noted, Paul's reading of Isaiah results in his understanding that the poor response of the Jews to the gospel was part of God's overall purpose. In Rom 11:13–16, Paul expressed his hope that the people of Israel would see the salvation of the Gentiles and be provoked into turning toward the gospel and "swell the ranks of the remnant" (*Romans*, 2:575–76).

citation of Isa 8:14 on the other hand is further from the LXX rendering and closer to the Hebrew, though the exact source is difficult to identify.[24]

The Isa 8:14 and 28:16 citations occur in the diatribe of Rom 9:30–10:4. The diatribe serves to address an objection inferred from the midrash of Rom 9. The objection reflects the antithetical parallel in Paul's description of the Gentiles and Israel in reference to the obtaining of righteousness. The Gentiles obtained righteousness without pursuit, while ironically the Jews failed to obtain righteousness with pursuit.[25] Jewett summarized the unit well when he wrote, "The entire argument deals with the 'present situation of Israel' in failing to recognize Christ as the goal of the Law, in whom there is righteousness for everyone who has faith."[26]

As others have noted, Paul's conflation of the texts is centered on the function and identity of the "stone."[27] For Paul, the stone laid in Zion is the work of God in Christ.[28] The larger contexts of both Isa 8:14 and 28:16 includes a sharp contrast between a self-reliance and a reliance upon God alone. As noted in the analysis of Isa 28, the woe oracle warned Judah against trusting in foreign powers as opposed to God. The same contextual meaning concerning misplaced trust is present also in Paul's use of Isa 8:14 and 28:16. The repetition of Isa 28:16 in Rom 10:11 also demonstrates that Paul's major motif in using the Isaiah text in Rom 9:33 is one of trust. The same dual function of the stone as judgment for unbelief and salvation for faith observed in the rhetoric of Isa 28 is present also in Paul's rhetoric in Rom 9.

24. In reference to Paul's quote of Isa 28:16, he used τίθημι instead of ἐμβάλλω, and dropped "foundation" in reference to stone. He also changed the aorist subjunctive form of the verb καταισχύνω in the LXX to a future passive form. In reference to Paul's quote of Isa 8:14, Paul dropped the negative and used synonymous terms for "stone of offense" and "rock of stumbling." Paul's conflation of the Isaiah passages also may reflect an adaptation from a pre-Pauline citation. Paul's citation of Isa 28:16 matches nearly exactly with the citation in 1 Pet 2:6. For further discussion, see Dunn, *Romans*, 2:583–84; Shum, *Paul's Use*, 212–19; Jewett, *Romans*, 612–13.

25. In support of identifying Rom 9:30–10:4 as a unit and understanding the unit's rhetorical function as a treatment of an inference from the midrash of Rom 9, see Dunn, *Romans*, 2:579–80; Jewett, *Romans*, 607.

26. Jewett, *Romans*, 608–9.

27. Moo, *Epistle to the Romans*, 628. Dunn, *Romans*, 2:584. Shum, *Paul's Use*, 216. Jewett, *Romans*, 613.

28. Some debate does exist concerning Paul's identity of the stone. The discussion has included the suggestions of the Law, Christ, and the gospel. The Law as a referent of the stone seems the most unlikely choice, and little difference exists between Christ and the gospel of Christ. Both contain a Christological emphasis. For further discussion of the possible interpretations, see Fitzmyer, *Romans*, 579; Jewett, *Romans*, 610–11.

Furthermore, the remnant was seen to be a major theme in Isaiah's development of the Immanuel motif of Isa 7–9. Paul's placement of the Isa 28 citation in close literary proximity to his introduction of the remnant in the catena of Rom 9:25–29 illustrates his awareness of Isaiah's close connection between the remnant and God's salvation of Israel as seen in the stone placed in Zion. Again, Paul's Isaiah citations echo themes from the larger Isaiah context.

Paul's interpretation of Isaiah's stone in Zion and its relation to the remnant of Israel directly involves the Gentiles as well. Paul's diatribe in Rom 9:30–32 demonstrates a clear attitude of inclusivism. More importantly, Paul's inclusive attitude toward the Gentiles is juxtaposed to God's salvation of the remnant of Israel such that the two necessarily are intertwined. Paul's repetition of Isa 28:16 in Rom 10:11 with the addition of πᾶς reflects his inclusive reading of Isa 28 in connection with the messianic program.[29] Jewett stated that the fusion of Isa 8:14 and 28:16 produced the "Christological ambivalence required for Paul's argument" concerning the divine action of God's placing the stumbling stone in Zion for the sake of the Gentile inclusion.[30] Again, Paul's rhetorical use of Isaiah reflects a clear attitude of inclusivism as opposed to particularism.[31]

Isaiah 52 and 53 in Romans 10

The context of Isa 52–53 resurfaces in Paul's argument through two direct citations. Paul cited Isa 52:7, ὡς ὡραῖοι οἱ πόδες τῶν εὐαγγελιζομένων [τὰ]

---

29. Paul's insertion of πᾶς in the Isa 28:16 citation is apart from any linguistic warrant in the LXX or MT. Fitzmyer argued that Paul's conflation of Isa 8:14 and 28:16 and additional changes to the Isaiah text reflect his disregard of the original context and efforts to accommodate the Scriptures to his context. In reference to the stone laid in Zion he concluded that Paul "makes the OT say almost the exact opposite of what it actually says" (*Romans*, 579–80, 592). Paul's interpretive insertion in the scriptural text is targumic in nature. This observation is not to agree with Fitzmyer's view concerning Paul's use of Scripture, but only to recognize that Paul's technique of changing the text would not have been judged as unusual in the synagogue context. Paul's conflation is not a disregard of the Isaiah context. Rather, Paul's conflated citation illustrates his reading of the larger context of Isa 7–9, in which the stone is connected to Isaiah's Immanuel motif.

30. Jewett, *Romans*, 613.

31. Paul's argument that Israel's disobedience has resulted in the salvation of the Gentiles also is reflected in the rhetorical function of his citation of Isa 29:10 in Rom 11:8. Paul described Israel's disobedience as a hardening of the heart and echoed the same term σκάνδαλον ("stumbling block") used in Rom 9:33 in his citation of Ps 69:22 in Rom 11:9.

ἀγαθά ("how timely are the feet of those who proclaim the good news"), in Rom 10:15 with the introductory formula καθὼς γέγραπται ("as it is written"), and Isa 53:1, κύριε, τίς ἐπίστευσεν τῇ ἀκοῇ ἡμῶν ("Lord, who has believed our message?"), in Rom 10:16 with the introductory formula Ἡσαΐας γὰρ λέγει ("for Isaiah says"). Paul's citation of Isa 53:1 agrees exactly with the LXX, which matches the MT with the exception of the addition of "Lord." On the other hand, Paul's citation of Isa 52:7 differs from both the LXX versions and the MT.[32] Paul's Isaiah citations in Rom 10:15–16 occur within a diatribe consisting of a series of rhetorical questions and scriptural responses contained in the unit of Rom 10:14–21. The objections constructed in the form of questions (vv. 14–15) express the interlocutor's excuse for Israel's disobedience to the proclamation of the gospel of Christ. With the string of scriptural citations (vv. 15–21), Paul refuted the excuses and placed the responsibility to respond to the gospel of Christ upon Israel. The unit functions as a criticism of Israel's disobedience and a proclamation that Israel has no excuse.[33]

Paul's rendering of Isa 53:1 in Rom 10:16 supports his argument that heralds indeed have been sent and Israel's rejection of the gospel of Christ is not entirely surprising because Isaiah already foretold this negative response. The language in Rom 10:16–17 echoes Paul's earlier statement in Rom 1:5. The close connection between Rom 1:5 and 10:16–17 is established through the repetition of the verb ὑπακούω, the close association between ὑπακούω and πίστις, and the contextual emphasis upon the apostolic proclamation of the εὐαγγέλιον. Paul's close association in Rom 10:15–17 between the concept of the obedience of faith as a response to the Messiah and Isa 52–53 is indicative of his reading of the larger context of Isaiah. Paul understood Isaiah's question to reflect the reality that some people actually will reject the

---

32. Paul omitted the phrase "on the mountains" and Isaiah's reference to "him who proclaims good news of peace," which are present in both the LXX versions and the MT. He also changed the number for πούς from singular, as in both LXX and MT, to plural. In conjunction with the Lucianic family of the LXX and against the MT, Paul included the article οἱ with πόδες and replaced ὥραν with ὡραῖοι. Jewett suggested that although the citation does not match any known text exactly, the citation of Isa 52:7 is closer to the Lucianic family of the LXX. In support of this argument, he noted that the citation retains the exact term for "timely" and the inclusion of the definite article for "feet" as seen in the Lucianic family text (*Romans*, 639). For further discussion of the sources for Paul's Isaiah citations in Rom 10:15–16, see Dunn, *Romans*, 2:621–22.

33. For further discussion on the identity and structure of Rom 10:14–21 as a unit in diatribe style, see Fitzmyer, *Romans*, 595; Moo, *Epistle to the Romans*, 662–63; Jewett, *Romans*, 635–37.

messianic servant. Paul clarified the ambiguity observed in Isa 52–53 concerning the identity of the people who reject the servant by suggesting that his fellow Jews are the ones who have heard and yet rejected (cf. Rom 10:21).

The slight variations to the text of Isa 52:7 in Paul's citation are significant in relation to the role of the Gentiles in God's proclamation of victory. Paul's omission of "the mountains" as the place of the heralding may reflect an effort to universalize the text beyond that of the geographic location of Mount Zion, where Isaiah expected the fulfillment to be centered. The declaration of good news in Isa 52:7 that Israel is about to experience the end of Babylonian captivity takes on new significance for Paul in Rom 10:15. Israel's salvation proclaimed in Isa 52–53 is echoed in Romans as contained in the preaching of the gospel of Christ. Paul and the apostolic preachers of the church are presented through the voice of Isaiah as the heralds of Israel's eschatological salvation. Paul's omission of the LXX phrase "the one preaching the message of peace" also reflects an effort to remove any potential for understanding the gospel in imperial terms. As Jewett noted, the phrase carries the same context as Pax Romana, which includes a peace that results in the subordination of all potential enemy nations.[34] In echoing the salvation proclaimed by the prophet in conjunction with the servant of Isaiah, the citation functions rhetorically in its new context as a scriptural support for the gospel about Christ and the salvation found through him. With his citation of Isa 52:7, Paul intentionally emphasized the voice of inclusivism and removed any potential for understanding Isaiah's good news in particularistic terms.

Isaiah 65 in Romans 10

Paul's references to Isaiah 52–53 in Rom 10:15–16 then were followed closely by the citation of Isa 65:1, εὑρέθην [ἐν] τοῖς ἐμὲ μὴ ζητοῦσιν, ἐμφανὴς ἐγενόμην τοῖς ἐμὲ μὴ ἐπερωτῶσιν ("I was found among those not seeking me, I revealed myself to those not inquiring of me"), in Rom 10:20 and Isa 65:2, ὅλην τὴν ἡμέραν ἐξεπέτασα τὰς χεῖράς μου πρὸς λαὸν ἀπειθοῦντα καὶ ἀντιλέγοντα ("all day long I stretched out my hands to a disobedient and rebellious people") in Rom 10:21. Both citations reflect the LXX reading with slight changes.[35] The Isaiah citations occur following

---

34. As Jewett noted, Paul's citation displays an "ecumenical emphasis" that derives from the "anti-imperial logic of the gospel" (*Romans*, 640).

35. The Isa 65:1 citation matches the LXX (closer to the A and Q versions according

a citation of Deut 32:21 and function as an answer to the question posed in Rom 10:19 concerning Israel's understanding of the message. The scriptural string closes out the unit of Rom 10:14–21 concerning Israel's failure to respond to the gospel of Christ.

Paul's introductory formulas to both Isaiah texts are unique and reflect his exegesis of the texts. In reference to Isa 65:1 Paul wrote, Ἡσαΐας δὲ ἀποτολμᾷ καὶ λέγει ("and Isaiah boldly says"). Paul's addition of the term "boldly" highlights the astonishing content of the text, namely that God has acted to reveal himself to people outside of Israel.[36] As has been acknowledged by other scholars, Paul's description of Isaiah's message as "bold" demonstrates Paul's awareness of the astonishing nature of the content of Isaiah 65:1.[37] As an introduction to the Isa 65:2 citation, Paul wrote, πρὸς δὲ τὸν Ἰσραὴλ λέγει ("and concerning Israel he says"). Although Paul's shift in focus toward Israel clearly serves to highlight Israel's disobedience, the exact nature of the disobedience is not as explicit in the citation. What was the nature of the disobedience that Paul had in mind?

Jewett suggested that Paul described the disobedience of Israel in Rom 10:16 as a rejection of the gospel.[38] Although Jewett is generally correct, his explanation falls short of considering the complete rhetorical function of the Isaiah texts and the significance of the introductory formulas.[39] Paul's

---

to Jewett) with the addition of ἐν before "those not seeking." The Isa 65:2 citation matches the LXX with a slight change in word order of "all day long" to the beginning for emphasis. For further discussion concerning the sources, see Schreiner, *Romans*, 573–74; Shum, *Paul's Use*, 226–27; Jewett, *Romans*, 647–49.

36. Although scholarly discussion has included some debate concerning the referent of "those who did not seek" in Rom 10:20, a considerable consensus has developed for the Gentiles as the referent. Furthermore, the introductory formula used with Isa 65:2, which references Israel, also supports a change in referent by Paul between Rom 10:20 and Rom 10:21. For further discussion, see Cranfield, *Critical and Exegetical Commentary*, 2.541; Shum, *Paul's Use*, 227–29; Jewett, *Romans*, 648.

37. Cranfield, *Critical and Exegetical Commentary*, 2.540; Jewett, *Romans*, 647.

38. Jewett, *Romans*, 649. Schreiner described the disobedience as Israel's refusal to return to God (*Romans*, 574). Cranfield suggested that Israel's disobedience is "strictly incidental," and Paul's central focus is God's mercy (*Critical and Exegetical Commentary*, 2:541). Although God's mercy to Israel is central to Paul's argument in Romans 9–11, the mention of Israel's disobedience is far from incidental for several reasons. For example, Paul's use of the Jewish Scriptures demonstrates his careful consideration of the exact form of his citations. If the mention of Israel's disobedience was in any way antithetical or even incidental to Paul's argument, his maintaining of the phrase would be odd. Furthermore, Israel's disobedience is echoed throughout the context of Romans 9–11.

39. Jewett argued that the Isaiah passages serve to confirm the charge of Rom 10:19

rhetorical use of the Isaiah texts in connection with his citation of Deut 32:21 suggests a more nuanced understanding of Israel's disobedience. Both Deut 32:21 and Isa 65:1 serve as an answer to the rhetorical question posed by Paul in Rom 10:19.

In Rom 10:19 Paul asked, "Did Israel not understand?" The use of the adjective πρῶτος in the introduction of Deut 32:21 (Rom 10:19) and the use of the conjunction δὲ in the introductions to the Isaiah texts (Rom 10:20–21) suggests a logical connection to the answer. The logic of Paul's answer can be paraphrased, Yes. First Moses said, "Israel will become angry and envious because of my action toward the Gentiles" (v. 19). Second Isaiah also boldly said concerning the Gentiles, "I will include the Gentiles in the my triumphant restoration of Zion" (v. 20), but concerning Israel Isaiah said, "Even though I continue to offer the same inclusion to Israel, their anger and zeal leads them to reject and disobey (v. 21)." For Paul, both Deut 32:12 and Isa 65:1–2 foretold the inclusion of the Gentiles. Israel's anger and envy of Paul's bold proclamation are a manifestation of Israel's disobedience to the gospel. Paul's point in the scriptural citation string (vv. 19–20) is not just that Israel has rejected the gospel, but that Israel has rejected the gospel because of its inclusive message.[40] As Shum suggested, the inclusion of the Gentiles into the people of God is one of the "distinct aspects of Paul's gospel."[41] For Paul, the Isaiah passages demonstrate that God reaches out to

that "there is no way a message that was producing such wide-ranging results would not have been heard by the Jews" (*Romans*, 648). Although Jewett did acknowledge a connection between Rom 10:19 and Rom 10:20–21 as the answer to the rhetorical question in Rom 10:19a, he failed to understand the nature of the answer for two reasons. First, he underestimated the significance of the introductory formulas to all three citations to the construction of Paul's answer. Second, the question that Jewett proposed Paul to answer with his citations in Rom 10:19–21 was answered already in Rom 10:18. The citation of Rom 10:18 confirms that they heard the gospel. The citations in Rom 10:19–21 confirms that they understood the gospel.

40. Paul's Isa 65:1–2 citation of the LXX with its addition of ἀντιλέγω also may reflect his emphasis upon the Jewish objection or argument against his inclusive gospel. The term ἀντιλέγω occurs elsewhere in the LXX to express a rejection of a spoken message (cf. 4 Macc 4:7, Sir 4:25) and on one occasion in Isaiah to express the servant's refusal to speak against God's prophetic message (cf. Isa 50:5). The concept in both Isa 65:2 and Rom 10:21 reflects the act of verbal objection and argument as an expression of refusal, which fits well with Paul's experience with his preaching of the gospel in the synagogue context. Paul's experience of rejection in the synagogue is witnessed in 2 Cor 11:24, where he wrote that he received thirty-nine lashes, which was the official punishment of the synagogue, on five occasions "from the Jews." For further discussion, see Harris, *Second Epistle*, 801; Martin, *2 Corinthians*, 376–77.

41. Shum, *Paul's Use*, 230.

both Jew and Gentile alike and for this reason the Jews reject and remain in disobedience.[42]

Although the referent of Isa 65:1–2 in the original context of Isaiah is clearly Israel, Paul's reading of the text may not be a complete abandonment of the original context. Shum suggested that Paul's reading of Isa 65:1 as a reference to Gentiles could have been influenced by the larger literary context of Isa 65–66. He concluded that Paul's exegesis of Isa 65:1 reflects "the entire Isaianic tradition concerning the nations."[43] If Isa 65 does function as an answer to the people's lament in Isa 63–64, then God's response that he has not been silent would fit well with Paul's rhetorical argument and use of Isaiah in Rom 10:14–18. Paul applied Isaiah's point in Isa 65:1–2, namely that the Lord has revealed himself to a sufficient degree to be found by people who were not even looking, to his present context.[44] According to Paul, the positive response of the Gentiles to the preaching of the gospel of Jesus Christ demonstrates Isaiah's point. Furthermore, the focus on identifying Israel in Isaiah 56–66, may also be a major concern for Paul in his use of Isaiah in Romans 9–11, as his comments in Rom 9:6–8 suggest. In conclusion, Paul's citation of Isa 65:1–2 in the context of Rom 10:14–21 demonstrates his inclusive reading of Isaiah.

Isaiah 29 in Romans 11

The diatribe style witnessed in Rom 9–10 continues into Rom 11:1–10, which contains midrash of various Jewish Scriptures including a citation from Isa 29. In Rom 11:8, Paul cited a brief portion of Isa 29:10 in

---

42. Paul's argument should not be understood as an absolute encompassing of all Jews. As he argued in Rom 11, a remnant among the Jews does exist. Furthermore, Paul's transposition of the phrase ὅλην τὴν ἡμέραν, which reflects his emphasis upon the continual state of God's offer of mercy to Israel, also provides a transition into his discussion of the remnant in Rom 11. Even while emphasizing Israel's disobedience in Rom 10:14–21, the remnant remains in Paul's thoughts. Paul's citation of Isa 65:2 reflects both the positive message of God's grace to Israel and the negative message of Israel's disobedience. Moo likewise rejected choosing between the two messages and suggested that both were important for Paul's argument (*Epistle to the Romans*, 669). For further discussion of the significance of the transposition within the context of Rom 10:14–21, see Jewett, *Romans*, 649.

43. Shum, *Paul's Use*, 227–29.

44. Moo made a similar observation. "As he did with Hos 1:10 and 2:23 in 9:25–26, Paul takes OT texts that speak of Israel and applies them, on the principle of analogy, to the Gentiles" (*Epistle to the Romans*, 669).

conjunction with Deut 29:4: ἔδωκεν αὐτοῖς ὁ θεὸς πνεῦμα κατανύξεως, ὀφθαλμοὺς τοῦ μὴ βλέπειν καὶ ὦτα τοῦ μὴ ἀκούειν, ἕως τῆς σήμερον ἡμέρας ("God gave to them a spirit of stupor, so that eyes do not to see, and ears do not hear, up to the present time") with the introductory phrase καθὼς γέγραπαται. Paul's reference to Isa 29:10 is indicated with his brief citation from the LXX of the phrase πνεῦμα κατανύξεως.[45] The unit of Rom 11:1–10 contains two related rhetorical questions (vv. 1, 7), which then were each followed by an answer and a scriptural proof. The thesis of vv. 1–6 that God has not rejected his people results in the rhetorical question in v. 7, which asks what happened to Israel if God did not reject them? The scriptural citations in Rom 11:8–10 function as proofs for Paul's thesis in v. 7 that God temporarily has hardened Israel.[46]

The same judgment of Judah and Jerusalem present in the larger context of Isa 28–29 is assumed in Paul's contextual use of Isa 29:10. As in Isa 28–29, Israel is held responsible for their own rejection of God in Rom 9–11 (cf. Rom 9:30–32; 10:16, 21). Paul's citation Isa 29:10 in conjunction with Deut 29:4 demonstrates that both the Law and the prophets witness to God's hardening of Israel in the past. According to Paul, the same hardening continued even up to his day. As some scholars have noted, Paul's use of πνεῦμα κατανύξεως also may reflect a temporary condition for Israel's stupor.[47] For Paul, Israel's rejection of the gospel of Jesus Christ is reflective of a hardness toward God that is indicative of their historical narrative and is only a temporary condition brought about by the divine initiative of God for the purpose of bringing salvation to the Gentiles (cf. Rom 11:11). While Paul's specific citation of Isa 29:10 does not display an explicit inclusivism or particularism, his close connection between the hardness of Israel in Rom 11:7–10 and the subsequent salvation of the Gentiles in Rom 11:11 displays an attitude of inclusivism in relation to his reading of Isaiah.

---

45. The phrase πνεῦμα κατανύξεως occurs in the LXX only in Isa 29:10. The conclusion that πνεῦμα κατανύξεως is a citation in reference to Isa 29:10 has been acknowledged widely. For examples, see Fitzmyer, *Romans*, 606; Byrne, *Romans*, 332; Dunn, *Romans*, 2:641; Jewett, *Romans*, 662. The presence of the motif of God's dulling of Israel in Isa 6:9–10 most likely is echoed also in Paul's citation of Isa 29:10 in Rom 11:8.

46. For further discussion of the rhetorical structure of Rom 11:1–10 as a unit consisting of two related rhetorical questions and answers, see Dunn, *Romans*, 2:633–34; Jewett, *Romans*, 651–52, 660–61.

47. Dunn, *Romans*, 2.649; Jewett, *Romans*, 662–63.

Isaiah 27 and 59 in Romans 11

The final Isaiah citation in Romans 9–11 occurs in Rom 11:26–27. The citation is a composite of Isa 59:20–21 and Isa 27:9 from the LXX with some slight changes: ἥξει ἐκ Σιὼν ὁ ῥυόμενος, ἀποστπεψει ἀσεβείας ἀπὸ Ἰακώβ. Καὶ αὕτη αὐτοῖς ἡ παρ' ἐμοῦ διαθήκη, ὅταν ἀφέλωμαι τὰς αμαρτίας αὐτῶν ("The deliverer will come from Zion; he will turn away ungodliness from Jacob. This is my covenant with them, when I take away their sins").[48] Paul introduced the conflated citation with the formula καθὼς γέγραπται. The conflated citation occurs within the unit of Rom 11:25–32, which functions as an explanation of the Gentile engrafting in Rom 11:23–24 and a conclusion to Paul's treatment of the problem of Israel in Rom 9–11.[49] In Rom 11:25–32, Paul offered the reason for his warning to the Gentile Roman readers against having an attitude of superiority over unbelieving Jews (Rom 11:13–22). For Paul, the reason is that God's salvific plan concerning Israel involves a mystery in which "all Israel will be saved."[50]

---

48. Paul omitted the καὶ from Isa 59:20–21 and changed the third person singular "his sin" of Isa 27:9 to third person plural. The phrase ἕνεκεν Σιων in the LXX was changed to ἐκ Σιὼν. Jewett pointed out that this omission of the second καὶ is significant in that Paul intentionally removed the possibility of interpreting the two actions as separate (*Romans*, 704).

49. For further discussion of Rom 11:25–32 as a unit as well as the unit's relationship to the immediate context of Rom 11:23–24 and the larger context of Rom 9–11, see Chilton, "Romans 9–11," 27–37; Fitzmyer, *Romans*, 618–20; Jewett, *Romans*, 695–96.

50. Debate exists concerning Paul's meaning with the claim καὶ οὕτως πᾶς Ἰσραὴλ σωθήσεται in Rom 11:26. Moo offered a helpful summary of the various suggested meanings of the clause in Rom 11:26a, which he described as "the storm center in the interpretation of Rom 9–11." He suggested at least three issues must be solved in reference to interpreting Rom 11:26a: the meaning of οὕτως, the reference of πᾶς Ἰσραήλ, and the time and manner of Israel's salvation (719–26). Scholarly consensus exists concerning the meaning of οὕτως as "in this way" in reference to the manner in which Israel will be saved, namely the process outlined in vv. 11–24 and summarized in v. 25. A hardening comes upon most of Israel whereby the Gentiles are included in the messianic salvation, which eventually results in Israel's jealousy and subsequent salvation through their acceptance of the gospel. Less consensus exists concerning the reference to "all Israel." Major suggestions include all Jews, a remnant of Jews, all Jewish and Gentile believers in Jesus Christ, or a corporate concept. The debate and resulting suggestions can be summarized with the question, Did Paul use the term Ἰσραήλ in Rom 11:26a in an ethnic sense or in a covenantal sense? Paul's statement in Rom 9:6, οὐ γὰρ πάντες οἱ ἐξ Ἰσραήλ οὗτοι Ἰσραήλ, demonstrates that he is comfortable applying both meanings. Paul's frequent use of Israel in Rom 9–11 as a reference to ethnic Israel, his overall contextual argument concerning the engrafting of Gentiles into the covenant with Israel, and his focus upon covenant as the central identity marker of Israel suggest a more diachronic

Paul and the Synagogue

In support of his claim concerning the inclusion of the Gentiles and the eventual salvation of Israel in Rom 11:25–26, Paul offered the conflated citation in Rom 11:26–27. The Isaiah citations in Rom 11:26–27 function as a catalyst for Paul's central concluding statement, "And thus all Israel will be saved" in Rom 11:26.[51] Jewett described the citation as "providing confirmation of Paul's disclosure of the mystery of Israel's future salvation."[52] The same paradox concerning Israel observed in the analysis of Isaiah is echoed in Paul's discussion of contemporary Israel in Rom 9–11. Paul's citation of Isa 27:9 with its focus on the removal of sin in conjunction with Isa 59 and its covenant language demonstrates his conviction that God's faithfulness to the covenant remains central to the solution of the paradox. Paul's conflated citation of Isa 27 and Isa 59 draws together both aspects of Isaiah's paradox (i.e., Israel's covenant promises and Israel's sinful state) along with a proposed solution, which is expressed in Paul's innovative rendering of Isa 59:20–21.[53]

Christopher Stanley proposed that the conflated citation in Rom 11:26–27 was a pre-Pauline adaptation. He argued that the nature of the changes, the terminology in the citation such as "Zion" and "covenant," and the description of Israel's problem as "sin" are all unique in Pauline literature and argue against Pauline origin. He suggested that Paul had drawn his quotation from an already conflated Jewish oral tradition, which was adapted to express a particular interpretation, rather than directly from the Jewish Scriptures. Stanley described the particular interpretation as the expectation that God will come to Zion (or arise in Zion), liberate the land and the people of Israel from foreign domination, and then execute judgment on the nations.

---

and corporate understanding of Israel in Rom 11:26a. For purposes of this research, πᾶς Ἰσραήλ is interpreted as corporate Israel in a diachronic sense made up of both Jewish and Gentile believers in Jesus Christ. For support of the corporate interpretation, see Fitzmyer, *Romans*, 623; Dunn, *Romans*, 2:681; Moo, *Epistle to the Romans*, 723. For support of an ethnic interpretation, see Cranfield, *Critical and Exegetical Commentary*, 2.576–77; Mounce, *Romans*, 225; Jewett, *Romans*, 701–2.

51. Shum rejected the view that the Isaiah citations are critical to the interpretation of Paul's statement concerning Israel's salvation in Rom 11:26. Although he suggested that the citations serve only as a proof text for Paul's statement, he also stated that the citations serve "as showing the source from which Paul drew his inspiration about Israel's future" (*Paul's Use*, 243). Watson's argument concerning the relationship of a citation to an antecedent also should be considered (*Paul*, 43–53).

52. Jewett, *Romans*, 702.

53. Jewett noted that the presence of God's removal of Jacob's guilt in both oracles of Isaiah provided Paul with the opportunity according to the rules of Jewish exegesis to substitute Isaiah's definition of the covenant as consisting of the gift of the Spirit and divine messages in Isa 59:21 with Isa 27:9 (*Romans*, 705).

He based his description of the Jewish interpretation on the relationship of the conflated texts to the overall context of Isaiah and external evidence of similar traditions in Second Temple Jewish literature.[54]

Stanley's argument concerning a pre-Pauline origin to the conflated citation offers a viable solution to the question concerning the motivation behind the change from ἕνεκεν Σιων to ἐκ Σιών. The change could be motivated by a Jewish interpreter's desire to contextualize the text to the Diaspora context.[55] With no other external textual evidence to suggest that the combination of these two Isaiah texts were pre-Pauline, the argument that the shift was a pre-Pauline Diaspora contextualization remains possible at best. The nature of the conflated citation, whether Pauline in origin, and the change in prepositions still raise the question of Paul's rhetorical use of a scriptural text with a Zion-centered expectation. Accepting Stanley's argument that the conflated citation gives voice to a "particular interpretation of Yahweh's coming," regardless of the origin as Pauline or pre-Pauline, offers fertile ground for exploration of Paul's rhetorical use of the citation. When the surrounding context of Rom 9–11 is considered in conjunction with Stanley's suggestion that the citation reflects a particular Jewish interpretation of God's coming, a more likely rhetorical function of the citation beyond that of simple support for the claim in Rom 11:26 becomes apparent.

A significant question that needs to be asked is, How does Paul's conflated citation demonstrate the mystery as Paul articulated in Rom 11:25 and summarized in Rom 11:26? According to Rom 11:28, the point of stumbling for his fellow Jews concerning the gospel is the inclusion of the Gentiles. In Rom 11:28, Paul described the people of Jacob as enemies of the gospel because of the Gentile believers.[56] Paul's conflated Isaiah citation

---

54. Stanley, "Redeemer," 118–42.

55. Shum disagreed with Stanley's conclusion that the conflated citation was pre-Pauline in origin. He argued for a Pauline origin for two reasons: (1) the absence of any evidence that these two texts were combined outside of Romans, and (2) the probability of Paul's access to the Isaiah text due to his writing while in Corinth. He suggested that the change from ἕνεκεν Σιων to ἐκ Σιών reflects the influence of "certain Jewish eschatological expectations" on Paul (*Paul's Use*, 236–39). Jewett suggested that the change was motivated by a desire to make the passage less offensive to the Gentiles and less misleading concerning his argument that no distinction exists between Jew and Gentile (*Romans*, 704). Although Jewett's explanation coincides well with the overall rhetorical purpose of Romans, the lack of "Zion" language in Pauline literature outside of two scriptural citations in Romans still raises the question of Paul's use of the text.

56. The prepositional phrase δι' ὑμᾶς is best translated as a causal phrase in parallel to διὰ τοὺς πατέρας.

functions as a polemic against the expression, noted by Stanley, of a particular expectation in Judaism concerning God's coming and deliverance of Israel. As is rendered in Paul's conflated citation and is present in the Isaiah context, God will save Israel as deliverer, and he will uphold the covenant by the removal of their sins. The crucial point in Paul's rendering of Isaiah is that God will not accomplish this salvation through a national ethnocentric restoration at the expense of the Gentile nations, but through the inclusion of the Gentile nations. Paul's rendering of ἐκ Σιὼν instead of ἕνεκεν Σιων reflects the heightening of the inclusive voice that results from Paul's reading of the larger context of Isaiah in conjunction with the Zion tradition. As the deliverer goes out from Zion, through the ministry of Jesus the Messiah and the extended mission to the Gentiles, Paul expects the jealousy of Israel to ensue (Rom 11:11). The result will be a wide-scale acceptance of the gospel by Paul's fellow Jews on the basis of faith. Paul's rendering of ἐκ Σιὼν reflects his gospel's element of inclusivism.

Isaiah 45 in Romans 14

In Rom 14:11, Paul cited Isa 45:23 nearly verbatim from the LXX, ζῶ ἐγω, λέγει κύριος, ὅτι ἐμοι κάμψει πᾶν γόνυ καὶ πᾶσα γλῶσσα ἐξομολογήσεται τῷ θεῷ ("As I live," says the Lord, "every knee will bend and every tongue will confess to God"), with the introductory formula γέγραπται γάρ.[57] The citation functions as a scriptural proof for Paul's exhortation of inclusivism within the Roman churches as observed in the unit of Rom 14:1–12.[58]

In Rom 14:1–12, Paul addressed the specific problem of division between "the weak" and "the strong" in the Roman churches over the cultural and traditional issues of dietary laws and holy days.[59] The more conservative-

---

57. The only difference in Paul's citation from the LXX version of Isa 45:23 is his transposition of ἐξομολογήσεται and πᾶσα γλῶσσα. Furthermore, Paul conflated the phrase ζῶ ἐγω, λέγει κύριος to his Isa 45:23 citation. Though the phrase may be a citation of Isa 49:18, the frequent occurrence of the phrase throughout the LXX (cf. Jer 22:24; Ezek 5:11; 14:16; 16:48; 17:16; 18:3; 20:31; Zeph 2:9) may suggest also that Paul is citing a common prophetic introductory formula meant to bolster authority and has no particular text in mind.

58. For further support of identifying Rom 14:1–12 as a unit, see Achtemeier, *Romans*, 214; Dunn, *Romans*, 2:796–77; Moo, *Epistle to the Romans*, 834–35; Jewett, *Romans*, 831–33.

59. The application of the terms ἀσθενέω ("weak") and δυνατός ("strong") in the Roman churches most likely did not originate with Paul but with the Roman Christians who considered themselves the strong. Jewett suggested that the epithet "the weak"

minded weak, who held to traditional Jewish dietary laws and specific holy days, were condemning the more liberal-minded strong, who rejected the necessity of such practices. At the same time, the strong were despising the weak for their traditionalist practices. Paul responded by refusing to take sides and affirming the legitimacy of both expressions of Christianity. He exhorted the strong to welcome the weak and cease taking advantage of their position, and he exhorted the weak to stop condemning the strong for their freedom (Rom 14:1–3). The theological justification that Paul gave for his exhortations was that every believer is responsible to the Lord, and he will cause the believer to stand in the eschatological judgment (Rom 14:4–9).[60] Paul then affirmed the believer's individual accountability to the Lord in Rom 14:10–12 with the accompanying scriptural citation from Isaiah.

Paul described the believer not with cultural identity markers but with the identity markers of acknowledgment (ἐξομολογήσεται, v. 11) and thanksgiving (εὐχαριστεῖ, v. 6). The occurrences of these terms in Rom 14 reverberate from the earlier occurrences of εὐχαριστέω in Rom 1:21 and ὁμολογέω in Rom 10:9–10. In Rom 1:18–32, the wrath of God is revealed against those who refuse to acknowledge God or give thanks to him and instead engage in idolatry. Similarly in Rom 10:9–13, the acknowledgment of Jesus as Lord is the defining marker of one who trusts in him; and Paul closely tied this confession to the sovereignty of God over all. The implication of Paul's argument is that the judgment and condemnation of one believer upon another over an "opinion" (διαλογισμός) is an act of idolatry because the act fails to acknowledge the sovereignty of God as judge. As Dunn noted, when the Roman believers judged one another, they were "usurping the authority of God alone, falling into the same old trap of idolatry."[61]

In the rhetoric of Rom 14:1–12, Paul maintained the same emphasis upon God's sovereignty observed in Isa 45 while emphasizing the inclusive voice also observed in Isa 45. For Paul, Isaiah's declaration that every tongue will acknowledge the Lord applies not only to Jewish believers but to Gentile believers as well. Paul's rhetorical use of Isa 45:23 is reflective of the larger original Isaiah context, which envisions a Gentile conversion alongside Israel's restoration. The particularistic voice observed in Isa 45:14

---

functioned as a caricature imposed on the subordinate group by the more dominant group (*Romans*, 834–35). For further support, see Dunn, *Romans*, 2:797–98.

60. Jewett noted that the phrase "he will stand" is technical Pauline language for eschatological perseverance (*Romans*, 842).

61. Dunn, *Romans*, 2:809.

is nowhere echoed in Rom 14:1–12.[62] Paul's citation of Isa 45:23 reflects the same inclusive reading of Isaiah observed in his other Isaiah citations.

Isaiah 11 in Romans 15

Paul's citation of Isa 11:10 in Rom 15:12 is nearly verbatim with the LXX, ἔσται ἡ ῥίζα τοῦ Ἰεσσαὶ καὶ ὁ ἀνιστάμενος ἄρχειν ἐθνῶν, ἐπ' αὐτῷ ἔθνη ("The root of Jesse will come, and he who rises to rule the nations, in him the nations will hope").[63] The scriptural citation comes at the end of a catena including 2 Sam 22:50; Ps 18:49; Deut 32:43; and Ps 117:1 and concludes the *probatio* (Rom 1:18–15:13) of Romans.[64] The catena was introduced with the standard formula καθὼς γέγραπαται, and the Isaiah citation was introduced with καὶ πάλιν Ἡσαΐας λέγει ("again Isaiah says"). The scriptural citations in the catena clearly are linked by the repetition of καὶ πάλιν at the beginning of each quotation. Furthermore, the scriptural citations are linked also by the repetition of the terms ἔθνος and λαός and by the thematic repetition of praise. The relationship of the Gentiles to Israel in the context of messianic expectation is the central focus of the catena.[65]

---

62. Jewett wrote, "To bend the knee and utter public praise and acknowledgment are typical expressions of homage and obeisance in the ancient world" (*Romans*, 852). Dunn likewise argued that ἐξομολογήσεται was used in the usual LXX sense of acknowledgment, confession, and praise and the term reflects a larger Gentile conversion to the God of Israel (*Romans*, 2:809–10).

63. Both the καὶ "and" and the phrase ἐν τῇ ἡμέρᾳ ἐκείνῃ ("in that day") of the LXX were omitted in Paul's citation. For further discussion of the source, see Dunn, *Romans*, 2:850; Shum, *Paul's Use*, 252–53; Jewett, *Romans*, 896.

64. For further discussion of the identification of the *probatio* in Romans as Rom 1:18–15:13, see Wuellner, "Paul's Rhetoric," 142; Jewett, *Romans*, 29–30, and idem, "Following the Argument of Romans," 272–77. Though Schreiner did not deny the literary unity of Rom 1:18–15:13 within the structure of Romans, he did disagree with the analysis of Paul's letters with Greco-Roman rhetoric. He argued that the analysis with Greco-Roman rhetoric forces categories upon the data (*Romans*, 23–24). The legitimacy of analyzing Paul's letters with Greco-Roman rhetorical categories is justified by the significant influence of rhetoric within Hellenistic society. For further support of the significance of Greco-Roman rhetoric in first-century Hellenistic society and of the influence upon Paul, see Mack, *Rhetoric*, 28–31; Richards, *Paul and First-Century*, 123; Jewett, *Romans*, 29–30. As noted previously, Jewett's identification of the rhetorical structure of Romans is accepted for this research.

65. The inclusion of the Gentiles as the central point of the catena has been recognized widely in scholarly discussions. For example, see Dunn, *Romans*, 2:848; Chae, *Paul as Apostle*, 59; Schreiner, *Romans*, 755–56; Shum, *Paul's Use*, 251–54; Jewett, *Romans*, 895–97.

The central focus of the catena concerns the Gentiles, yet the citations are not all repetitions of the same point. Paul's logical argument builds from one citation to the next until the argument culminates with the final point in the citation of Isa 11:10.[66] Israel's praise ἐν ἔθνεσιν ("*among* the Gentiles") is reflected in the citation of 2 Sam 22:50 and Ps 18:49 in Rom 15:9. The chorus of praise is taken up by the Gentiles μετὰ τοῦ λαοῦ αὐτοῦ ("*with* his people") in the citation of Deut 32:43 in Rom 15:10. The praise reflected in Deut 32:43 is described further as directed toward God and inclusive of πάντα τὰ ἔθνη ("all Gentiles") in the citation of Ps 117:1 in Rom 15:11. The inclusion of all the Gentiles proclaimed in the catena up to this point is set within a messianic context, which defines the nature of the Gentile obedience as one of voluntary hope in God in the citation of Isa 11:10.

Interestingly, the theme of praise is present explicitly in all the citations except Isa 11:10. The more inclusive voice present throughout the catena is used to interpret the nature of the rule of the root of Jesse. For Paul, the Gentiles will praise God not out of forced submission, but because according to Isa 11:10 they will hope in him. As Jewett noted, Paul's contextualization of Isa 11:10 within the catena served to nullify the "chauvinistic potential of Israel's military dominance over the Gentiles in Isaiah's wording."[67] Rather than a threatening day of judgment in which the Gentiles would be forced to obey the Messiah, Paul's recontextualization of Isa 11:10 proclaims a missionary fulfillment to the Gentiles.[68] Paul's citation and rhetorical use of Isa 11:10 demonstrate clearly an inclusive reading of Isa 11.

Isaiah 52 in Romans 15

The final Isaiah citation in Romans is Isa 52:15b in Rom 15:21, οἷς οὐκ ἀνηγγέλη περὶ αὐτοῦ ὄψονται, καὶ οἳ οὐκ ἀκηκόασιν συνήσουσιν ("those who were not told about him will see, and those who have not heard will understand"). The citation matches the LXX, which differs slightly from

---

66. Jewett also noted the argumentative progression within the catena (*Romans*, 892–96).

67. Jewett, *Romans*, 895.

68. Paul's recontextualization of Isa 11:10 should not be understood as a complete abandonment of Isaiah's original context. As was observed in the analysis of Isa 10–11, both the voice of inclusivism and the voice of particularism are present in the context of Isa 11. Paul's recontextualization of Isa 11:10 reflects his reading of the larger context of Isaiah and subsequent emphasis of the inclusive voice witnessed throughout Isa 1–11.

the MT.⁶⁹ The Isaiah citation occurs at the end of the Rom 15:14–21 unit in which Paul discussed his apostolic calling and strategy.⁷⁰ Paul's citation of Isa 52:15 in Rom 15:21 constitutes the fourth direct citation from the context of the servant song of Isa 52:13—53:12, which suggests the significance of Isaiah's servant motif in Romans.⁷¹

In the *peroratio*, Paul recapitulated the urgency of his call from the *exordium*.⁷² Paul's call is expressed in Rom 15:17–18 as a service to God to bring about an obedience of the Gentiles to God. He expressed his strategy in Rom 15:19–20 and stressed that his goal was to proclaim the gospel in places where Christ was not known.⁷³ The Isaiah citation in Rom 15:21 then functions rhetorically as a scriptural proof for Paul's call and strategy. The placement of the Isaiah citation in the *peroratio* demonstrates the close connection between Paul's understanding of his call to the Gentiles and the prophetic witness of Isaiah.

As the analysis of Isa 52 demonstrated, considerable ambiguity exists in the Isaiah text concerning the identity of the servant, the identity of the people whose sins the servant carries, and the relationship between the servant and the nations. Paul's contextualization of Isa 52:15 in Romans

---

69. According to the MT, "for what has not been told to them, they will see; and what they did not hear they will understand." The LXX adds περὶ αὐτοῦ in order to make the reference to the servant clearer.

70. Jewett identified Rom 15:14–21 as the first pericope of the *peroratio* of Rom 15:14—16:24 (*Romans*, 900–902). For further support of identifying Rom 15:14–21 as a unit, see Dunn, *Romans*, 2:854; Byrne, *Romans*, 434–35; Schreiner, *Romans*, 885–86. Fitzmyer suggested Rom 15:14–24 (*Romans*, 710). Mounce suggested Rom 15:14–22 (*Romans*, 265).

71. The other three Isaiah citations are Isa 52:5 in Rom 2:24, Isa 52:7 in Rom 10:15, and Isa 53:1 in Rom 10:16. The texts of Isa 52:5 and 7 are not within the Servant Song of Isa 52:13–53:12 but are in close proximity. Furthermore, Paul's connection of Isa 52:7 and 53:1 in Rom 10:15–16 demonstrates his reading of Isa 52:1–12 and Isa 52:13—53:12 as thematically related.

72. The recapitulation is observed in the thematic and vocabulary parallels between the *exordium* (1:1–12) and *peroratio* (15:14—16:16 + 16:21–23). For example, Paul's work in leading the nations to obedience (εἰς ὑπακοὴν ἐθνῶν) in Rom 15:18 is recapitulated from Rom 1:5, the description of his service to the gospel (ἱερουργοῦντα τὸ εὐαγγέλιον) in Rom 15:16 is paralleled in Rom 1:9, and the close connection between the themes of grace and apostolic call in Rom 15:15–16 is repeated from Rom 1:5.

73. Notice should be given to Paul's use of traditional Jewish language to describe his call and strategy. For example, Paul used priestly language (ἱερουργοῦντα τὸ εὐαγγέλιον) to describe his call, and he also invoked the formula "signs and wonders" (σημείων καὶ τεράτων) as an authentication of his mission. For further discussion of this observation, see Dunn, *Romans*, 2:860, 862–63; Schreiner, *Romans*, 889–90, 893; Jewett, *Romans*, 910–11.

results in considerable clarity concerning these exegetical issues. Paul clearly defined the servant (περὶ αὐτοῦ in the Isaiah citation) as Christ and the people whose sins he carries as both Jews and Gentiles. Paul identified the people who have not been told and who have not heard in Isa 52:15 as primarily Gentiles, and he defined the message that they will see and understand as the gospel of Christ, which he proclaimed.

The same description of the messianic figure as the שֹׁרֶשׁ ("root") in Isa 11:10 is repeated in Isa 53:2, offering the potential for understanding the servant as the same messianic figure. The close literary proximity between Paul's citations of Isa 11:10 (Rom 15:12) and Isa 52:15 (Rom 15:21) illustrates his larger contextual reading of Isaiah and his messianic connection between the two Isaiah units. Paul's Isaiah citations in Rom 15 also demonstrate his observance of the inclusive voice within the context of Isaiah's messianic expectation. Furthermore, Paul's rhetorical use of Isa 52 maintains a close connection between his own mission to the Gentiles and Isaiah's messianic expectation. Paul believed his mission to the Gentiles to be the eschatological fulfillment of Isaiah's prophetic vision of God's salvation.

Inclusivism and ὑπακοὴν πίστεως in Rom 1:5

The placement of Isa 11:10 at the close of the catena and the placement of the catena at the close of the *probatio* are significant for several reasons. First, the placement of a catena of Jewish Scripture at the close of the *probatio* demonstrates the importance of Paul's reading of Scripture and the authority of the Scriptures in Paul's overall argument. Second, the book of Isaiah figures prominently in Paul's scriptural discussion of the gospel. Third, the central theme of inclusivism concerning the Gentiles in the catena at the close of the *probatio* indicates the centrality of the theme to the *probatio* as a whole.[74]

The centrality of the inclusion of the Gentiles in Paul's presentation of the gospel in Romans can be seen in the echo of the issue in the *exordium*, *propositio*, and *peroratio*. Paul's connection between the gospel and the inclusion of the Gentiles is reflected in his self-described call to the Gentiles

---

74. The significance of the Gentiles in the catena and the centrality of the theme to the argument of Romans were suggested also by Dunn (*Romans*, 2:844-45, 848) and Jewett (*Romans*, 887, 897). Schreiner rejected Dunn's view that Rom 15:7-13 is a detached summary of the entire letter, and instead argued that Rom 15:7-13 both functions as a conclusion of 14:1-15:6 and contains a summary of the letter (*Romans*, 753).

in the *exordium* (Rom 1:5), his description of the gospel as applying to both Jew and Gentile in the *propositio* (Rom 1:16), and his summary of the letter in the *peroratio* (Rom 15:16). Paul's claim that his gospel was proclaimed "beforehand by the prophets" (Rom 1:2) is supported in the catena in the close of the *probatio* (Rom 15:9–12). As the analysis above demonstrated, Paul's rhetorical use of Isaiah demonstrates his consistent inclusive reading. Should these observations impact the interpretation of ὑπακοὴν πίστεως in the *exordium*? Both the close literary proximity of the catena to the *peroratio* and the practice of introducing the expanded themes from the *peroratio* in the *exordium* suggest so.

A phrase very similar to εἰς ὑπακοὴν πίστεως ἐν πᾶσιν τοῖς ἔθνεσιν in Rom 1:5 is also present in Rom 15:18 εἰς ὑπακοὴν ἐθνῶν. As Jewett argued, the phrase in Rom 15:18 recapitulates the phrase in Rom 1:5 and even the entire preceding argument.[75] Although Schreiner simply defined the obedience as "the conversion of the Gentiles," the argument of inclusivism in the catena suggests a more nuanced understanding of Paul's use of the phrase.[76] Paul intentionally defined the obedience of the Gentiles in the catena with an inclusive reading of the Scriptures before he repeated the phrase from Rom 1:5 in Rom 15:18. For Paul, the obedience of the Gentiles in Rom 15:18 is a specific *kind of* conversion, namely a voluntary conversion that results in an entrance into the covenant on equal terms with Jews. The phrase in 15:18 is a shortened form of the phrase in Rom 1:5. The phrase "obedience of faith among all the Gentiles," like the shorter form in Rom 15:18, reflects the argument of inclusivism in the catena.

As Paul's use of Isaiah demonstrates, he read Isaiah as a whole and consistently emphasized the inclusive voice over the particularistic voice. The phrase ὑπακοὴν πίστεως encapsulates Paul's solution to the tension between the voices of inclusivism and particularism in Isaiah. As Garlington and others have recognized, a synonymous understanding of "faith" and "obedience" was acknowledged commonly in relation to the covenant in Second Temple Judaism. He concluded that *faith* was another term often used to describe one's voluntary obedience to God's covenant and was practically inconceivable apart from Jewish identity.[77] Paul's use of the terms

---

75. Jewett, *Romans*, 909.

76. Schreiner, *Romans*, 768.

77. Garlington's work established the continuity between the terms *faith* and *obedience* within Paul's Jewish heritage concerning a number of works in Second Temple Jewish literature. For further examples, see Garlington, *Obedience of Faith*, 4, 247, 254.

ὑπακοὴν πίστεως together in Rom 1:5 cannot be divorced from his Jewish background. He accepted some elements of the nationalistic attitude as seen in Isaiah and emphasized in the Targum, namely the salvation of the remnant of Israel and the future obedience of the Gentiles. His solution to the tension in Isaiah was to understand the promised salvation toward Israel reflected in the voice of particularism as fulfilled in conjunction with the voice of inclusivism. Paul's application of ὑπακοὴν πίστεως to the Gentiles in Rom 1:5 and within the larger context of Romans reflects an inclusion of the Gentiles into the covenant between God and Israel apart from an ethnic Jewish identity. Despite their disobedience, Israel maintains the eschatological role of bringing the Gentiles to glorify God as prophesied by Isaiah through the remnant. Thus, according to Paul, the covenant promises with Israel are maintained through the accomplishment of Israel's primary purpose to bring salvation to the nations.

Conclusion

The analysis offered above concerning Isaiah in Romans suggests at least three significant conclusions for this research. First, Romans witnesses an emphasis of the inclusive voice over the particular voice regarding the tension observed in the book of Isaiah. Paul's inclusivistic reading of Isaiah was reflected in each of the Isaiah citations analyzed and was expressed explicitly in the majority of the citations (cf. Isa 1 and 10 in Rom 9, Isa 8 and 28 in Rom 9 and 10, Isa 52 and 53 in Rom 10, Isa 65 in Rom 10, Isa 27 and 59 in Rom 11, Isa 11 in Rom 15, Isa 52 in Rom 15). Even when an attitude of inclusivism was not explicitly expressed in conjunction with the Isaiah citation, Paul's rhetoric was observed to be more congruent to inclusivism than to particularism (cf. Isa 52 in Rom 2, Isa 59 in Rom 3, Isa 29 in Rom 11, Isa 45 in Rom 14). In a couple of the Isaiah citations observed, Paul made intentional changes to the text in order to heighten the inclusive voice over the particularistic voice (e.g., Isa 52 and 53 in Rom 10, Isa 27 and 59 in Rom 11).[78] When faced with any ambiguity or tension between the voices in Isaiah concerning

---

78. Paul's inclusive interpretation of Isaiah also was observed in the rhetorical use of Isaiah in Rom 9:27–29 in conjunction with his rhetoric concerning Pharaoh as an exemplar of God's sovereignty in showing grace to the undeserved. Furthermore, the analysis of Paul's rhetorical use of Isa 65:1–2 in conjunction with Deut 32:21 in Rom 10:19–21 demonstrated that the inclusive nature of Paul's gospel was central to Paul's argument in Romans because he saw the inclusive message as the primary reason for the wide-scale Jewish rejection of his gospel of Christ.

the role of the Gentiles in relation to Israel's salvation, Paul deemphasized the particularistic voice and emphasized the inclusive voice. Paul's rhetorical use of Isaiah demonstrated a consistent inclusive reading of the text.

Second, Romans witnesses a close connection between inclusivism and Paul's expectation of the messianic program. Though the connection between the messianic figure and the role of the nations already exists in the Isaiah text, the analysis resulted in the observation that Paul often emphasized the connection and at times made the connection through the conflation of various Isaiah texts.[79] Furthermore, the paradox concerning Israel observed in Isaiah remained a central concern in Romans. In both Isaiah and Romans, the messianic program is presented as the solution, and the existence of the remnant demonstrates God's faithfulness to the covenant. Paul's significant contribution to Isaiah's vision of a messianic salvation of Israel with an inclusion of the nations was his understanding of the relationship between the two as expressed in his declaration of the "mystery" (Rom 11:25–32). The analysis indicates that for Paul discussion of Isaiah's messianic program necessarily entails discussion of the Gentile place in that program.

Third, the inclusive interpretation of Isa 11:10 in the catena of Rom 15:9–12 was influential on Paul's use of εἰς ὑπακοὴν ἐθνῶν in Rom 15:18 and the parallel phrase εἰς ὑπακοὴν πίστεως ἐν πᾶσιν τοῖς ἔθνεσιν in Rom 1:5. Paul's contextualization of the obedience of the Gentiles in the catena functioned to clarify any ambiguity present in the context of Isa 11 concerning the role of the nations in relation to Israel's salvation. Furthermore, the same close connection between Paul's messianic expectation and his inclusive interpretation of the Isaiah text witnessed elsewhere in Romans is observed also in his contextualization of the Isa 11:10 citation within the catena. For Paul, Isa 11:10 exemplifies Isaiah's inclusive voice in relation to the messianic program.

Although the parallel between the phrases in Rom 1:5 and 15:18 and the influence of inclusivism upon Paul's use of the phrases are apparent, the question of the origin of ὑπακοὴν πίστεως still remains. The term *obedience* is conspicuously absent from the catena of Rom 15:9–12. Can an answer to the question of Paul's coinage of the phrase be found in an intertextual comparison between the Isaiah Targum and Romans?

---

79. For example, Paul's conflation of Isa 8:14 and 28:16 in Rom 9:33 demonstrated his messianic interpretation of both texts, which functioned rhetorically in Rom 9 as a proof for Paul's argument concerning the inclusion of the Gentiles as a stumbling stone for national Israel. Paul's connection between the inclusion of the Gentiles and the stone of Isa 8 and 28 is absent in both Isaiah contexts.

5

An Intertextual Dialogue

Introduction

Based on the above analysis of the textual contexts in reference to the parallel passages between Isaiah, the Isaiah Targum, and Romans, the possibility of an intertextual relationship between the Isaiah Targum and Romans can be explored. Vocabulary and thematic parallels between the Isaiah Targum and Romans should be expected due to each text's intertextual relationship with the same base text (i.e., Isaiah). The probability of a direct intertextual relationship would be indicated by the presence of vocabulary or thematic similarities occurring in both Romans and the Isaiah Targum, but absent in the Isaiah text. The presence of parallel or polemic at the rhetorical level would also further indicate a higher probability of a direct intertextual relationship. If a direct intertextual relationship exists, then the relationship would be found not only at the thematic and linguistic level but also at the rhetorical level.

Analysis

The previous analysis led to several intertextual observations concerning the relationship of Isaiah and the Isaiah Targum and the relationship of Isaiah and Romans. The Isaiah Targum and Romans deviated in regard to the tension observed between the presence of the particularistic voice and the inclusive voice in Isaiah. In the Isaiah Targum, the voice of particularism was emphasized in conjunction with the meturgeman's messianic program concerning the covenant and salvation of Israel. In Romans, the voice of inclusivism was emphasized in conjunction with the meturgeman's messianic program concerning the covenant and salvation of Israel. With these intertextual observations in mind, the question remains: Does an intertextual dialogue exist between the Isaiah Targum and Romans?

Isaiah Targum 52 and Romans 2

Paul's emphasis on Israel's blame for the Gentiles' blasphemy stands in stark contrast to the heightened particularism seen in *Tg. Isa.* 52. A parallel can be observed between Romans and the Isaiah Targum in reference to the term "boast," which is absent in the Hebrew and LXX texts. The meturgeman changed the term ילל ("wail") of the Hebrew text of Isa 52:5 to שבח ("boast" or "praise").[1] The meturgeman's alteration of the text resulted in the description of the blasphemy of the Gentile rulers as "boasting" or "praise." His alteration fits well the overall particularistic context of *Tg. Isa.* 52–53. For the meturgeman, the boasting of the Gentile nations over Israel's exile and subjugation is the reason for God's pronounced imminent salvation of Israel (*Tg. Isa.* 52:5) and judgment and captivity of the nations (*Tg. Isa.* 52:15; 53:3, 7, 11).

In contrast, Paul accused the people of Israel rather than the Gentiles of καυχάομαι ("boasting") with the rhetorical question in Rom 2:23. According to Paul, Jewish "boasting" in the law while breaking the law was the reason for the Gentiles' blasphemy. The boasting against God's name placed in the mouths of the Gentiles in the Isaiah Targum was shifted polemically to the mouths of Jews in Romans. The polemic difference between the Isaiah Targum and Romans in the rhetorical function of the parallel term "boast" may indicate a direct intertextual relationship. Although an attitude of inclusivism is not explicitly present in Paul's citation, his rhetorical use of the citation is opposed to the particularistic attitude witnessed in the Isaiah Targum.

---

1. The term ילל occurs eleven times in the Hebrew text (MT) of Isaiah, always with the idea of "wail" or "lament." The meturgeman followed the MT by using ילל in all but the Isa 52:5 occurrence. The term שבח occurs thirty-seven times in the Isaiah Targum and always within a context of praise. The distinct pattern of usage of the two terms in the Isaiah Targum indicates an intentional rhetorical shift by the meturgeman.

Isaiah Targum 59 and Romans 3

The Isa 59:7–8 citation in Rom 3:15–17 and the immediate context of Rom 3 contain no vocabulary parallels with the Isaiah Targum that are not present already in the Isaiah text. Despite the absence of parallel vocabulary that is unique to Romans and the Targum, an observation concerning the different rhetorical contexts of Romans and the Targum in reference to Isa 59:7–8 could prove helpful. The most significant difference concerning the contextual use of Isa 59:7–8 between the Targum and Romans is the identification of the antecedent of the pronouns, which results in two different applications of Isa 59:7–8. In the Targum, Israel is clearly the antecedent of the pronouns. For the meturgeman, the people of Israel are the ones who rush to do evil, shed blood, and lack the knowledge of the way of peace. For Paul, both Jew and Greek alike are the clear antecedents of the pronouns. Paul's catena in Rom 3:10–18 serves to demonstrate that the sin problem highlighted in Isaiah's paradox in Israel is applicable also to all humankind.

Israel's question presented by the interlocutor betrays an underlying assumption of exceptional status over the Gentiles based on possession of the covenant promises and the law. Paul's response to the interlocutor's question and underlying assumption is that the present state of sin evidenced among the Jews is no different than that of the Gentiles. If Israel sinned despite their possession of the law as evidenced in the larger context of Isaiah, then the problem is not in the possession or lack of possession of the law. Paul's reasoning is that equal status in sin voids any right to boasting in national or ethnic exceptionalism. The meturgeman, on the other hand, maintained an attitude of particularism in Isa 59, which demonstrates his underlying assumption of national exceptionalism.

Both the meturgeman and Paul recognized and highlighted Israel's central question concerning God's faithfulness to the covenant. Both recognized the paradox present in Isaiah between the reality of Israel's sin and God's promises in the covenant. Both agreed that God's judgment upon Israel was because of Israel's sin and rebellion. The divergence between the meturgeman and Paul is observed in their understanding of the implications of the presence of sin in Israel. The meturgeman maintained his attitude of particularism despite the paradox by reasoning that Israel's possession of the law and covenant results in exceptionalism. For the meturgeman, Israel's sin carries the consequence of judgment, but the covenant promises possessed in the law imply a status in God's salvation not afforded to the Gentiles. For Paul, the very presence of the paradox nullifies the boasting that results from an attitude of exceptionalism.² The divergence witnessed between Paul and the meturgeman in reference to inclusivism and particularism in Isa 59 does not indicate necessarily a direct intertextual relationship. A more interesting hermeneutical divergent and possible intertextual relationship between the meturgeman and Paul may be observed in their readings of God's solution to the paradox in the later half of Isa 59, as will be discussed more fully below.

Isaiah Targum 1, 10 and Romans 9

As was stated previously, the context of the *Tg. Isa.* 10 reflects a strong particularism. In the Isaiah Targum, the people who are judged in the earth were described as "the wicked," and the remnant was described as those of Israel who did not sin or have repented of sin. According to the Targum, the deliverance of the remnant from captivity will coincide with the shattering of the Gentiles by the Messiah (*Tg. Isa.* 10:27). In contrast, Paul's expansion with the Hosea citations to include Gentiles in "my people" is strongly reflective of inclusivism. The subsequent link of the Isaiah passages to the Hosea passages serves to add an inclusive element to the remnant theology reflected in Paul's use of Isaiah.³ The meturgeman and Paul have entirely different interpretations of Isaiah's portrayal of the nations' role in relation to the messianic salvation of the remnant of Israel.

---

2. At this point, Paul has not offered fully a solution to the paradox in Israel. Whereas in the Isaiah Targum the call for repentance to the law is offered as the solution, Paul offered a different solution in Rom 3:21–26. Paul's proposed solution then was developed more fully in reference to Israel's paradox in Rom 9–11. Furthermore, the absence of the term Ἰσραήλ "Israel" and the presence of the term Ἰουδαῖος "Jew" in Paul's carefully constructed diatribe should be noted. Paul framed his dialogue with the interlocutor concerning the paradox of Israel as seen in Isa 59 within the linguistic field of ethnic and nationalistic vocabulary (i.e., "Jew" and "Greek") and specifically avoided the use of "Israel." This omission of "Israel" is striking. At this point in his argument, Paul may be differentiating between the nationalistic identity of the Jews and the identity of scriptural Israel and by implication severing ethnic identity from the identity of Israel.

3. Shum argued that Paul's use of Hosea and attachment to the Isaiah texts demonstrates a "deeper theological understanding of the passages." He suggested that although the Hosea text originally did refer to Israelites, the overall context of Hosea indicates that the determining factor for God's acceptance of Israel was his unconditional mercy. The emphasis upon God's mercy in Rom 9:14–24 suggests that Paul followed the logic that if the mercy given to Israel was unconditional, then God's mercy cannot be based simply on ethnicity. For further discussion, see Shum, *Paul's Use*, 208. The underlying concept of mercy as the determining factor of the restoration is present also in Isa 14:1.

An Intertextual Dialogue

In reference to a possible intertextual relationship between *Tg. Isa.* 10 and Rom 9, an interesting parallel occurs with the mention of Pharaoh in conjunction with Isa 10:22–23. As noted previously, both the meturgeman and Paul introduced the exodus motif and a specific reference to Pharaoh. While Egypt is mentioned in Isa 10:26, the motif is absent in Isa 10:22–23, and the term *Pharaoh* is nonexistent in Isa 10. While Romans and the Isaiah Targum share the vocabulary parallel that is not present in Isa 10:22–23, the rhetorical use of the parallel material in each text is very different. In the Targum, the exodus event serves as an example of the destruction that will come to Israel's oppressors as a part of the messianic program. More specifically, God's defeat of Pharaoh serves as an example of the Messiah's defeat of the Gentiles. In Romans, Pharaoh serves as an example of God's sovereignty in showing mercy to the undeserved, both Jew and Gentile. The use of Pharaoh as an example in both Romans and the Targum in the same context of Isa 10:22–23 in conjunction with the absence of the term Pharaoh in Isa 10 is suggestive of a possible intertextual relationship. Paul's rhetorical use of Pharaoh is polemic to the particularistic interpretation witnessed in the Targum. The presence of a polemic concerning parallel at the rhetorical level is more suggestive of an intertextual relationship.

Isaiah Targum 8, 28 and Romans 9–10

While Romans contains no linguistic parallels to the Targum not already present in Isaiah, both texts do emphasize the theme of Israel's trust. The meturgeman innovatively expanded the people's mocking of the prophet's message to focus upon Israel's misplaced trust with the addition of סבר. While "hope" remains the best translation of סבר in *Tg. Isa.* 28:10, the term also reflects Israel's trust in God's salvation throughout the Isaiah Targum.[4] In Romans, trust is the central focus of the call to Israel (Rom 9:33) in reference to God's salvation and also is correlated closely to hope.[5] When

---

4. For example, in reference to Israel in *Tg. Isa.* 17:7, the statement דישראל יסברן ועינוהי למימר קדישא ("His eyes will *hope in the Memra of* the Holy One of Israel") occurs in parallel to the phrase "*a man will rely on the work of* his maker." The term סבר also occurs in contexts depicting Israel waiting with hopeful anticipation for God's messianic salvation, which is portrayed in nationalistic terms (cf. *Tg. Isa.* 26:8; 40:31; 49:23; 52:14; 64:4).

5. Paul's close association of πίστις ("trust") and ἐλπίς ("hope") can be seen in Rom 4:18; 5:2; 9:30–33; 15:12–13. These examples illustrate that the vocabulary of the πιστ- and ἐλπι- roots serves as Paul's linguistic field for expressing the believer's proper response to the gospel of God's messiah.

addressing Isaiah's paradox concerning Israel, both the meturgeman and Paul expressed the problem as one of misplaced trust, and both utilized the term *hope* as the central expression of that trust. Apart from this commonality, the meturgeman and Paul went in very different directions with their suggestions of the proper object of Israel's trust.

A comparison of Paul's rhetorical use of Isa 8 and 28 in Rom 9:33 and the meturgeman's contextual rendering of both texts reveals markedly different interpretations. For the meturgeman, the stone in *Tg. Isa.* 8:14 (i.e., the Lord as avenger) and the stone appointed in Zion in *Tg. Isa.* 28:16 (i.e., the terrible Gentile king) both function as God's judgment upon Israel. The stones in both Targum contexts bring only judgment. Unlike Paul, the meturgeman avoided interpreting Isaiah's stones in messianic terms, because in Isaiah the stones in both contexts bring judgment to Israel.[6] In the Isaiah Targum, the Messiah is primarily an agent of restoration for Israel. The Messiah will save the righteous remnant, which the meturgeman defined as those who return to and obey the law. The meturgeman's association of the stone with a Gentile king as opposed to the Messiah reflects his nationalistic expectation of the messianic program. In no way can the Messiah be associated with bringing judgment and destruction upon Israel.

For Paul, the stones present in Isa 8:14 and 28:16 function as an act of God in Christ that results in the potential of either judgment or salvation of Israel. In Romans, Israel stumbled over the stone because they pursued a law of righteous, which Paul further described as a pursuit by works instead of by faith. Unlike the meturgeman's interpretation, Paul also interpreted the possibility of a positive outcome of salvation in connection to the stones in Isaiah. Paul carried the same positive and negative message of Immanuel seen in Isa 7–9 into the context of Isa 28 through the linkage of the catchword "stone."

The messianic deliverance in the contexts of *Tg. Isa.* 8 and 28 was portrayed in particularistic terms. The meturgeman maintained a clear distinction between God's work in bringing judgment as portrayed in the

---

6. Both Dunn and Jewett's suggestion that the Isaiah Targum witnesses to a messianic interpretation of the stone laid in Zion in Isa 28 is incorrect. Jewett further cited Strack and Billerbeck's citation of *Tg. Isa.* 28:16 as support, but Strack and Billerbeck offered the Targum rendering only as a parallel reading to the MT and LXX, not necessarily as a messianic explanation of the stone. See Str–B 3.276; Dunn, *Romans*, 2:584; Jewett, *Romans*, 613. While the meturgeman did introduce a messianic motif in his rendering of Isa 28, he differentiated between stone, which he interpreted as God's judgment through a Gentile king (i.e., Vespasian) in *Tg. Isa.* 28:16, and the messianic salvation, which he described in *Tg. Isa.* 28:5–6.

stones and the salvation brought by the Messiah upon the remnant's return to the law. Alongside the Messiah's deliverance of Israel, the meturgeman included the destruction of the Romans. For the meturgeman, the hope of Israel expressed the expectation of a national deliverance by the Messiah along with a particularistic attitude toward the Gentiles. Paul, on the other hand, portrayed the Messiah's deliverance of the remnant in inclusive terms. His insertion of πᾶς in the Isa 28:16 citation in Rom 10:11 expands on the rhetorical point made with the citation of the same text in the diatribe of Rom 9:30–33. According to Paul, Isa 8:14 does not only witness to the messianic salvation of Israel but the salvation of the Gentiles as well. For Paul, the hope of Israel expressed the expectation of a worldwide deliverance of both Jew and Gentile.[7]

The absence of vocabulary or thematic parallels not already present in the Isaiah text makes the conclusion for a direct intertextual relationship in reference to the citations of Isa 8:14 and 28:16 between Romans and the Targum uncertain. More certain is the observation that Paul and the meturgeman had widely different interpretations of the stone passages in Isa 8 and 28. Paul associated the stone with the Messiah, while the meturgeman avoided the association due to his nationalistic expectation of the messianic program. The same divergence in attitude concerning the Gentiles' place in relation to the messianic program (i.e., inclusivism and particularism) observed in the previous analysis continues in reference to Isa 8 and 28.

Isaiah Targum 52–53 and Romans 10

While the meturgeman and Paul share a similar messianic interpretation of the servant in Isa 52–53, they differ widely in reference to their

---

7. Dunn argued that Paul used the phrase νόμον δικαιοσύνης in Rom 9:31 to "evoke the typical Jewish understanding of the law as a goal to be pursued" and as a standard of God's covenant demand of righteousness. He further argued that Paul was opposed, not to an understanding of the law as defining righteousness, but rather to the defining of covenant righteousness in ethnocentric terms as strictly Jewish (*Romans*, 2:581). As Moo noted, the interpretation of the phrase has become significant in recent discussions of Paul's view of the law (*Epistle to the Romans*, 622). While a full exegesis of the phrase is beyond the scope of this research, a potential implication is worth noting. If Dunn is correct with his interpretation of the phrase νόμον δικαιοσύνης in Rom 9:31, then Paul's reading of Isaiah in Rom 9:33 would be a direct polemic against the particularistic expectation of the messianic program as witnessed in the Isaiah Targum. For further discussion of the phrase νόμον δικαιοσύνης in Rom 9:31, see Thielman, *Paul and the Law*, 205–8; Byrne, *Romans*, 309–10, 313; Westerholm, *Perspectives*, 325–30; Watson, *Paul*, 332–33; Jewett, *Romans*, 610.

understanding of God's salvation in the messianic program. Paul's adjustments to the text of Isa 52:7 demonstrate an emphasizing of the universal scope of the good news of God's salvation and a removal of any possible particularistic overtones. On the other hand, the Targum witnesses a move in the opposite direction in limiting the proclamation to the "mountains *of the land of Israel*" (*Tg. Isa.* 52:7). According to the Targum, the salvation brought by the servant in Isa 52–53 is interpreted as applying strictly to Israel, while the Gentiles nations are made to suffer (*Tg. Isa.* 53:3, 8, 11).

An interesting vocabulary and thematic parallel, not present in the Isaiah text, can be observed between the Targum and Romans. In Romans, Paul called for an obedience of faith to the ῥήματος Χριστοῦ ("word of Christ"), which he defined as the gospel of Jesus proclaimed by the apostles to all the earth (cf. Rom 1:1–5; 10:8–9, 17–18).[8] In the Targum, the meturgeman called for an adherence to לפתגמוהי ("his words"), which he described as the performing of the law (cf. *Tg. Isa.* 53:5, 10). For the meturgeman, the good news is that God's salvation has come to Jerusalem and the nation of Israel can participate in the victory by obeying the Messiah's word, which is the law of God. For Paul, the good news is that God's salvation has come to all the earth, and anyone can participate in the victory by responding to the word of Christ, which is the gospel preached concerning Jesus' death and resurrection. The theme of the Messiah's word was a central expression for both the meturgeman and Paul in reference to the salvation proclaimed by Isaiah, yet they differed widely in their definition of the Messiah's word.[9]

The triumph of the Lord in Isa 52:1–12, which was associated with the deliverance brought by the Messiah in the Targum (*Tg. Isa.* 52:13), was connected in Romans to the gospel of God reflected in Jesus' messianic program (Rom 1:1). The presence of a shared vocabulary and thematic parallel (i.e., the word(s) of the Messiah) in reference to Isa 53, not present in the Isaiah text, suggests a possible intertextual relationship between the Targum and Romans. The difference concerning the definition of the parallel suggests that the nature of the possible relationship would be polemic. Likewise, the inclusivism reflected in Paul's Isaiah citations stands in strong contrast to the overt particularism reflected in the context of *Tg. Isa.* 52–53.

8. The genitive construction of ῥήματος Χριστοῦ is best interpreted as an objective genitive. For further discussion in support of the object genitive, see Moo, *Epistle to the Romans*, 666; Jewett, *Romans*, 642.

9. The plural "words" in the Targum reflects the Messiah's teaching of the law as the antecedent, and the singular "word" in Romans reflects the gospel message proclaimed by Paul and the other apostles of the church as the antecedent.

An Intertextual Dialogue

Isaiah Targum 65 and Romans 10

A comparison of the Isaiah Targum and Romans in reference to Isa 65:1–2 portrays strikingly different renderings. The meturgeman rendered Isa 65:1 in such a way that Isaiah's original implication that God is found by those not seeking him is entirely absent. Isaiah's statement regarding the availability of God was transformed by the meturgeman into an accusation against Israel for not praying or seeking God correctly. Paul on the other hand rendered Isa 65:1 in such a way as to demonstrate the reality of God's self-revelation to the Gentiles. While their renderings of Isa 65:1–2 differ, neither Paul nor the meturgeman abandoned the rhetoric of Isaiah's original context. Both Paul and the meturgeman rendered Isaiah's rhetoric as an address to the contextual situation of their audiences. The rhetorical address offered by both the meturgeman and Paul reflect an awareness of Isaiah's larger context concerning Isa 65 as a response to the people's lament in Isa 63:7—64:11. A lament concerning the perception of God's favorable treatment of the Gentiles and unfavorable treatment of Israel was expressed in the larger contexts of *Tg. Isa.* 63–65 and Rom 10.[10] Both the meturgeman and Paul addressed the same question raised in Isa 63–65 concerning God's faithfulness in light of the favorable treatment of the Gentile nations within their respective historical contexts, but they responded with very different answers.

The meturgeman responded that God temporarily has judged Israel for their refusal to keep the law but fully intends to restore Israel upon their repentance to the law, while simultaneously judging the Gentile nations. According to the meturgeman, God's faithfulness to Israel's covenant is maintained and will be demonstrated through the messianic restoration of Israel and simultaneous judgment of the Gentile nations. Paul responded that God's sovereign extension of grace to Gentiles does not nullify his faithfulness to Israel's covenant. To the contrary, the inclusion of the Gentiles into Israel's covenant is the demonstration of God's faithfulness to the covenant. In conclusion, Paul's explicit inclusive interpretation of Isa 65:1 stands in contrast to the overt particularism witnessed in the surrounding literary context of *Tg. Isa.* 65.

Despite the rhetorical differences between the Targum and Romans, an interesting thematic parallel can be noted in reference to God's

---

10. For examples, see *Tg. Isa.* 63:17–19; 64:12. The same lament concerning the perception of God's favorable treatment of the Gentiles and unfavorable treatment of Israel is present also in Rom 9–10 with Paul's rhetorical questions (9:30–31; 10:14–15) and subsequent answers (9:32–33; 10:16–21).

self-revelation. Paul's declaration in Rom 10:20 that God has revealed himself to Gentiles (i.e., ἐμφανὴς ἐγενόμην) is strikingly similar to the motif of God's self-revelation in the Isaiah Targum. The meturgeman often used the term גלי ("to reveal") in reference to God's salvation of Israel and simultaneous judgment of the Gentile nations.[11] Paul's contextual use of Isa 65:1 and the occurrence of a revelatory motif as a central expression of God's salvation in the gospel of Jesus Christ in the *propositio* of Romans may echo the same revelatory motif observed in the Isaiah Targum, albeit with an inclusive understanding as opposed to a particularistic understanding.[12]

Isaiah Targum 29 and Romans 11

Not surprisingly, the same messages of judgment upon Israel for their disobedience and of future restoration of Israel present in Isa 29 also are witnessed to in the contexts of *Tg. Isa.* 29 and Rom 10–11. A difference can be observed between Romans and the Isaiah Targum in reference to the rendering and contextualization of Isa 29:10. The meturgeman rendered the Hebrew רוח תרדמה ("a spirit of sleep") with רוח דטעו ("a spirit of error"), which resulted from the removal of the prophets, scribes, and teachers.[13]

11. For examples of the meturgeman's use of גלי in reference to God's act of salvation of Israel and simultaneous judgment of the Gentile nations, see *Tg. Isa.* 1:24; 2:19, 21; 3:13; 12:5; 14:22; 19:1, 21; 24:23; 25:10; 26:11, 15, 21; 28:21; 30:7, 30; 31:4, 5; 33:7, 10, 21; 34:5; 35:4; 40:9, 10; 42:13, 14; 49:22; 51:9, 14; 52:1, 7, 10; 53:1; 59:17; 60:1, 2; 62:11; 63:1, 15; 66:14. The same motif of God's self-revelation as a description of God's acting on behalf of Israel is present in other Targums as well. For example, see *Tg. Hab.* 1:1, 13; 2:7, 15; 3:1, 3, 4, 6, 8, 9, 10, 12, 13, 15; *Tg. Joel* 4:12.

12. While the statement ἐμφανὴς ἐγενόμην ("I revealed myself") is present in the LXX, the revelation motif also occurs in Rom 1:16–18 with a different term (i.e., ἀποκαλύπτω). The presence of the revelation motif in the *propositio* (Rom 1:16–17) suggests that that motif is a significant aspect of Paul's rhetoric in Romans, while the different expressions (i.e., ἐμφανὴς ἐγενόμην in Rom 10:20 and ἀποκαλύπτω in Rom 1:16–18) suggest that Paul's use of the theme is not dependent upon the occurrence of ἐμφανὴς ἐγενόμην in the LXX Isa 65:1. Paul's description of the power of God in reference to both salvation and wrath was described as "being revealed" (Rom 1:16–18) and parallels the similar motif of "revelation" in the Targums. Not only was Paul's use of the revelatory motif in Romans a possible reflection of the targumic motif, but Paul's citation of the LXX Isa 65:1–2 also may be have been influenced by his intention to echo that same motif from Rom 1.

13. The meturgeman offered a rendering of Isa 29:10 that differs from both the Hebrew and the LXX. He wrote, "For the Lord *cast among* you a spirit of *error*, and has *hidden himself from* you; the prophets, *the scribes and the teachers who were teaching* you *the teaching of the law* he has *hidden.*"

An Intertextual Dialogue

The meturgeman's focus upon the removal of the prophets, scribes, and teachers is in no way present in Paul's rhetoric. The analysis of the Isa 29:10 citation in the context of Rom 11 demonstrated an attitude of inclusivism, and the analysis of the context of *Tg. Isa.* 29 demonstrated an attitude of particularism; but these attitudes toward the Gentiles have been observed throughout the texts. The lack of any thematic or vocabulary parallels in reference to Isa 29:10 beyond any elements already present in Isaiah between Romans and the Isaiah Targum suggests the absence of a direct parallel in reference to Isa 29:10.

Isaiah Targum 27, 59 and Romans 11

A comparison of the context of *Tg. Isa.* 27 and 59 with the context of Rom 11 demonstrates that God's faithfulness to Israel's covenant remains a central concern in both texts. The texts differ in reference to how God would maintain faithfulness to the covenant. In the Targum, the Lord promises to "keep *for them the covenant of their fathers*" (*Tg. Isa.* 27:3), which was described as Israel's national restoration and domination over their Gentile enemies (*Tg. Isa.* 27:3). In Romans, God's faithfulness to Israel is described as a covenant of the removal of the ungodliness from Jacob through the inclusion of the Gentiles. While both the meturgeman and Paul interact with Isaiah's paradox concerning Israel's sin and covenant promises, a significant difference exists concerning their solutions.

The context of *Tg. Isa.* 27–29 witnesses a high degree of particularism concerning God's salvation of Israel and the subsequent destruction of the nations. The meturgeman expected the salvation of Israel to coincide with the Messiah's destruction of Israel's Gentile oppressors. For the meturgeman, the solution is Israel's return to the law. In contrast, Paul placed the Jewish tradition concerning God's deliverance through a messianic figure alongside the inclusion of the Gentiles. For Paul, the solution is Israel's acceptance of the gospel by faith in the same manner as the Gentiles.

As noted previously, the cause for the forgiveness of the sins in Isa 27:9 is obscure, and the phrase "by this" is difficult to interpret. According to the Isaiah text, the sins seem to be forgiven because of the removal of idolatry. The ambiguity was clarified in the Isaiah Targum. The removal of the deeds of idolatry will be the cause of the forgiveness of Israel's sins, which will lead to the judgment and destruction of the Gentile nations (*Tg. Isa.* 29:10–11). For Paul, the ἀσέβεια ("ungodliness") of Jacob is a zealous piety expressed in a hostile zeal toward Israel's perceived adversaries. In Rom 11:11–14, he argued that the zealous anger over the inclusion of the Gentiles, as seen in Israel's disobedience in the Isa 65:2 citation, eventually would lead to the conversion of Israel. "Thus in this way," as Paul claimed in Rom 11:25, God will ἀποστρέφω ("change") the "ungodliness" of Jacob into an acceptance of the gospel with its key component of Gentile inclusion.

The same expectation proposed by Stanley reflected in the possible pre-Pauline conflation of Rom 11:26–27 that God will come to Zion (or arise in Zion), liberate the land and the people of Israel from foreign domination, and then execute judgment on the nations is observed in the exegetical tradition of *Tg. Isa.* 27 and 59. Paul's reconfiguration of the particularistic Jewish expectation within the argument of Rom 11 appears in his understanding of "salvation." In Romans 11, the word takes on a whole new meaning. The salvation of Israel (Rom 11:25) will come about because of the inclusion of the Gentiles into the covenant, as opposed to their exclusion. Paul's reconfiguration of the Jewish interpretation of God's salvation is an inclusive polemic against an interpretation of particularism as witnessed in the exegetical tradition of the Isaiah Targum. Paul's expectation of God's coming ἐκ Σιών is not as a military conqueror of the nations for Israel's salvation as seen in the Isaiah Targum but as a gatherer of both the Gentile nations and Israel into the covenant.

While linguistic parallels are not present between the Isaiah Targum and Romans, apart from the Isaiah text already present, a thematic parallel can be observed between Paul's connection of the covenant term in Isa 59 with the removal of Israel's sin in Isa 27 and the meturgeman's insertion of covenant language in *Tg. Isa.* 27. The observation of this thematic parallel is not nearly persuasive enough to postulate a direct intertextual relationship. On the other hand, the conclusion can be drawn that Paul's inclusive reading of Isa 27 and 59 and his rhetorical use of the conflated citation is in direct polemic against the same particularistic, Zion-centered exegetical tradition witnessed in the parallel literary contexts of the Isaiah Targum.

Isaiah Targum 45 and Romans 14

When the contexts of Rom 14:1–12 and *Tg. Isa.* 45 are compared, several parallels emerge. Perhaps the most obvious parallel is that both the Targum and Romans reflect the same inclusive attitude. Both texts reflect the interpretation of Isaiah's proclamation "every knee would bow and tongue confess to God" as an expression of a Gentile conversion to God as opposed to a forced submission or subjugation. Furthermore, thanksgiving is linked closely to the confession of God's sovereignty in both contexts. In the Targum, the meturgeman inserted *"and they will give thanks"* as a description of the confession *"In truth, God is with you, there is no other God except him"* (*Tg. Isa.* 45:14). Likewise in Romans, Paul connected the believer's thanksgiving to God with Isaiah's proclamation that they will offer acknowledgment to God. Like the meturgeman, Paul's reading of Isa 45 reflects a close association between the acknowledgment of God's sovereignty and the expression of thanksgiving. Another parallel can be observed in the contrast drawn between idolatry and acknowledgment to God. While idolatry is present in Isa 45:16, the meturgeman emphasized the theme in *Tg. Isa.* 45:9 in a contrast between the attitude of idolatry and the expression of thanks and acknowledgment of God in *Tg. Isa.* 45:14. Likewise, when Paul's rhetoric in Rom 14:1–12 is placed in the context of his arguments in Rom 1:18–32 and Rom 10:9–13, the same contrast between idolatry and acknowledgment of God is present in reference to Isa 45.

While the parallels suggest a similar reading of Isa 45 between the meturgeman and Paul, they are not suggestive necessarily of a direct textual relationship. The element of idolatry, though emphasized in both the Targum and Romans, is present in Isa 45:16. The presence of the thankfulness theme in both the Targum and Romans is perhaps the strongest suggestion of some level of direct intertextual relationship because the theme is absent in the context of Isa 45. However, the presence of the thankfulness theme by itself is not weighty enough to conclude a direct textual relationship. Furthermore, the meturgeman's and Paul's similar inclusive interpretation of Isa 45 is not suggestive necessarily of a direct textual relationship either, because the voice of inclusivism was present already in the original text. Alongside the observation of the parallel inclusive interpretations of Isa 45, the overall Amoraic context of in *Tg. Isa.* 45 should be noted.

Isaiah Targum 52 and Romans 15

As was discussed in the previous analysis of *Tg. Isa.* 52 and Rom 2 as well as *Tg. Isa.* 52–53 and Rom 10, Paul and the meturgeman share a similarity in their messianic interpretation of the servant but differ widely in reference to their understanding of the messianic program. The same attitude of inclusivism observed in Paul's other citations from Isa 52–53 is evident also

Paul and the Synagogue

in Rom 15:14–22. Likewise the same particularistic attitude observed in *Tg. Isa.* 52–53 is reflected in the meturgeman's rendering of Isa 52:15. When Paul's citation and the meturgeman's rendering of Isa 52:15 are compared to the MT and LXX texts, significant differences are observable.

Some ambiguity exists in reference to the correct text of Isa 52:15a. The MT contains the reading "so he will sprinkle (נזה) many nations," while the LXX contains the reading "so many nations will marvel (θαυμάζω) at him." The meturgeman rendered the text "so he will scatter (בדר) many peoples."[14] According to the Targum, the incredulity of the many nations in Isa 52:14–15 at the appearance of the servant is interpreted as the Messiah's scattering of the nations and exalting of national Israel at his arrival. As noted previously, the disfigurement of the servant in the Isaiah text is transferred by the meturgeman to the nation of Israel. In *Tg. Isa.* 52:15, the meturgeman expects a reversal of fortunes between Israel and the Gentile nations. When the Messiah arrives he will return Israel and exile the nations. According to the meturgeman, the event that the nations were not told about and did not see is the exaltation of Israel. The exaltation of Israel is the cause of their astonishment and silence. Again, the meturgeman's rendering of the Isaiah text demonstrates a close connection between particularism and his messianic expectation.

On the other hand, Paul's rendering of Isa 52:15b reflects his consistent inclusive reading of Isaiah. According to Paul, the event that the nations were not told about and did not see is the suffering and exaltation of the Messiah on their behalf. Paul's contextualization of Isa 52:15 in Rom 15:14–22 reflects his understanding that the Messiah's work is not to save national Israel at the expense of the nations but to save all who would believe. Paul's omission of Isa 52:15a may be an effort to avoid any possible import of a particularistic voice in order to prevent a particularistic perception of the Isaiah text. Paul's contextualization of Isa 52:15b serves to clarify the ambiguity observed in the Isaiah text concerning the identity

---

14. The LXX rendering is to be preferred over the MT as the most likely original reading of the text. The term "sprinkle" is unusual for the context and does not fit the parallelism in Isa 52:14–15. The startling of many nations in Isa 52:15, on the other hand, does parallel the many who are appalled at the servant in Isa 52:14. The suggestion has been made that the MT reading may be from an identical root related to Arabic "startle." For further discussion of this possibility, see Watts, *Isaiah 34–66*, 225; Oswalt, *Book of Isaiah 40–66*, 374. For arguments in support of the LXX as the stronger witness to the original text, see Watts, *Isaiah 34–66*, 225; Oswalt, *Book of Isaiah 40–66*, 374. For arguments in support of the MT as the witness to the original text, see Motyer, *Prophecy of Isaiah*, 426.

An Intertextual Dialogue

of the servant, the nature of his mission, and the identity of the people who are appalled at the servant's appearance and whose iniquities are carried by the servant. While Romans and the Targum contain a similar messianic interpretation of Isaiah's servant not already found in the Isaiah text, Paul's inclusive messianic interpretation of Isa 52:15 is in direct contrast to the particularistic interpretation witnessed in the Targum.

Isaiah Targum 11 and Romans 15

When Paul's rhetorical use of Isa 11:10 is compared to the context of *Tg. Isa.* 11:10, both similarities and differences concerning the relationship of the Gentiles to the messianic rule can be identified. Like the meturgeman, Paul connected the "Root of Jesse" with the Messiah. For both Paul and the meturgeman, the messianic program clearly involves a rule over the Gentiles. The major difference between them is their understanding of the Messiah's rule. The meturgeman expressed an expectation of the destruction of the nations as a part of the messianic program. The obedience of the kingdoms in *Tg. Isa.* 11:10 is a forced obedience due to military conquest. Paul expressed a Gentile inclusion as a part of the messianic program. For Paul, the Gentiles' obedience to the Messiah's rule is a voluntary expression of trust and hope.

The tension in Isaiah concerning the relationship of the Gentiles to the restoration of Israel as discussed previously with the terms *particularism* and *inclusivism* can be seen even in the various Jewish translations of Isa 11:10. The texts are offered here for the purpose of comparison.

> והיה ביום ההוא שרש ישי אשר עמד לנס עמים אליו גוים ידרשו והיתה מנחתו כבוד: "It will be in that day that the root of Jesse will stand as a banner to the peoples, toward him the nations will seek, and his place of rest will be glorious." (MT Isa 11:10)

> καὶ ἔσται ἐν τῇ ἡμέρᾳ ἐκείνῃ ἡ ῥίζα τοῦ Ἰεσσαὶ καὶ ὁ ἀνιστάμενος ἄρχειν ἐθνῶν, ἐπ'αὐτῷ ἔθνη ἐλπιοῦσιν καὶ ἔσται ἡ ἀνάπαυσις αὐτοῦ τιμή. "It will be in that day that the root of Jesse will come and arise to rule the nations, in him Gentiles will hope and the place of his rest will be honorable." (LXX Isa 11:10)

> ויהי בעידנא ההוא ברבריה דישי דעתיד דיקום את לעממיא ליה מלכון ישתמעון ויהי אתר בית־משרוהי ביקר: "It will be in that *time* that *the son of the son of* Jesse *who is about to* stand as a banner to the peoples, to him

113

> *Kingdoms will be obedient*, and the place of his dwelling will be glorious." (*Tg. Isa.* 11:10)
>
> ἔσται ἡ ῥίζα τοῦ Ἰεσσαὶ καὶ ὁ ἀνιστάμενος ἄρχειν ἐθνῶν, ἐπ'αὐτῷ ἔθνη ἐλπιοῦσιν. "The root of Jesse will come and arise to rule the nations; in him Gentiles will hope." (Isa 11:10 in Rom 15:12)

The Hebrew text reflected in the MT is the most indefinite of all the translations concerning the exact nature of the relation of the nations to the root of Jesse. As was pointed out in the analysis of Isa 11, the context of the chapter contains an ambiguity concerning Isaiah's attitude to the nations. Although the seeking of the nations after the Root of Jesse can be read inclusively, the particularistic voice is present also in Isa 11:11–16. The LXX and the Targum diverge in their interpretations of the ambiguity. Inclusivism is emphasized in the LXX, and particularism is emphasized in the Targum. The meturgeman's use of the *ithpeel* form of שמע in *Tg. Isa.* 11:10 suggests the concept of obedience rather than hearing and possibly could reflect the more nuanced meaning of surrendering to an enemy.[15] Consideration of the particularistic attitude in the immediate context of *Tg. Isa.* 11 supports a more nuanced interpretation.[16] In comparison, Paul's choice to cite the LXX is itself a move toward an inclusive interpretation.

The texts themselves echo the larger Jewish discussion concerning the nature of the relationship of the Gentiles to God, Israel, and the covenant. The significance of the Scriptures, Isaiah in particular, in that discussion is evident in Second Temple Jewish literature. Recognition of the tension between particularism and inclusivism in the Isaiah text can be observed through the various interpretations concerning the Gentile issue within Second Temple Jewish literature. Christopher D. Stanley stated that alongside Isaiah's "simple hope for political restoration" grew at least three complete narrative scenarios concerning the relationship of God's salvation of Israel to the Gentile nations. His description of the three narratives can be categorized as either particularistic or inclusive in nature. He argued that these traditions then were developed further in the literature of the Second Temple period. For example, he suggested that an interest in the

---

15. Jastrow, "שמע," *Dictionary*, 1599.

16. The *ithpeel* form of שמע in the Targum can be passive, communicating the meaning "to hear" (e.g., *Tg. Isa.* 9:7; 15:4; 60:18; 65:19), or reflexive, communicating the meaning "to obey" (e.g., *Gen Tg. Onq.* 49:10, 16, *Deut Tg. Neof.* 33:5, *Tg. Hos.* 3:5, *Psa Tg. Ket.* 18:45). While the *ithpeel* form of שמע often is used in the Targums to communicate the idea of voluntary or willing obedience, the argument here is that the context of *Tg. Isa.* 11 suggests a forced obedience that results from a military conquering.

Isaianic traditions concerning Israel's deliverance and the Gentile nations could be seen already in the LXX.[17] Garlington noted several observations of both particularism and inclusivism within Second Temple literature. For example, he concluded that the connection between faith and obedience in Sirach assumed a particularistic attitude. Particularism then received a "boost forward" in 2 Maccabees, even though a Gentile's confession toward God still is envisioned as a possibility. He also concluded that a more inclusivistic approach to the Gentiles is witnessed in Tobit and Judith, where inclusion of the Gentiles is accepted as entirely possible.[18]

Michael A. Knibb noted that the importance of Isaianic traditions in the Second Temple period is witnessed in the prominence of Isaianic traditions in the Apocrypha and Pseudepigrapha. For example, the influence of Isaianic tradition can be seen with Isa 52:7–12 in *Psalms of Solomon* and *Jubilees*.[19] The good news proclaimed in Isa 52 concerning the exaltation of Zion is central in *Pss. Sol.* 11:1–9. Craig Evans suggested that an allusion to Isa 52:11 lies behind the command to Israel to "separate yourselves from the Gentiles, and do not eat with them" in *Jub.* 22:16.[20] The Isaianic traditions also influenced the texts of Qumran. For example, Isa 31:8 was cited within an eschatological context of the exaltation of Zion in the context of 1QM XI–XII. The text of Isa 31:8 was interpreted as a prophecy that would result in the destruction of Jerusalem's enemies and the subjugation of the Gentile nations. In 1QM XI–XII, the nations were described as "brought in" to Jerusalem in order to "serve" and "bow down" before Zion.[21]

The brief survey offered here demonstrates that the discussion and debate concerning the role of the Gentiles are witnessed throughout the Second Temple literature. Some texts witness to an emphasis of particluarism, and some texts witness to an emphasis of inclusivism. Furthermore,

---

17. Stanley offered numerous examples from the LXX of translational changes to a particularistic interpretation (e.g., Isa 10:17–23; 11:11, 16; 35:8–10; 42:1; 49:6; 66:12) as well as nationalistic readings in *1 En.* 91:7–17, *Pss. Sol.* 17:21–32, and Bar. 4:21–25:9 (*Arguing*, 126–32).

18. For Garlington's discussion and conclusions of these texts, see Garlington, *Obedience of Faith*, 65–185.

19. Knibb, "Isaianic Traditions," 633.

20. Evans, "Function of Isaiah," 657.

21. Isa 31:8 cited in 1QM XI, 11–12. See also 1QM XII, 10–20. Translations of Qumran texts are the writer's own unless otherwise stated. All Qumran texts are from *Qumran Non-Biblical Texts*. For English translations, see Vermes, *Complete Dead Sea Scrolls*; Wise et al., eds., *Dead Sea Scrolls*.

the LXX, the Qumran War Scroll, *Jubilees*, and the *Psalms of Solomon* witness to the prominence of the Isaian traditions within the discussion. The texts also witness to a connection between particularism and the expected messianic program, as seen in the Isaiah Targum. Given the nature of the discussion concerning the Gentiles and the prominence of the Isaian tradition in that discussion during and prior to the first-century CE, the suggestion that Paul was aware of both the discussion and the tension in Isaiah is more than plausible. Paul's rhetorical use of Isaianic texts demonstrates both an awareness of discussion concerning the tension in Isaiah within Second Temple Judaism and his own resolution of the tension.

Paul's rhetorical use of Isaiah in Romans reflects his engagement of the discussion.[22] Both similarities and differences are observable between Paul's interpretation of the tension and interpretations evidenced in other contemporary texts dealing with Isa 11. For example, Paul's connection between the Isa 11:10 citation and the Messiah in the context of Rom 15 parallels the same connection made in the targumic rendering of Isa 11. Paul's consistent interpretation of inclusivism in reference to Isaiah stands in sharp contrast to the particularistic interpretation in the Targum and the larger historical discussion. The similarities noted between Paul's use of Isaiah and the Isaiah Targum are not unique to the texts alone but can be found within larger Judaism. These similarities and differences by themselves simply demonstrate Paul's position in the discussion and the polemic nature of his rhetorical use of Isaiah toward the traditional voice of particularism witnessed in the Targum. Only the presence of material common to the Isaiah Targum and Romans yet absent in the text of Isaiah would indicate a more direct intertextual relationship. Can any parallel material common to the Isaiah Targum and Romans yet absent in the text of Isaiah be observed?

The Isaiah Targum and ὑπακοὴν πίστεως in Rom 1:5

When Paul's phrase ὑπακοὴν πίστεως is compared to the Targum text, the parallel with the term "obedience" becomes apparent. Only in the Isaiah Targum's translation of Isa 11:10 is the relationship of the Gentiles to the Messiah described as one of obedience. The common presence of the term as

---

22. Strack and Billerbeck's observation that the phrase "among all the Gentiles" in Rom 1:5 reflects Paul's universalism in opposition to particularism as witnessed in the "alten Synagoge" parallels the understanding of Rom 1:5 as Paul's engagement with a particularism witnessed in the synagogue context. See Str-B, 3.22.

An Intertextual Dialogue

a description of the relationship of the Gentiles to the Messiah in both the Targum (i.e., שמע) and Romans (i.e., ὑπακοή) in connection with Isa 11:10 indicates a more direct relationship. Furthermore, the linguistic construction of εἰς ὑπακοὴν πίστεως in Rom 1:5 may reflect an Aramaic influence. Paul's stylistic pattern in Romans for communicating purpose with the εἰς preposition is to use the εἰς preposition with the infinitive.[23] Paul's highly unusual use of εἰς ὑπακοὴν πίστεως to communicate purpose in Rom 1:5 requires some explanation.[24] The closest Aramaic equivalent to Paul's construction of the purpose clause (i.e., εἰς with the anarthrous noun ὑπακοή) would be the lamed infinitive of שמע with an anarthrous noun.[25] Just such a purpose clause construction exists in the Aramaic Testament of Levi (4Q213 f1i:9), which reads, ועל כרסי די יקר לה מותבי]ן למשמע מלי חכמתה ("They will cause him to sit upon the throne of honor to hear his words of wisdom").[26]

The significance of the influence of the catena of Rom 15:9–12, and more particularly the Isa 11:10 text, upon Paul's definition and use of the phrase ὑπακοὴν ἐθνῶν in Rom 15:18 and in ὑπακοὴν πίστεως Rom 1:5 is now more noticeable. The exegetical tradition observed in the Targum rendering of Isa 11:10 has influenced Paul's use of ὑπακοὴν ἐθνῶν. The significant difference between Paul and the meturgeman was their understanding of the nature of the obedience. Paul's expansion of the phrase in

23. See the Appendix for the syntactical use of εἰς in Romans.

24. The weight of the argument for purpose in reference to εἰς ὑπακοὴν πίστεως in Rom 1:5 is not on the syntactical construction but on the larger context of Romans. Paul elsewhere expressed his call as apostle as a call specifically to the Gentiles (cf. Rom 11:13). Others have recognized Paul's use of the prepositional phrase εἰς ὑπακοὴν πίστεως in Rom 1:5 as a means of conveying the purpose for his apostolic call. For example, see Fitzmyer, *Romans*, 237; Byrne, *Romans*, 37, 40; Moo, *Epistle to the Romans*, 51; Jewett, *Romans*, 110. The use of the preposition εἰς with a noun would be an unusual construction for purpose, since εἰς with a noun syntactically under normal circumstances is a result construction. However, the observation that εἰς ὑπακοὴν πίστεως, a phrase coined by Paul, is unparalleled in ancient Jewish literature also must be given exegetical weight in determining the hermeneutical possibilities.

25. Stevenson noted, "In OJ an infinitive dependent on a governing verb is nearly always preceded by ל, even when there is no preposition in the Hebrew text" (*Grammar*, 53).

26. A similar occurrence of the Aramaic construction (i.e., the lamed infinitive of שמע with an anarthrous noun) as a purpose clause can be found in the Targums as well (e.g., *Tg. Onq. Judg* 5:16). Although the *peal* form in 4Q213 f1i:9 does not exactly parallel the *ithpeel* form in *Tg. Isa.* 11:10, the occurrence of the Aramaic construction of the lamed infinitive of שמע with an anarthrous noun as a purpose clause in an equivalent Jewish Literary Aramaic text does demonstrate the availability and use of the construction within the period of Second Temple Judaism. Vermes dated the Qumran Testament of Levi to the mid-first century BCE (*Complete Dead Sea Scrolls*, 557).

Rom 1:5 with the insertion of the genitive πίστεως was his polemic effort to redefine the nature of the obedience from one of subjection and forced compliance to one of voluntary hope.[27]

Conclusion

The analysis offered above concerning the Isaiah Targum and Romans suggests at least three significant conclusions. First, the Isaiah Targum and Romans contain analogous interpretations of significant Isaian themes. For example, both the Targum and Romans exhibit a messianic interpretation of the root of Jesse and Isaiah's servant, as well as an awareness and treatment of Israel's paradox. Second, material common to the Isaiah Targum and Romans yet absent in the text of Isaiah, observed in reference to several texts, suggests a direct intertextual relationship. The parallel occurrence of the term and theme of boasting in reference to Isa 52, the application of Pharaoh in reference to Isa 10, and the treatment of the word(s) of the Messiah in reference to Isa 53 all substantiate the possibility of a direct intertextual relationship. Even more important for this research is the employment of the term *obedience* as a description of the nations' relationship to the messianic program in reference to the key text of Isa 11:10. Third, the rhetorical use of the Isaiah citations in Romans consistently reflects a polemic rhetoric in support of inclusivism against a particularism as witnessed in the Isaiah Targum. Paul's rendering of several Isaiah texts (e.g., Isa 59:20 in Rom 11:26; Isa 65:1-2 in Rom 10:20-21) and consistent rhetorical use of Isaiah citations imply intentional polemic against particularistic readings of Isaiah. The three observations establish the existence of parallel material unique to Romans and the Targum and of a direct polemic of that material at the rhetorical level, which signifies a direct intertextual relationship between exegetical traditions in the Isaiah Targum and Romans.

---

27. Further work may indicate that the construction of each element of the phrase εἰς ὑπακοὴν πίστεως ἐν πᾶσιν τοῖς ἔθνεσιν ὑπὲρ τοῦ ὀνόματος αὐτοῦ, in Rom 1:5 was motivated by the catena of Rom 15:9-12. For example, the phrase ἐν πᾶσιν τοῖς ἔθνεσιν may reflect the scriptural citations in Rom 15:10-11, and the phrase ὑπὲρ τοῦ ὀνόματος αὐτοῦ may reflect the scriptural citations in Rom 15:9.

Conclusion

WAS PAUL'S COINAGE OF ὑπακοὴν πίστεως motivated by a larger first-century discussion concerning the Hebrew Scriptures in relation to the Gentile debate? The exploration of the intertextual field in reference to the book of Isaiah, the Isaiah Targum, and Romans has resulted in an affirmative answer. The analysis of Isaiah demonstrated the presence of the voices of both inclusivism and particularism. The analysis further resulted in the observation of an ambiguous relationship between the two voices, effectuating a tension in the Isaiah text. The tension created by these two voices within the Isaiah text influenced the interpretational discussion within Second Temple Judaism concerning the relationship of the Gentiles to the Lord and his coming messianic program, making possible divergent readings of Isaiah's attitude toward the Gentile nations.

The divergence in readings of Isaiah is observable in the comparison between the Isaiah Targum and Romans. The analysis of the Isaiah Targum demonstrated an intentional emphasizing of the particualristic voice and deemphasizing of the inclusive voice. The analysis of Paul's use of Isaiah in Romans demonstrated an intentional emphasizing of the inclusive voice over the particualristic voice. The significance of the book of Isaiah in the Jewish discussion concerning the Gentiles witnessed within Second Temple Jewish literature provided ample motivation for Paul's prominent use of Isaiah in Romans for rhetorical effect in his effort to engage the discussion concerning the Gentile's relationship to the messianic program.

Was Paul's coinage of ὑπακοὴν πίστεως intertextually connected with the exegetical tradition contained in the Isaiah Targum? The common occurrence of the term *obedience* in connection with Isa 11:10 in both Romans and the Isaiah Targum apart from the other ancient translations suggests an affirmative answer. Beyond the parallel reference to the obedience of the nations in relation to Isa 11:10, parallel material in conjunction with other Isaiah texts also was observed between the Isaiah Targum and Romans. These thematic and vocabulary parallels, which were not present in the original Isaiah text, are emblematic of some type of intertextual relationship. When the parallels between the Isaiah Targum and Romans are observed at the rhetorical level, the intertextual relationship could be identified as more direct.

The exegetical tradition concerning the attitude of particularism and the messianic expectation observed throughout the Isaiah Targum reflect the Tannaitic period. The Tannaitic milieu of the exegetical tradition observed in *Tg. Isa.* 11 allows for the possibility of the historical circumstance of an intertextual relationship between Romans and the targumic tradition. The major difference between the Isaiah Targum and Romans is the rhetorical use and meaning of the "obedience of the Gentiles." Paul's rhetorical use of ὑπακοὴν πίστεως is direct polemic to the exegetical tradition as witnessed in *Tg. Isa.* 11:10. The genesis of Paul's phrase ὑπακοὴν πίστεως was not found in the LXX or MT versions of Isa 11:10, but rather in the intertextual dialogue of Paul's inclusive reading of Isaiah against the particularistic reading of the Isaiah Targum.

In conclusion, the syntactical force of the genitive is best understood as epexegetical. According to Paul, πίστις defines the ὑπακοη of the nations and expresses a specific *kind of* Gentile conversion. Paul's coinage of ὑπακοὴν πίστεως in Rom 1:5 functions rhetorically as a polemic against a first-century Jewish particularism, which includes submission of the Gentiles as evidenced in the Isaiah Targum. The Pauline hermeneutic of ὑπακοὴν πίστεως is the articulation of the position of inclusivism in response to the targumic tradition of particularism concerning the nature of the conversion of the Gentiles.

At least several implications follow from this intertextual research. First, the proposed five-step methodology demonstrates a viable path for further research concerning the intertextual relationship between the Targums and the NT. As noted previously, the conjunction of the literary perspective and the historical perspective concerning the Targums has resulted in a problem of methodology for Targum and NT studies. As an augment to Chilton's four types of comparisons and three types of historical analogies, this five-step intertextual method offers advancement to field of Targum and NT research.

Second and in reference to Targum research specifically, the consolation motif could be offered as a possible addition to Chilton's list of

Conclusion

targumic theologoumenon as means for further identification of the exegetical frameworks in Targum literature. The analysis of the Isaiah Targum resulted in the observation of the meturgeman's intentional and repeated insertion of the consolation motif in connection to the literal restoration of Jerusalem. While not the central focus of this research, the consolation motif was observed through the analysis of the Isaiah Targum in connection primarily to the Tannaitic framework. Further analysis of the Targums would be required in order to substantiate or deny the viability of the consolation motif as a targumic theologoumenon.

Third, an intertextual approach focused on the rhetorical use of the Jewish Scriptures by the NT authors holds significant value for exegesis of NT literature. The analysis demonstrates that Paul's reading of Isaiah had significant influence upon his rhetorical argument in Romans. Paul's Isaiah citations were more than proof texts. The citations functioned as the source for much of his argument. Determining how a NT author is interpreting a given Jewish Scripture citation and its context can aid further in understanding his discourse.

Fourth, the analysis indicates a significant synagogue influence upon Paul. The intertextual relationship observed between the Isaiah Targum and Romans indicates his continued preoccupation with the exegetical traditions from the synagogue context. When the antithesis to his rhetorical argument concerning the relation of the gospel to the Gentiles in Romans is identified, the nature of the letter's intertextual field becomes more apparent. In Romans, Paul engaged the Jewish exegetical traditions of the synagogue as evidenced in the Isaiah Targum. Paul's literary dialogue with the Jewish exegetical traditions as evidenced in the Isaiah Targum coincides with his continued historical interaction with the synagogue throughout his apostolic career. The intertextual study offered here contains a relevancy to the scholarly debate concerning the most dominant cultural context to the historical Paul and the most profitable cultural background study for understanding the Pauline epistles.[1] While the Hellenistic background to Paul should not be ignored, neither should his Jewish background. This research suggests that the still largely unexplored synagogue milieu may prove to be a fruitful avenue for Pauline scholarship, and the Targums are one of the best windows into the historical world of exegetical traditions of the first-century Jewish synagogue.

---

1. For a recent example of the scholarly discussion of the dominant cultural context of the historical Paul in terms of Judaism or Greco-Roman culture and of the extent to which Paul was Hellenized, see Capes et al., *Rediscovering*, 40–41.

Appendix

Εἰς In Romans

Construction	Syntax	Text
εἰς + anarthrous noun	Relationship	(Rom 1:1) εἰς εὐαγγέλιον
εἰς + anarthrous noun	Purpose	(Rom 1:5) εἰς ὑπακοὴν
εἰς + anarthrous noun	Relationship	(Rom 1:16) εἰς σωτηρίαν
εἰς + anarthrous noun	Measure	(Rom 1:17) εἰς πίστιν
εἰς + anarthrous noun	Relationship	(Rom 3:22) εἰς πάντας
εἰς + anarthrous noun	Result	(Rom 3:25) εἰς ἔνδειξιν
εἰς + anarthrous noun	Reference	(Rom 4:3) εἰς δικαιοσύνην
εἰς + anarthrous noun	Reference	(Rom 4:5) εἰς δικαιοσύνην
εἰς + anarthrous noun	Reference	(Rom 4:9) εἰς δικαιοσύνην
εἰς + anarthrous noun	Reference	(Rom 4:22) εἰς δικαιοσύνην
εἰς + anarthrous noun	Reference	(Rom 5:8) εἰς ἡμᾶς
εἰς + anarthrous noun	Result	(Rom 5:16) εἰς κατάκριμα
εἰς + anarthrous noun	Result	(Rom 5:16) εἰς δικαίωμα
εἰς + anarthrous noun	Result	(Rom 5:18) εἰς κατάκριμα
εἰς + anarthrous noun	Result	(Rom 5:18) εἰς δικαίωσιν
εἰς + anarthrous noun	Measure	(Rom 5:18) εἰς πάντας
εἰς + anarthrous noun	Measure	(Rom 5:18) εἰς πάντας
εἰς + anarthrous noun	Result	(Rom 5:21) εἰς ζωὴν αἰώνιον
εἰς + anarthrous noun	Measure	(Rom 6:3) εἰς Χριστὸν Ἰησοῦν
εἰς + anarthrous noun	Result	(Rom 6:16) εἰς ὑπακοήν
εἰς + anarthrous noun	Result	(Rom 6:16) εἰς θάνατον
εἰς + anarthrous noun	Result	(Rom 6:16) εἰς δικαιοσύνην
εἰς + anarthrous noun	Reference	(Rom 6:17) εἰς ὃν

Appendix

εἰς + anarthrous noun	Measure	(Rom 6:19) εἰς ἁγιασμόν
εἰς + anarthrous noun	Measure	(Rom 6:22) εἰς ἁγιασμόν
εἰς + anarthrous noun	Result	(Rom 7:10) εἰς ζωήν
εἰς + anarthrous noun	Result	(Rom 7:10) εἰς θάνατον
εἰς + anarthrous noun	Reference	(Rom 8:7) εἰς θεόν
εἰς + anarthrous noun	Measure	(Rom 8:15) εἰς φόβον
εἰς + anarthrous noun	Measure	(Rom 8:18) εἰς ἡμας
εἰς + anarthrous noun	Relationship	(Rom 8:28) εἰς ἀγαθόν
εἰς + anarthrous noun	Reference	(Rom 9:8) εἰς σπέρμα
εἰς + anarthrous noun	Relationship	(Rom 9:17) εἰς αὐτὸ
εἰς + anarthrous noun	Reference	(Rom 9:21) εἰς τιμὴν
εἰς + anarthrous noun	Reference	(Rom 9:21) εἰς ἀτιμίαν
εἰς + anarthrous noun	Reference	(Rom 9:22) εἰς ἀπώλειαν
εἰς + anarthrous noun	Reference	(Rom 9:23) εἰς δόξαν
εἰς + anarthrous noun	Measure	(Rom 9:31) εἰς νόμον
εἰς + anarthrous noun	Pred. Acc.	(Rom 10:1) εἰς σωτηρίαν
εἰς + anarthrous noun	Result	(Rom 10:4) εἰς δικαιοσύνην
εἰς + anarthrous noun	Measure	(Rom 10:12) εἰς πάντας
εἰς + anarthrous noun	Measure	(Rom 10:14) εἰς ὃν
εἰς + anarthrous noun	Measure	(Rom 10:18) εἰς πᾶσαν
εἰς + anarthrous noun	Pred. Acc.	(Rom 11:9) εἰς παγίδα
εἰς + anarthrous noun	Pred. Acc.	(Rom 11:9) εἰς θήραν
εἰς + anarthrous noun	Pred. Acc.	(Rom 11:9) εἰς σκάνδαλον
εἰς + anarthrous noun	Pred. Acc.	(Rom 11:9) εἰς ἀνταπόδομα
εἰς + anarthrous noun	Measure	(Rom 11:24) εἰς καλλιέλαιον
εἰς + anarthrous noun	Measure	(Rom 11:32) εἰς ἀπείθειαν
εἰς + anarthrous noun	Measure	(Rom 11:36) εἰς αὐτὸ
εἰς + anarthrous noun	Reference	(Rom 12:10) εἰς ἀλλήλους
εἰς + anarthrous noun	Reference	(Rom 12:16) εἰς ἀλλήλους
εἰς + anarthrous noun	Relationship	(Rom 13:4) εἰς τὸ ἀγαθόν
εἰς + anarthrous noun	Result	(Rom 13:4) εἰς ὀρὴν
εἰς + anarthrous noun	Reference	(Rom 13:6) εἰς αὐτο
εἰς + anarthrous noun	Reference	(Rom 13:14) εἰς ἐπιθυμίας
εἰς + anarthrous noun	Reference	(Rom 14:1) εἰς διακρίσεις
εἰς + anarthrous noun	Result	(Rom 14:9) εἰς τοῦτο
εἰς + anarthrous noun	Reference	(Rom 14:19) εἰς ἀλλήλους

Appendix

εἰς + anarthrous noun	Result	(Rom 15:4) εἰς τὴν ἡμετέραν διδασκαλίαν
εἰς + anarthrous noun	Result	(Rom 15:7) εἰς δόξαν
εἰς + anarthrous noun	Result	(Rom 15:18) εἰς ὑπακοὴν
εἰς + anarthrous noun	Measure	(Rom 15:25) εἰς Ἰερουσαλὴμ
εἰς + anarthrous noun	Measure	(Rom 15:28) εἰς Σπανίαν
εἰς + anarthrous noun	Measure	(Rom 15:31) εἰς Ἰερουσαλὴμ
εἰς + anarthrous noun	Reference	(Rom 16:5) εἰς Χπιστόν
εἰς + anarthrous noun	Relationship	(Rom 16:6) εἰς ὑμας
εἰς + anarthrous noun	Reference	(Rom 16:19) εἰς πάντας
εἰς + article + noun	Measure	(Rom 1:25) εἰς τοὺς αἰωνας
εἰς + article + noun	Reference	(Rom 4:20) εἰς ἐπαγελίαν
εἰς + article + noun	Measure	(Rom 5:2) εἰς τὴν χάριν
εἰς + article + noun	Measure	(Rom 5:15) εἰς τοὺς πολλοὺς
εἰς + article + noun	Measure	(Rom 6:3) εἰς τὸν θάνατον
εἰς + article + noun	Measure	(Rom 6:4) εἰς τὸν θάνατον
εἰς + article + noun	Measure	(Rom 6:19) εἰς τὴν ἀνομίαν
εἰς + article + noun	Measure	(Rom 8:21) εἰς τὴν ἐλευθερίαν
εἰς + article + noun	Measure	(Rom 9:5) εἰς τοὺς αἰῶνας
εἰς + article + noun	Measure	(Rom 10:6) εἰς τὸν οὐρανόν
εἰς + article + noun	Measure	(Rom 10:7) εἰς τὴν ἄβθσσον
εἰς + article + noun	Measure	(Rom 10:18) εἰς τὰ πέρατα
εἰς + article + noun	Measure	(Rom 11:36) εἰς τοὺς αἰῶνας
εἰς + article + noun	Manner	(Rom 12:3) εἰς τὸ σωφρονεῖν
εἰς + article + noun	Relationship	(Rom 15:2) εἰς τὸ ἀγαθόν
εἰς + article + noun	Reference	(Rom 15:16) εἰς τὰ ἔθνη
εἰς + article + noun	Measure	(Rom 15:24) εἰς τὴν Σπανίαν
εἰς + article + noun	Relationship	(Rom 15:26) εἰς τοὺς πτωχοὺς
εἰς + article + noun	Reference	(Rom 16:19) εἰς τὸ ἀγαθόν
εἰς + article + noun	Measure	(Rom 16:27) εἰς τοὺς αἰῶνας
εἰς + infinitive	Purpose	(Rom 1:11) εἰς τὸ στηριχθῆναι
εἰς + infinitive	Purpose	(Rom 3:26) εἰς τὸ εἶναι
εἰς + infinitive	Purpose	(Rom 4:11) εἰς τὸ εἶναι
εἰς + infinitive	Purpose	(Rom 4:11) εἰς τὸ λογισθῆναι
εἰς + infinitive	Purpose	(Rom 4:16) εἰς τὸ εἶναι

Appendix

εἰς + infinitive	Result	(Rom 4:18) εἰς τὸ γενέσθαι
εἰς + infinitive	Purpose	(Rom 6:12) εἰς τὸ ὑπακούειν
εἰς + infinitive	Result	(Rom 7:4) εἰς τὸ γενέσθαι
εἰς + infinitive	Result	(Rom 7:5) εἰς τὸ καρποφορῆσαι
εἰς + infinitive	Purpose	(Rom 8:29) εἰς τὸ εἶναι
εἰς + infinitive	Result	(Rom 10:10) εἰς δικαιοσύνην
εἰς + infinitive	Result	(Rom 10:10) εἰς σωτηρίαν
εἰς + infinitive	Purpose	(Rom 11:11) εἰς τὸ παραζηλῶσαι
εἰς + infinitive	Purpose	(Rom 12:2) εἰς τὸ δοκιμάζειν
εἰς + infinitive	Purpose	(Rom 15:8) εἰς τὸ βεβαιῶσαι
εἰς + infinitive	Purpose	(Rom 15:13) εἰς τὸ περισσεύειν

Bibliography

Aageson, James W. *Written Also for Our Sake: Paul and the Art of Biblical Interpretation.* Louisville: Westminster John Knox, 1993.
Achtemeier, Paul J. *Romans: A Bible Commentary for Preaching and Teaching.* Interpretation. Atlanta: Knox, 1985.
Aland, Barbara, et al. *The Greek New Testament.* 4th ed. Stuttgart: Deutsche Bibelgesellschaft, 1998.
———. *Novum Testamentum Graece.* 27th ed. Stuttgart: Deutsche Bibelgesellschaft, 2001.
Alverez, Andrea E. "The Restoration of Israel and Its Messiah: The History of Interpretation of Isaiah 61:1–2." MA thesis, Trinity Western University, 2004.
Aune, David. "Romans as a Logos Protreptikos." In *The Romans Debate*, edited by Karl P. Donfried, 278–96. Rev. and exp. ed. Peabody, MA: Hendrickson, 1991.
Baltzer, Klaus, *Deutero-Isaiah: A Commentary on Isaiah 40–55.* Hermeneia. Minneapolis: Fortress, 2001.
Beal, Timothy K. "Glossary." In *Reading between Texts: Intertextuality and the Hebrew Bible*, edited by Danna Nolan Fewell, 21–24. Louisville: Westminster John Knox, 1992.
———. "Ideology and Intertextuality: Surplus of Meaning and Controlling the Means of Production." In *Reading between Texts: Intertextuality and the Hebrew Bible*, edited by Danna Nolan Fewell, 27–31. Louisville: Westminster John Knox, 1992.
Beattie, D. R. G., and J. McNamara, editors. *The Aramaic Bible: The Targums in Their Historical Context.* JSOTSupp 166. Sheffield: JSOT Press, 1992.
Beker, J. Christiaan. *Paul the Apostle: The Triumph of God in Life and Thought.* Philadelphia: Fortress, 1980.
Black, Matthew. *An Aramaic Approach to the Gospels and Acts.* Oxford: Blackwell, 1967.
Bowker, John. *The Targums and Rabbinic Literature: An Introduction to Jewish Interpretation of Scripture.* Cambridge: Cambridge University Press, 1969.
Buchanan, George Wesley. *Introduction to Intertextuality.* Mellen Biblical 26. Lewiston, NY: Mellen Biblical, 1994.
Byrne, Brendan. *Romans.* Sacra Pagina 6. Edited by Daniel J. Harrington. Collegeville, MN: Liturgical, 1996.
Campenhausen, Hans von. *The Formation of the Christian Bible.* Translated by J. A. Baker. Mifflintown, PA: Sigler, 1997.
Capes, David B. *Old Testament Yahweh Texts in Paul's Christology.* Tübingen: Mohr, 1992.
Capes, David B., et al., *Rediscovering Paul: An Introduction to His World, Letters and Theology.* Downers Grove, IL: InterVarsity, 2007.

Catto, Stephen K. *Reconstructing the First-Century Synagogue: A Critical Analysis of Current Research*. Edited by Mark Goodacre. Library of New Testament Studies 363. New York: T. & T. Clark, 2007.

Chae, Daniel Jong-Sang. *Paul as Apostle to the Gentiles: His Apostolic Self-Awareness and Its Influence on the Soteriological Argument in Romans*. Carlisle, UK: Paternoster, 1997.

Charles R. H., editor. *The Apocrypha and Pseudepigrapha of the Old Testament in English*. Vol. 2. London: Oxford University Press, 1913.

Childs. Brevard S. *Isaiah*. Old Testament Library. Louisville: Westminster John Knox, 2001.

Chilton, Bruce D. "From Aramaic Paraphrase to Greek Testament." In *From Prophecy to Testament: The Function of the Old Testament in the New*, edited by Craig A. Evans, 23–43. Peabody, MA: Hendrickson, 2004.

———. *A Galilean Rabbi and His Bible: Jesus' Use of the Interpreted Scripture of His Time*. Good News Studies 8. Wilmington, DE: Glazier, 1984.

———. *The Glory of Israel: The Theology and Provenience of the Isaiah Targum*. Edited by David J. A. Clines, Philip R. Davies, and David M. Gunn. JSOTSupp 23. Sheffield: JSOT Press, 1982.

———. *The Isaiah Targum: Introduction, Translation, Apparatus, and Notes*. Vol. 11 of *The Aramaic Bible*. Edited by Kevin Cathcart, Michael Maher, and Martin McNamara. Collegeville, MN: Liturgical, 1987.

———. *Judaic Approaches to the Gospels*. International Studies in Formative Judaism and Christianity 2. Atlanta: Scholars, 1994.

———. *Profiles of a Rabbi: Synoptic Opportunities in Reading about Jesus*. Brown Judaic Studies 177. Atlanta: Scholars, 1989.

———. "Romans 9–11 as Scriptural Interpretation and Dialogue with Judaism." *Ex Auditu* 4 (1988) 27–37.

Cranfield, Charles E. B. *A Critical and Exegetical Commentary on the Epistle to the Romans*. 2 vols. International Critical Commentary. Edinburgh: T. & T. Clark, 1977–79.

Dalman, Gustaf. *Grammatik des jüdisch-palästinische Aramäisch*. Leipzig: Hinrichs, 1894.

Davidson, Robert. "Universalism in Second Isaiah." *Scottish Journal of Theology* 16 (1963) 167–83.

Davies, Glenn N. *Faith and Obedience in Romans: A Study in Romans 1–4*. JSNTSupp 39. Sheffield: JSOT Press, 1990.

Davies, W. D. *Paul and Rabbinic Judaism: Some Rabbinic Elements in Pauline Theology*. London: S. P. C. K., 1958.

Le Déaut, Roger. *The Message of the New Testament and the Aramaic Bible (Targum)*. Rev. ed. Translated by Stephen F. Miletic. Rome: Biblical Institute, 1982.

Dodd, C. H. *The Epistle of Paul to the Romans*. Moffatt New Testament Commentary. New York: Harper & Brothers, 1932.

Dunn, James D. G. *Romans*. Word Biblical Commentary 38a–38b. Dallas: Word, 1988.

———. *The Theology of Paul the Apostle*. Grand Rapids: Eerdmans, 1998.

Elliger, Karl, and William Rudolph, editors. *Biblia Hebraica Stuttgartensia*. 4th corr. ed. Edited by Adrian Schenker. Stuttgart: Deutsche Bibelgesellschaft, 1983.

Etheridge, J. W. *The Targums of Onkelos and Jonathan ben Uzziel on the Pentateuch: With the Fragments of the Jerusalem Targum from the Chaldee*. New York: KTAV, 1968.

Bibliography

Evans, Craig A. "The Aramaic Psalter and the New Testament." In *From Prophecy to Testament: The Function of the Old Testament in the New*, edited by Craig A. Evans, 44-91. Peabody, MA: Hendrickson, 2004.

———. "The Function of Isaiah in the New Testament." In *Writing and Reading the Scroll of Isaiah: Studies in Interpretive Tradition*, 651-91. Supplements to Vetus Testamentum 2. New York: Brill, 1997.

———. "Old Testament in the Gospels." In *Dictionary of Jesus and the Gospels*, edited by Joel B. Green and Scot McKnight, 579-90. Downers Grove, IL: InterVarsity, 1992.

Evans, Craig A., and James A. Sanders, editors. *Paul and the Scriptures of Israel*. JSNTSupp 83. Sheffield: Sheffield Academic, 1993.

Fitzmyer, Joseph A. Review of *The New Testament and the Palestinian Targum to the Pentateuch* by Martin McNamara. *Theological Studies* 29 (1968) 321-26.

———. *Romans: A New Translation with Introduction and Commentary*. Anchor Bible 33. New Haven: Yale University, 1993.

Flesher, Paul V. M., editor. *Targum Studies: Targum and Peshitta*. Vol. 2 Atlanta: Scholars, 1992.

Flesher, Paul V. M., and Bruce D. Chilton. *The Targums: A Critical Introduction*. Waco: Baylor University Press, 2011.

Gamble, Harry. *The Textual History of the Letter to the Romans*. Studies and Documents 42. Grand Rapids: Eerdmans, 1977.

Garlington, Don B. *"The Obedience of Faith": A Pauline Phrase in Historical Context*. Wissenschaftliche Untersuchungen zum Neuen Testament 38. Tubingen: Mohr, 1991.

Gordon, Robert P. *Studies in the Targum to the Twelve Prophets: From Nahum to Malachi*. Supplements to Vetus Testamentum 51. New York: Brill, 1994.

Gray, George Buchanan. *A Critical and Exegetical Commentary on the Book of Isaiah I-XXVII*. Vol. 1. International Critical Commentary. Edinburgh: T. & T. Clark, 1980.

Harrington, Daniel J. Review of *Targum and Testament* by Martin McNamara. *Catholic Quarterly* 34 (1973) 253-54.

Harris, Murray J. *The Second Epistle to the Corinthians*. The New International Greek Testament Commentary. Grand Rapids: Eerdmans, 2005.

Hays, Richard B. *The Conversion of the Imagination: Paul as Interpreter of Israel's Scripture*. Grand Rapids: Eerdmans, 2005.

———. *Echoes of Scripture in the Letters of Paul*. New Haven: Yale University, 1989.

Hays, Richard B., Stefan Alkier, and Leroy A. Huizenga, editors. *Reading the Bible Intertextually*. Waco: Baylor University Press, 2009.

Hayward, Robert. "Red Heifer and Golden Calf: Dating Targum Pseudo-Jonathan." In *Targum Studies*, edited by Paul V. M. Flesher, 1:9-32. Atlanta: Scholars, 1992.

———. *The Targum of Jeremiah*. Vol. 12 of *The Aramaic Bible*. Edited by Kevin Cathcart, Michael Maher, and Martin McNamara. Wilmington, DE: Glazier, 1987.

Herntrich, Volkmar. *Der Prophet Jesaia: Kapitel 1-12*. Das Alte Testament Deutsch 17. Göttingen: Vandenhoeck & Ruprecht, 1957.

Hollenberg, D. E. "Nationalism and 'The Nations' in Isaiah XL-LV." *Vetus Testamentum* 19 (1969) 23-36.

Irvine, Stuart A. *Isaiah, Ahaz, and the Syro-Ephraimitic Crisis*. SBL Dissertation 123. Edited by David L. Petersen. Atlanta: Scholars, 1990.

Jastrow, Marcus. *Dictionary of the Targumim, the Talmud Babli and Yerushalmi, and the Midrashic Literature*. Peabody, MA: Hendrickson, 2005.

Jewett, Robert. "Following the Argument of Romans." In *The Romans Debate*, edited by Karl P. Donfried, 265-77. Rev. and exp. ed. Peabody, MA: Hendrickson, 1991.

———. *Romans*. Hermeneia. Minneapolis: Fortress, 2007.

Kahle, Paul. *The Cairo Geniza*. London: Oxford University Press, 1941.

Kaiser, Otto. *Isaiah 1-12: A Commentary*. Old Testament Library. Philadelphia: Westminster, 1972.

Käsemann, Ernst. *Commentary on Romans*. Translated and edited by Geoffrey W. Bromiley. Grand Rapids: Eerdmans, 1980.

Kaufman, Stephen A. "Dating the Language of the Palestinian Targums." In *The Aramaic Bible: Targums in Their Historical Context*, edited by D. R. G. Beattie and M. J. McNamara, 118-41. Sheffield: JSOT Press, 1994.

———. "On Methodology in the Study of the Targums and Their Chronology." *Journal for the Study of the New Testament* 23/1 (1985) 117-24.

Kebede, Aschalew. "How Can the Concepts of Universalism and Nationalism in the Book of Isaiah Be Reconciled?" PhD diss., New Orleans Baptist Theological Seminary, 2002.

Kim, Johann D. *God, Israel, and the Gentiles: Rhetoric and the Situation in Romans 9-11*. SBL Dissertation 176. Atlanta: SBL, 2000.

Klein, Michael L. *The Fragment-Targums of the Pentateuch: According to Their Extant Sources*. Vol. 2. Rome: Biblical Institute, 1980.

Klein, William W., Craig L. Blomberg, and Robert L. Hubbard. *Introduction to Biblical Interpretation*. Rev. ed. Dallas: Word, 1993.

Knibb, Michael A. "Isaianic Traditions in the Apocrypha and Pseudepigrapha." In *Writing and Reading the Scroll of Isaiah: Studies in Interpretive Traditio*, edited by Craig C. Boyles and Craig A. Evans, 633-50. Supplements to Vetus Testamentum 2. New York: Brill, 1997.

Kristeva, Julia. *Revolution in Poetic Language*. Translated by Margaret Waller. New York: Columbia University Press, 1984.

Levey, Samson H. "The Date of Targum Jonathan to the Prophets." *Vetus Testamentum* 21/2 (1971) 186-96.

Lindblom, Johannes. *The Servant Songs in Deutero-Isaiah: A New Attempt to Solve an Old Problem*. Lund, Sweden: Gleerup, 1951.

Lods, Adolphe. *The Prophets and the Rise of Judaism*. Edited by C. K. Ogden. Translated by S. H. Hooke. History of Civilization. London: Routledge, 1955.

Lohse, Eduard. *Die Texte aus Qumran*. München: Kösel, 1964.

Longenecker, Richard N. *Biblical Exegesis in the Apostolic Period*. 2nd ed. Grand Rapids: Eerdmans, 1999.

Mack, Burton L. *Rhetoric and the New Testament*. Minneapolis: Fortress, 1990.

Martin, Ralph P. *2 Corinthians*. Word Biblical Commentary 40. Waco: Word, 1986.

McKenzie, John L. *Second Isaiah*. Anchor Bible 20. Garden City, NY: Doubleday, 1968.

McLay, R. Timothy. "Biblical Texts and the Scriptures for the New Testament Church." In *Hearing the Old Testament in the New Testament*, edited by Stanley E. Porter, 38-58. Grand Rapids: Eerdmans, 2006.

McNamara, Martin. *The New Testament and the Palestinian Targum to the Pentateuch*. Rome: Pontifical Biblical Institute, 1969.

———. *Palestinian Judaism and the New Testament*. Edited by Robert J. Karris. Good News Studies 4. Wilmington, DE: Glazier, 1983.

———. *Targum and Testament Aramaic Paraphrases of the Hebrew Bible: A Light on the New Testament*. Shannon, Ireland: Irish University Press, 1972.

Bibliography

———. *Targum and Testament Revisited. Aramaic Paraphrases of the Hebrew Bible: A Light on the New Testament*. 2nd ed. Grand Rapids: Eerdmans, 2010.
Michel, Otto. *Der Brief an die Romer*. Göttingen: Vandenhoeck & Ruprecht, 1955.
Miller, James C. "'The Obedience of Faith,' the Eschatological People of God, and the Purpose of Romans." PhD diss., Union Theological Seminary, 1999.
Moo, Douglas J. *The Epistle to the Romans*. New International Commentary on the New Testament. Grand Rapids: Eerdmans, 1996.
Motyer, J. Alec. *The Prophecy of Isaiah: An Introduction and Commentary*. Downers Grove, IL: InterVarsity, 1993.
Mounce, Robert. *Romans*. New American Commentary 27. Nashville: Broadman & Holman, 1995.
Oswalt, John N. *The Book of Isaiah*. 2 vols. New International Commentary on the Old Testament. Grand Rapids: Eerdmans, 1986, 1993.
Qumran: Non-Biblical Texts on CD-ROM. CD-ROM, Accordance Version 4.4.3, 2006.
Richards, E. Randolph. *Paul and First-Century Letter Writing: Secretaries, Compositions and Collection*. Downers Grove, IL: InterVarsity, 2004.
Sanders, E. P. *Paul and Palestinian Judaism: A Comparison of Patterns of Religion*. Minneapolis: Fortress, 1977.
Sandmel, Samuel. "Parallelomania." *Journal of Biblical Literature* 81/1 (1962) 1–13.
Schodde, G. H. "Interpretation." In *The International Standard Bible Encyclopedia*, 3: 1489–90.
Schreiner, Thomas R. *Romans*. Baker Exegetical Commentary on the New Testament. Grand Rapids: Baker, 1998.
Shepherd, Michael B. "Targums, the New Testament, and Biblical Theology of the Messiah." *Journal of the Evangelical Theological Society* 51/1 (2008) 43–58.
Shum, Shiu-Lun. *Paul's Use of Isaiah in Romans: A Comparative Study of Paul's Letter to the Romans and the Sibylline and Qumran Sectarian Texts*. Wissenschaftliche Untersuchungen zum Neuen Testament 156. Tübingen: Mohr, 2002.
Smith, Gary V. *Isaiah 1-39*. The New American Commentary 15A. Edited by E. Ray Clendenen. Nashville: Broadman & Holman, 2007.
Smolar, Leivy, and Moses Aberbach. *Studies in Targum Jonathan to the Prophets*. The Library of Biblical Studies. Edited by Harry M. Orlinsky. New York: KTAV, 1983.
Sperber, Alexander, editor. *The Former Prophets according to Targum Jonathan*. Vol. 2 of *The Bible in Aramaic Based on Old Manuscripts and Printed Texts*. Leiden: Brill, 1959.
———. *The Latter Prophets according to Targum Jonathan*. Vol. 3 of *The Bible in Aramaic Based on Old Manuscripts and Printed Texts*. Leiden: Brill, 1962.
Stamps, Dennis L. "The Use of the Old Testament as a Rhetorical Device: A Methodological Proposal." In *Hearing the Old Testament in the New Testament*, edited by Stanley E. Porter, 9–37. Grand Rapids: Eerdmans, 2006.
Stanley, Christopher D. *Arguing with Scripture: The Rhetoric of Quotations in the Letters of Paul*. New York: T. & T. Clark, 2004.
———. "The Redeemer Will Come 'ἐκ Σιών': Romans 11.26–27 Revisited." In *Paul and the Scriptures of Israel*, 118–42. JSNTSupp 83. Sheffield: Sheffield Academic, 1993.
Stenger, William Richard. "The Rebuke Tradition." In *Targum Studies*, edited by Paul V. M. Flesher, 1:33–59. Atlanta: Scholars, 1992.
Stevens, Gerald L. "The Literary Background and Theological Significance of ΟΡΓΗ ΘΕΟΥ in the Pauline Epistles." ThD diss., New Orleans Baptist Theological Seminary, 1981.

Stevenson, William B. *Grammar of Palestinian Jewish Aramaic*. Ancient Language Resources. Eugene, OR: Wipf & Stock, 1999.

Stowers, Stanley K. *A Rereading of Romans: Justice, Jews, and Gentiles*. New Haven: Yale University Press, 1994.

Strack, Hermann L. and Paul Billerbeck. *Kommentar zum Neunen Testament aus Talmud und Midrasch*. 6 vols. München: Beck, 1922–1961.

Stuhlmacher, Peter. *Paul's Letter to the Romans: A Commentary*. Translated by Scott J. Hafemann. Louisville: Westminster John Knox, 1994.

Targum Jonathan to the Prophets. CD-ROM, Accordance Version 4.4.3, 2006.

Thielman, Frank. *Paul and the Law: A Contextual Approach*. Downers Grove, IL: InterVarsity, 1994.

Thiselton, Anthony C. *New Horizons in Hermeneutics: The Theory and Practice of Transforming Biblical Reading*. Grand Rapids: Zondervan, 1992.

Toney, Carl N. *Paul's Inclusive Ethic: Resolving Community Conflicts and Promoting Mission in Romans 14–15*. Wissenschaftliche Untersuchungen zum Neuen Testament 252. Tubingen: Mohr, 2008.

Torrey, Charles Cutler. *The Second Isaiah: A New Interpretation*. Edinburgh: T. & T. Clark, 1928.

Vermes, Geza. *The Complete Dead Sea Scrolls*. Rev. ed. London: Penguin, 2004.

Wagner, J. Ross. "'Who Has Believed Our Message?' Paul and Isaiah 'in Concert' in the Letter to the Romans." PhD diss., Duke University, 1999.

Walker, William O. *Interpolations in the Pauline Letters*. JSNTSupp 213. London: Sheffield Academic, 1993.

Watson, Francis. *Paul and the Hermeneutics of Faith*. New York: T. & T. Clark, 2004.

Watts, John D. W. *Isaiah*. 2 vols. Word Biblical Commentary 24–25. Waco: Word, 1985–1987.

Wedderburn, A. J. M. *The Reasons for Romans*. Edinburgh: T. & T. Clark, 1991.

Westerholm, Stephen. *Perspectives Old and New on Paul: The "Lutheran" Paul and His Critics*. Grand Rapids, Eerdmans, 2004.

Westermann, Claus. *Isaiah 40–66*. Old Testament Library. Translated by David M. H. Stalker. London: SCM, 1969.

Whybray, R. N. *Isaiah 40–66*. New Century Bible Commentary. Grand Rapids: Eerdmans, 1981.

———. *The Second Isaiah*. Old Testament Guides. Sheffield: JSOT Press, 1983.

Wildberger, Hans. *Isaiah: A Commentary*. 3 vols. Translated by Thomas H. Trapp. Minneapolis: Fortress, 1990.

Wise, Michael O., Martin G. Abegg, Jr., and Edward M. Cook, editors. *The Dead Sea Scrolls: A New Translation*. Rev ed. New York: HarperCollins, 2005.

Witherington, Ben, III. *The Paul Quest: The Renewed Search for the Jew of Tarsus*. Downers Grove, IL: InterVarsity, 1998.

Wright, N. T. *The New Testament People of God*. Vol. 1 of *Christian Origins and the Question of God*. Minneapolis: Fortress, 1992.

Wuellner, Wilhelm. "Paul's Rhetoric of Argumentation in Romans: An Alternative to the Donfried-Karris Debate over Romans." In *The Romans Debate*, edited by Karl P. Donfried, 128–46. Rev. and exp. ed. Peabody, MA: Hendrickson, 1991.

York, Anthony D. "The Dating of Targumic Literature." *Journal for the Study of Judaism* 5 (1974) 49–62.

———. "The Targum in the Synagogue and the School." *Journal for the Study of Judaism* 10 (1979) 74–86.

Young, Edward J. *The Book of Isaiah 1-18*. New International Commentary on the Old Testament 1. Grand Rapids: Eerdmans, 1965.

www.ingramcontent.com/pod-product-compliance
Lightning Source LLC
Chambersburg PA
CBHW070911160426
43193CB00011B/1431